ATHEISM

and

FAITHEISM

ATHEISM

and

FAITHEISM

ROBERT M. PRICE

Pitchstone Publishing
Durham, North Carolina

Pitchstone Publishing
Durham, North Carolina
www.pitchstonepublishing.com

Most of the chapters in this volume were previously published as essays or presented as conference papers. For more, see the "Credits" at the end of this volume.

10 9 8 7 6 5 4 3 2 1

Library of Congress Cataloging-in-Publication Data

Names: Price, Robert M., 1954- author.
Title: Atheism and faitheism / Robert M. Price.
Description: Durham, North Carolina : Pitchstone Publishing, 2017. | Includes
  bibliographical references.
Identifiers: LCCN 2017024460| ISBN 9781634311342 (pbk. : alk. paper) | ISBN
  9781634311366 (epdf) | ISBN 9781634311373 (mobi)
Subjects: LCSH: Christianity. | Religions.
Classification: LCC BR96 .P725 2017 | DDC 230—dc23
LC record available at https://lccn.loc.gov/2017024460

To Jeff Lowder, the atheist Tom Cruise

CONTENTS

INTRODUCTION

This collection of my essays represents opinions and theories floated at various stages of my career. I have been at various times an agnostic, an exponent of Liberal Protestant theology, a non-theist, a secular humanist, a religious humanist, a Unitarian-Universalist wannabe, an unaffiliated Universalist, and a Fellow of the Jesus Seminar. Am I forgetting anything? Any way you cut it, my name is Legion. These chapters show me thinking out loud, or rather, thinking in print. I have grouped them by subject area. The initial section, "Criticizing Christianity," is three times the size of any of the others. Why? Because they are the products of my extrication of myself, step by step, from Born Again Christianity in which I dwelt for some dozen years. I had to think it out carefully and in detail, and from numerous angles. I share these writings in case they may be useful to others engaged in the same struggle. C.S. Lewis said that he wasn't asking anyone to accept Christianity against his better judgment, if the arguments didn't seem convincing. Well, I say the same from the other side: I am merely trying to account for my decisions and opinions. I will not mind if you reject my views. I only hope to provoke your developing thoughts. Let a hundred flowers bloom!

I have a few things to say about the various great religions and their founders. I guess I am not a very good atheist because I continue to love these faiths. I admire and cherish them as endlessly fascinating creations/expressions of the human spirit. You *have* to do that if you claim to be a humanist, don't you? Surely humanists are at least partly anthropologists, right? Nothing human can be alien to us. To me, religion is art. And there is an art to studying religion. I once had to withdraw from an atheist educational program because I was expected to share the director's disdainful and mocking attitude toward the various religions. You don't have to believe in them, any of them, in order to love them. And you can never really understand a faith unless you look at it with empathy, in order to see what its adherents see in it.

I love theology, too. At the time I wrote some of these essays I considered myself an adherent of Radical (Deconstructive and Death-of-God) theology. Sometimes I still do. I prefer Nietzsche's proclamation that God is dead to the straight-laced party line of purely secular atheism. But I have gladly written from the standpoint of old-time Freethought, too, and I gladly include some of those pieces, too.

But, as you know, I am the Bible Geek, and the Bible is my main focus of interest. So naturally I have chosen a hand full of my biblical studies. I can't keep awake reading much of today's scholarly pedantry. But I am careful to get my ducks in a row, to adhere to the standards of professional scholarship, even while being venturesome and speculative.

Again, I see my job not as framing dogmas but just to raise questions and possibilities you might not have considered before. I love it when other scholars do me that favor. So I'm trying to repay that debt by paying it forward.

—Robert M. Price

PART ONE: CRITICIZING CHRISTIANITY

1

MUST WE TAKE A LEAP
OF FAITH? (HAVE WE ALREADY?)

I want to respond briefly to a challenge frequently issued by well- meaning religious believers to the rest of us. In fact I am sure most readers will have been confronted personally with this challenge, namely, that a leap, or at least a step beyond reason is required if one is to live a full and well-directed life. The believer does not mean to violate reason, since reason is deemed fine as far as it goes. It just is not perceived as going far enough. It is held that the living of human life requires fundamental answers beyond the kind available from mere logic. Thus, the challenge continues, a leap (or step) of faith toward belief in the Bible (or Reverend Moon, or whatever) is advisable. Only so can we be sure of the meaning of life, the proper moral code, etc. Fair enough. In the interests of friendly dialogue and mutual understanding, I want to take these claims seriously, and to indicate where I believe they fail to convince.

THE LIMITS OF REASON

First, in what way is reason said to be deficient? This claim is made in three different forms.

Sometimes the charge denotes the doctrine of the "noetic effects of the fall," an implication drawn by some Calvinists (e.g., Cornelius Van Til) from the larger doctrine of "total depravity." Reality, it is held, truly operates according to reason and logic; the trouble is that sin has so blinded and warped the rational faculty of man that his logical capacity is a very poor one, and is fundamentally distorted. Otherwise, it would be plain to everyone that the Bible is the Word of God, etc. This argument is not to be taken too seriously, for its allegation must apply equally to the logical faculty of the one making the charge, at least so long as his words are understandable, however unconvincing, to the unbeliever. (If the Calvinist's "pre-fall" reason were regenerated and restored, would we "sinners" even be able to understand him?) Besides, since the only "reason" we know, the only "logic" we refer to by using that word, is being proscribed here, the result is the same as if we were simply being told to abandon reason in favor of a gnostic mysticism. And this is in fact what we are being told to do.

A second form of the "not reason alone" claim is that "post-fall" reason is still functional and healthy in itself, but that we unbelievers are "suppressing the truth in unrighteousness." The facts are supposed to be plain, an open-and-shut case as a matter of fact. Reason alone should lead any open-minded person to believe in the Bible (or the *Divine Principle*, or whatever). The trouble is that unbelievers are *not* open-minded. We are really just throwing out a smokescreen to avoid repenting, because we've got something to hide. "Men love darkness rather than light, for their deeds are evil."

Therefore, only repentance and faith will take away the veil, and allow right belief to prevail. Again, this claim may quickly be brushed aside. It is a bald-faced *ad hominem* argument. It merely charges one with bad faith instead of actually dealing in logical refutation.

A third, and more weighty, form of the argument is that there is too much more to reality and to human life to allow us to remain content with what reason can provide unaided. Indeed isn't it easy to agree that the error of "scientism" is its imperious arrogance in ruling that only the quantifiable is real? Weren't the original logical positivists properly taken to task for not admitting that there are always other "language games" besides that of the scientifically demonstrable, in which statements may be judged meaningful? So the basic premise seems justified. Yet the way in which it is employed by the apologist for faith may seem more controversial.

Sometimes this challenge is brought to bear when there is no contesting the relevant facts. Suppose an evangelist or revivalist is challenging his hearers to begin a vital "personal relationship" with Christ. It is assumed that the audience is already *nominally* Christian, as is implied in the remark, "You may know *about* Christ, but do you really *know* him?" That is, even if one accepts the cognitive claims about Christ, there is more at stake in the situation. Volition, existential commitment, is just as important. Will you commit yourself to what you know with your mind? This is a point well taken. We run into difficulties, however, when those to whom the challenge is directed do *not* assume the cognitive validity of the religious claims. Suppose we do not already believe that Christ or the Bible is the revelation of ultimate Truth? Will existential commitment (a leap of faith) be adequate to carry us across the chasm of intellectual uncertainty? Blaise Pascal in his famous "Wager" said yes. So did William James in his deliberations on "the will to believe." I want to examine the reasoning here, because there is more to it than first appears, yet there is finally *less* to it than there is supposed to be!

INTELLECTUAL HONESTY

Thomas Henry Huxley held that it is actually immoral to accept intellectual convictions for which we do not have sufficient reason. Now of course one might be mistaken in an honest judgment of the facts, accepting for sufficient what is really insufficient reason. What Huxley meant to censure was what we commonly call "intellectual dishonesty," the witting acceptance of a rational-type position on other-than-rational, and thus *inappropriate*, grounds. The "leap of faith" appeal seems to be telling us that just such a jump is navigable and justifiable, since we need answers that reason alone cannot provide. We may (indeed must) readily admit that reason is but a formal instrument and that logic is always employed after presuppositions have been established. That is, of course, what *pre*supposition means, after all.

But as "unbelievers" in revelation, we decline to leap, and this for two reasons. First, the logic of the argument assumes that there is only one "there" to leap to from "here."

Pascal says that if Christian dogma is true, then you have the devil to pay if you do *not* "wager" in Christ's favor. But if it is false, then a "mistaken" wager will cost you nothing and will on the other hand provide happiness and security (albeit ultimately illusory, but so what?) for this life. Yet what if Christianity is false, but Islam is true? Uh- oh! You're headed for hell! There are just too many possible directions in which to leap. And after the leap had been made, it would seem to have been the right choice, *ipso facto*. How could it seem otherwise, if the leap were really one of faith? But on this side of the chasm what guide have we? The "bet" Pascal wanted us to make is not the "sure thing" he thought it was. One could lose one's shirt, and at precisely the point when one made of asbestos might come in handy!

Another reason not to leap beyond reason to faith in a revelation is that this is not really allowed even by that extrarational margin recognized just above. For if in life we must sometimes go beyond reason, would it not seem that our goal in so doing would be itself extra- (or pre-) rational? Yet the revelation provided by an inspired scripture or creed *is* rational in nature ("propositional revelation") however stridently it claims exemption from rational verification. Here is that inappropriateness of criteria that spells intellectual dishonesty.

Of course, there are types of religion, e. g., mysticism or Liberal theology, wherein that religious "something more" does not pretend to take the form of privileged cognitive knowledge. For instance, for Paul Tillich revelation is an unveiling, *but not a rational explanation*, of the "Mystery of Being itself." This kind of revelation claim, that of mysticism, is indeed "more than rational" and does deserve serious attention. I only mean to challenge those who would ask us to accept a rational-type belief on other than-rational grounds (i.e., faith).

A PLACE TO STAND

At any rate, we say we are declining to take the leap advocated by believers. Yet they may reply that we have leapt already, merely by taking the position we hold, for "not to decide *is* to decide." In other words, it is impossible to stand in the middle. We inevitably leap to one side or the other. We act on the assumption that the religion in question is true, or on the assumption that it is not true, no matter how agnostic (and thus technically neutral) we may claim to be. Living on the basis of *any* presuppositions is supposed to be a leap of faith. We all leap, then; we can do nothing else—so why be ashamed of leaping to the side of Christ or the Bible, etc.? The problem with this seemingly cogent point is that it depends on an equivocal use of the term "faith." Is the "faith" of the one who simply declines to believe in revelation on the same level with the "faith" that does believe?

No, it is not, as religious apologists themselves quite clearly recognize in other contexts. For instance, the New Testament is clear that the kind of faith in view is nothing like the "faith" that, e.g., I really exist, that my body is substantial, that the chair I am sitting in will not collapse under me. Instead, we are told that "faith is the substantiation of things hoped for, the evidence of things *unseen*" (Hebrews 11:1). The apostle Paul says that "we walk by faith, *not by sight*" (2 Corinthians 5:7). This distinction is crucial. Faith in revelation is not faith in the inevitably evident. It is not the acceptance of those everyday realities which would take more faith to deny, the realities we cannot help but believe. Faith in the religious sense is that eulogized in the Gospel of John, "Blessed are those who have not seen, yet have believed" (John 20:29b). Or as Matthew puts it, faith is in realities which "flesh and blood hath not revealed unto thee, but rather my Father in heaven" (Matthew 16:17). By contrast, no leap is necessary to attain the perhaps unspectacular certainties of the agnostic. So without leaping we are already standing someplace.

What the religious person is really asking us to do is to leap from the common ground of mundane existence occupied by everyone, to a higher ground where life's answers are available to believers. But we ask if there is really any ground higher enough to merit attempting the climb. For perhaps where we stand now is not so bereft of the moral truths we are supposed to go seeking afar off, in some revelation. Let us look at some of the realities self-evident where we already stand. I have already mentioned those intuitive certainties which it would take a leap of faith to deny: my own existence, that of my physical body, the reality of my physical environment, etc. (Even Descartes admitted that his doubt of these things was only hyperbolic, all for argument's sake.) I believe we may add to the list certain moral truths, e. g., that persons deserve respect, that love is good, that honesty is obligatory, that truth is valuable. The crucial point is that these moral certainties seem to be intuitively established *prior* to any leap to "higher ground." The religious apologist himself implicitly recognizes this when he urges that one *ought* to make the best available choice of possible revelations, presuppositions, directions in which to leap. He appeals to an implicit moral obligation to find and honor the truth. He assumes that prior to accepting the "revealed moral standards" he offers, the unbelievers will recognize the need to find moral truth. And he is right—we do! But then why urge us to look further? The basic urges to truth, love, and righteousness to which he appeals seem to us as undeniable as our perceptions that we exist in a real world. It would take faith to *deny* them. Intuition yields these convictions; what more has faith to offer? We fail to see why other ground would be higher than that which we already occupy. "Do not say in your heart, 'Who will ascend into heaven?' or 'Who will descend into the deep?' For the word is near you; it is in your mouth and in your heart" (Deuteronomy 30:14).

SAVING KNOWLEDGE

At this point our religious friend will naturally suggest another angle from which to view the problem. If he is willing to grant the unbeliever his moral seriousness, even the workable adequacy of his moral stance, another question would seem to remain outstanding. What if there is some "saving truth" available only to faith, and without which one will be damned? If this were true, the believer suggests with obvious cogency, wouldn't it be good to know it? The "blissful ignorance" of the agnostic might one day turn out to be anything *but* blissful. (Remember our asbestos shirt.) If the question "whence morality?" is settled, the question of salvation still needs attention. A leap of faith might still be in order.

In answer, we must pose a counter-question. If God is a God of truth who requires honesty (and what creed denies it?), would he make salvation dependent upon an act of faith which some cannot make with intellectual integrity? Remember, we have already argued that to attain unto some alleged "saving/revealed truth" by a leap of faith would be impossible to do with intellectual integrity since it seems to entail accepting rational-type claims on other-than-rational grounds. If one must demur from the evangelist's offer of faith, because one is zealous for honesty, will the God of truth condemn him? If our well-intentioned religious friend finds himself answering (however reluctantly) "yes," then we must reject his offer as incoherent. For then it cannot really be the God of truth that we are being asked to obey!

Fundamentalists may have a rejoinder at the ready: "But the truth is often narrow and no one objects!" For instance, no pilot veers off his landing pattern because it would be narrow-minded to do otherwise. No one complains if a disease can be cured by only one treatment, so long as treatment is available at all. A point well taken, to be sure, but this is not the point at issue.

On the one hand, the line of reasoning just summarized does effectively refute the common liberal bias against the notion that one religion might be superior to others. (Is anyone really prepared to maintain that Buddhism or Judaism is not superior to the Rastafarian drug-cult?) Theoretically, there is certainly no reason that there might not be only one way of salvation, with non- believers in that religion being badly mistaken.

On the other hand, whether those non-believers (skeptics or believers in false religions) are damned by virtue of their ignorance is quite another question! And on this not even all Evangelical Christians are agreed. Some will allow some latitude for "those who have never heard the gospel."

But it is pretty well agreed that the rest of us are in trouble, whether we have simply declined to accept faith, or having once embraced it, now reject it.

Let us urge the religious believer to reconsider this position. Suppose that there is in fact one true plan of salvation and that we are "missing the boat" (however conscientiously) by not accepting it. Our doubts are not negative but positive since, as Paul Tillich would say, they are affirmations of Truth. We reject this or that candidate for "truth" because we will be satisfied with nothing but the truth and are afraid that many notions do not pass muster as truth. We could not with intellectual integrity accept them. And if we have mistakenly cast aside as glass what turns out to be the gem of revelation, because we honestly could not recognize it as such, will we be *damned* for it? We would think better of a God of truth. So we admit to the religious person concerned for our eternal destiny, that he might in fact have the truth (as might a thousand other sectarians), but that the bare possibility is not cogent evidence. And, from his vantage point, we would suggest that he keep in mind the warning of Virginia Ramey Mollenkott: "Failing to recognize that faith is a gift and not exclusively a product of the human will, certain conservative Christians refuse to believe in the integrity of a man who says that he cannot believe" (*Adamant and Stone Chips*, p. 88). Even if we are wrong, we may not be damned.

Finally, in answer to our religious friends, we agnostics and unbelievers must deny that the limits of reason compel us to accept their claims for special "revealed truth" inaccessible by normal channels. We cannot see how the gap can be leapt with intellectual honesty. We deny that our refusal so to leap is in itself a leap. We are not convinced that a leap of faith would supply any lack, for we perceive no lack. Like the religious believer, we already love the truth, and so we fear no reprisals from the God of truth, if such there be. And we humbly acknowledge that there is always truth yet to find. But we feel ourselves on safer ground if we seek it in a manner that it may be found—that of rational inquiry. We wish to "test all things and hold fast to that which is good" (1 Thessalonians 5:21).

2

MASOCHISM AND PIETY

Surely one of the most bizarre and astonishing religious tracts to appear in recent years is a little leaflet called *The Whipping*. In summarizing *The Whipping* some rather startling historical and literary parallels will become apparent. Then I will pose some intriguing questions for Christian spirituality and sexuality that arise from it.

THE WHIPPING

The pamphlet opens with a boy's defensive words to his father, "It wasn't my fault, Dad. We got in a fight and that kid called me a liar. . . and then he called my mother a bad name." To this protestation of familial honor, Dad's only response is an ominous one. "Bill's father closed the bedroom door and began to take off his belt." The trouble seems to be that in the heat of battle, Bill had used profanity.

Dad proceeds to inform Bill as to the real gravity of his crime. "When the Son of God hung on the cross at Calvary, He was dying there because you swore this morning . . . when the nails were driven into his hands, it was because you swore." However, despite the fact of Christ's atonement, Bill's parents had warned him he'd be punished if he swore again. Hadn't his mom forced him to memorize, "Thou shalt not take the name of the Lord thy God in vain"?

But instead of a punishment, Bill is about to receive a kinky object lesson about the vicarious atonement:

"W. . . What are you going to do, Dad?"

"Here, take my belt, Bill. Don't look so surprised. I want you to whip me!"

Bill's father took off his shirt and kneeled by the bed.

"But your back is bare, " stammered Bill. "The belt would hurt. You didn't do anything wrong, Dad. I can't hit you."

"You must be punished for swearing, Bill. And as you hit me I want you to realize that you hurt Jesus more, more than you're hurting me. Raise the belt!"

"I—I can't, Dad. Please, I'll never swear again. Please! "

"You must be punished, Son. And I'm going to bear the punishment something like Jesus bore your punishment on the cross. Go ahead, Bill!"

The belt came down with a crack and a red welt appeared.

"Again!" Again the belt came down.

"Harder!"

"Again!"

"Please, Dad!"

"Again!" Another red mark appeared on his back.

"I can't hurt you any more, Dad. I see what you've been trying to show me, how Jesus suffered for me on the cross, even for my swearing. I didn't know He loved me so. But I love Him now, and I love you too, Dad."[1]

VICTORIAN PORNOGRAPHY

Though the *prima facie* intention of this leaflet is to demonstrate the love of Jesus as it is expressed in the atonement, a form-critical analysis reveals that something quite different is going on here. In both structure and subject matter, *The Whipping* resembles nothing so much as the genre of Victorian pornography known as "flagellation literature." Indeed, the parallels are striking.

Steven Marcus devotes a whole chapter of his *The Other Victorians* to the large mass of flagellation pornography. He points out that while such material might be thinly veiled as medical monographs, lyric poems, comic operettas, or historical treatises, "they regularly break down into small, disconnected units, and the natural form, so to speak, of the genre is the anecdote."[2] Precisely such an anecdote is embodied in *The Whipping*.

As to specifics, Marcus describes how "a person is accused of some wrongdoing.. This person is most often a boy; sometimes he is a man acting or impersonating a boy."[3] In *The Whipping*, Bill is accused by his father, and the roles are reversed, whereupon Dad in effect impersonates the boy. "The accuser is almost invariably some surrogate for [the boy's] mother."[4] In the leaflet, Dad is shown carrying out the punishment for Bill's violation of his mother's warning.

While Marcus says that "an adult male figure, father or schoolmaster, occurs very infrequently, " he also shows how the accuser /disciplinarian is portrayed in masculine, even phallic, terms.[5] Latent homosexuality is thus implied. *The Whipping*, as were some few of the Victorian works, is explicit about the male-male scenario.

After the accusation is made, the one to be whipped defends himself (e.g., "No indeed, ma'am, I never insulted my momma, upon my honour, I did not.")[6] This protest soon turns to supplication for mercy, but to no avail. "The accused is then seized. He is . . . tied down to a bed. . . . His clothes are then lowered or raised. . . in order to expose his buttocks, and the whipping takes place. It is invariably accompanied by talk, usually dialogue."[7] All these elements, with merely idiomatic variations, are present in *The Whipping*.

The only material departure from the standard flagellation format would seem to be the fact of Dad's substituting himself for Bill. Of course, the main point of this development is to serve the theological purpose of the tract. It is after all an illustration of the vicarious atonement of Christ. But the departure is not so great as it might first appear. Marcus admits that, "In this literature, anybody can be or become anybody else. . . . There is, in the first place, an enormous amount of conscious acting or role playing throughout the literature; everyone is impersonating someone else. 'She embraced me,' runs a typical passage, 'and pressing my hand with transport, begged I would suffer her to represent my niece.' The playacting is frequently undertaken simultaneously by both parties. 'She instantly, by desire, assumed the character of Flirtilla's Governess.'"[8] In the same way, Bill (albeit reluctantly) portrays Dad, while Dad (with some apparent relish) plays the part of Bill.

MEDIEVAL PENANCE

No less revealing is the congruency of *The Whipping* with another historical precedent—that of the thirteenth-century flagellant movements active across Europe. Bands of fifty to five hundred penitents, specially uniformed and carrying whips and spikes, would embark on a month-long pilgrimage of punishment. The goal of these "self-immolating redeemers," as Norman Cohn calls them, was to atone with their blood for the sins of their countrymen. In this way they hoped to fend off impending plagues and disasters. Cohn describes the typical flagellant troupe, which "marched day and night, with banners and burning candles, from town to town." Upon arrival, "they would arrange themselves in groups before the church and flog themselves for hours on end."[9]

Again the parallels cannot but arrest one's attention. Just as these medieval ascetics sought to supplement Christ's blood atonement with their own, so does Dad, who says "You must be punished, Son. And I'm going to bear the punishment something like Jesus bore your punishment on the cross." Note that Dad is no longer simply illustrating Jesus' vicarious atonement; now he himself is bearing Bill's punishment.

And what of the results? "The impact which [the flagellants'] public penance made upon the general population was great. Criminals confessed, robbers restored their loot and usurers the interest on their loans, enemies were reconciled and feuds forgotten."[10] Likewise, Bill renounces his "crime" ("I'll never swear again!"), and he and his father are reconciled ("I love you, too, Dad.").

THE "HUMILIATE ME" CULT

Now all these correspondences might simply be called coincidental, perhaps unfortunate, perhaps amusing. But they are not simply coincidental. Instead, *The Whipping* is just a particularly clear instance of a trend long present in Fundamentalist piety—what someone has called the "'Humiliate Me' Cult." According to this form of spirituality, the believer takes a kind of morbid delight in suffering. The key scriptural passage here is 2 Corinthians 12:10: "For the sake of Christ, I delight in weaknesses, in insults, in hardships, in persecutions, in difficulties." For the record, these "difficulties" included the following: "Five times I received from the Jews the forty lashes minus one. Three times I was beaten with rods. . . ." (2 Corinthians 11:24–25)

Fundamentalist pietism has not balked at the path of discipleship thus marked out. This fact may be illustrated with a few quotes taken at random from the popular devotional booklet *Our Daily Bread*. "Sometimes in God's great wisdom He allows us to feel the sting and misery of our selfish, disobedient ways, that we may learn through the pain and humiliation that the Lord knows what is best."[11] "He wisely scourges and chastens every wayward child that He may form in him the character of the Crucified."[12] "Be sure you learn the lesson He is seeking to teach you, for His 'smiting' is always profitable if properly received."[13] "As we sometimes hold a crooked rod over the fire to straighten it, so God often holds us over the fire of affliction to straighten and temper us."[14]

"If you have prayed to know God's will, do not be surprised if He prods you with the thorns of trial and the rod of spiritual correction in order to properly direct your steps."[15]

> God uses for His glory those people and things which are the most perfectly broken. . . . Only if your evil pride is crushed and your spirit is contrite can God save and use you. Even as the crushed grape gives forth its liquid treasure, so only a broken and contrite heart can yield the fragrant perfume of holiness.[16]

The sadistic character of God, and the masochism inculcated in the believer, are made even plainer in these three analogies:

> A piece of wood bitterly complained because its owner kept whittling, cutting, and filling it with rifts and holes; but the master quietly replied, "What I am doing may make you think I am destroying you, but soon you will see it is the MAKING of you. I am changing you from a worthless black stick of ebony into a lovely flute whose music will charm the souls of men." So too, God the Master Craftsman uses the knife, file, and drill of trial upon us."[17]

> I am told that occasionally [an apple] tree seems to give all of its energy to growing wood and leaves, and consequently, bears little or no fruit. When the owner notices this, he takes an axe and makes a deep wound in its trunk close to the ground. Almost always that ugly gash produces a change. The next year the tree presents the husbandman with an excellent yield. It is the fruit of suffering! Oftentimes God's "trees" . . . are like that. He puts to us the axe of trial and the pruning knife of suffering.[18]

> A lady visiting Switzerland came upon a sheepfold. . . . One poor sheep [was] lying by the side of the road bleating in pain. . . . Its leg was injured. She asked the shepherd how it happened. "I had to break it myself," he answered sadly. "It was the only way I could keep the wayward creature from straying into unsafe places. From past experience I have found that a sheep will follow me once I have nursed it back to health." The woman replied thoughtfully, "Sometimes, we poor human sheep also want our own stubborn way...until the Good Shepherd sends sorrow and pain to arrest us.[19]

In all these cases, God expresses his love through drastically painful means, and the believer's response is to love God all the more for the suffering! Paul uses a sexual metaphor for the relationship between Christ and the

Church (Ephesians 5: 28- 33). Taking a leaf from his book, what kind of sexual relationship is implied by all the above examples? It is sadomasochism, and one suspects that it is no mere analogy.

UNDERGROUND SEX

Many have suggested that religious fervor is often repressed and sublimated libido. Weston LaBarre points out the obvious eroticism present in the writhing and moaning ecstasies of Holy-Roller Pentecostalism, not to mention the plain phallicism of the snake-handlers.[20] Philip M. Helfaer sees a zeal on the part of male Fundamentalists to evangelize other males as cloaking homosexual tendencies.[21] An unintentionally humorous example of the same thing is provided in the InterVarsity booklet *Sexual Freedom*. There, V. Mary Stewart describes her progress in setting aside her former life style of sexual abandon.

"The need to be always in a sexual relationship with someone was the best (or only) way I knew . . . to fill that 'God- shaped void.'"[22] One must at least wonder if the reverse were not really the case.

When Stewart advocates "doing spiritual calisthenics when it would be easier to grab onto an immediate, pleasant fantasy,"[23] isn't she really describing a sort of religious cold shower? Can she be oblivious to the repressed sexuality seeping through between the lines as she writes: *"The Lord is a very* gentle school master. . . . He never came down hard on me . . . He never *withdrew* his Spirit *capriciously or arbitrarily."*[24] *"Until we can open our tightly clenched* fists [or. . .?] *he cannot fill our* hands *full to overflowing."*[25]

If Fundamentalist fervor is to a noticeable degree the rechanneling of that sexual drive forbidden expression elsewhere, one must ask if morbid spirituality is not the rechanneling of a morbid sexuality.

To approach this issue from the other direction, one might consider not religion in the light of perversion, but rather perversion in the light of religion. Susan Sontag's essay "The Pornographic Imagination" makes exactly this linkage. She treats that classic of French pornography the *Story of O* in these terms. In the story, "O" becomes a "love slave" of one man, then another, who abuse her to the point of total submissiveness. One cannot help recalling the earlier illustrations of God axing the tree, gouging the stick, breaking the sheep's leg, all in order to "use" them, i.e., Christian believers.

"In the vision of the world presented by the *Story of O* the highest good is the transcendence of personality. The plot's movement is not horizontal, but a kind of ascent through degradation. [The heroine] wants to reach the perfection of becoming an object."[26] One can almost hear the strains of "Vessels only, blessed Master." Sontag herself sees the parallel in the self-abnegation required of Zen and Jesuit novices.

Is pietism then to be denigrated in its comparison to pornography? Or is pornography to be dignified in comparison to religion? To do the latter, as Sontag does, implies that to "transcend one's personality" through an "ascent through degradation" does serve some good purpose. However, to reject the masochistic piety of Fundamentalism as perverse stems from a prior rejection of its sexual counterpart. This huge question is not to be decided here, only defined. It is important to see that the spirituality and the sexuality of *The Whipping* are kindred expressions of the same instinct, and that they must stand or fall together.

NOTES

1. *The Whipping* (Grand Rapids: Faith, Prayer & Tract League, n.d.).

2. Stephen Marcus, *The Other Victorians, A Study of Sexuality and Pornography in Mid-Nineteenth Century England* (New York, New .American Library, 1977), p. 253.

3. Ibid., p. 255.

4. Ibid.

5. Ibid., p. 258.

6. Ibid., p. 256.

7. Ibid.

8. Ibid., p. 257.

9. Norman Cohn, *The Pursuit of the Millennium* (New York, Oxford University Press, 1972), p. 128.

10. Ibid.

11. *Our Daily Bread* (Grand Rapids, Radio Bible Class), March 1971.

12. *Our Daily Bread*, October 1969.

13. *Our Daily Bread*, February 1970.

14. *Our Daily Bread*, November 1970.

15. *Our Daily Bread*, April 1972.

16. *Our Daily Bread*, June 1970.

17. *Our Daily Bread*, May 1970.

18. *Our Daily Bread*, May 1970.

19. *Our Daily Bread*, April 1972.

20. Weston LaBarre, *They Shall Take Up Serpents* (New York, Schocken Books, 1974), p. 139.

21. Philp M. Hel£aer, *The Psychology of Religious Doubt. Boston*, Beacon Press, 1972), p. 132.

22. V. Mary Stewart, *Sexual Freedom* (Downers Grove: InterVarsity Press, 1974), p. 12.

23. Ibid., p. 18.

24. Ibid., p. 19.

25. Ibid., p. 20.

26. Susan Sontag, "The Pornographic Imagination," in Sontag, *Styles of Radical Will* (New York, Dell Publishing Company, 1978), p. 55.

3

PLASTER SANCTIFICATION

*"I have called pietism a scab, a suppuration of the best juices
of the spirit . . . Pietism is . . . the born and sworn enemy of true
scientific thinking. . . . The madness of pietism lies in the peculiarity
of its interest in religion. . . . The pietist is religious as if religion is his
trade, the pietist is he who goes around professing his religion, the pietist
is the man who smells for religion. . . . A pietist must be a hypocrite."*

—Friedrich Theodor Vischer

What's wrong with pietism? And is it the same thing as piety? I suspect maybe
it is not, and this would help explain something otherwise highly ironic about
this passage. For Vischer himself no doubt had a pious attachment of sorts to
the scholarly tradition of the Tübingen School to which he belonged. And so do
I. Was he, then, a hypocrite, as he says a pietist must be?

First, what exactly is offensive about pietism? About pietists? The ones
Vischer ran afoul of? Well, they must have sought in some way to stymie the
critical study of scripture. They always do, and it is not hard to see why. "We
must not criticize the scripture. We must allow it to criticize us! We dare not sit
in judgment on the Word of God!"

Pietism is all about self-improvement by reference to a Higher Power. AA
has direct roots in the Pietist movement and is a barely disguised version of
it, precisely as TM is a barely secularized version of Vedanta Hinduism. If you

laugh at Stuart Smalley, it is his sickening pietism you are laughing at. And that implies that pietism is a religiosity that lifts itself aloft, though that may not be very far off the ground, by means of slogans substituting for thought. And why? Because thought seems not to get you very far. So maybe chanting mantras will do it by self-hypnosis. For AA it may be "That's stinkin' thinkin'" or some such. For ecologists it's talk about "the planet, man." For Protestant pietists the slogans, the mantras, in short, the magic formulae are biblical "promises" of sanctification.

The Bible tells you you had better repent and improve yourself or face judgment. Christianity promises salvation from this prospect. Not by mere human effort, but by the grace of God. To effect this salvation, you must still do one crucial thing: you must call upon these promises. You must click on the icon. Because it is your faith in God's power that will let that power loose.

But then, if it is God's grace and your faith, where does the improvement of your life come in? What or who makes you better than you were, so your resume will pass muster at the last judgment? That is where the kindred doctrine of sanctification by faith comes in. There are "promises," i.e., Bible verses taken to mean that God will make you righteous and saintly despite your natural inclination to be a sinner. Again, he will not overwhelm you. You have to let him do it. You must "claim the promises," chant the formulae, for sanctification to occur.

And this is why the earnest pietist becomes a vicious opponent of the biblical critic. He sniffs with an unerring instinct that someone is at work devaluing the currency he needs to keep him afloat in the sin-free zone. "What? You mean these passages are mere opinions of mere mortals like me? They are not dictated from the Hestonian mouth of the Almighty? Then I cannot rely upon them in faith and trust, any more than I would the dubious preachments of some self-help paperback, and I am back to square one." And then any placebo effect the Bible references might once have had disappears. The jig is up. This is the single and sufficient rationale of the fundamentalist opposition to biblical criticism.

And in the course of that vehement opposition fundamentalists suddenly drop the mask of piety. At least no one else can see its features. They assume the role of sanhedrin inquisitors as if born to the role. "*Nail* some sense into 'em!" The sad fates of Spinoza, Strauss, Wellhausen, Bauer, Lüdemann, and others illustrate the wrath of the pious once aroused.

Why, do you suppose, can the pious slide so easily from the mode of devout to devourer? I venture to say it is because their sanctification, as it must be under the circumstances, was an illusion. We should have spotted the clue when we heard the news that they were sanctified by magical means, by faith and despite the evidence. The believer's virtue is to claim salvation in the absence of concrete evidence for salvation. And he equally claims sanctification despite the lack of worldly evidence. This may put him in the position of the failed believer in divine healing. He asked the deity to heal him, claimed the appropriate promise, and nothing seemed to happen. But it *must* have happened. And so it *did* happen: Satan must be counterfeiting the symptoms!! And if you seem un*sanct*ified, that, too, must be a trick of the light!

Harry Ironside, himself a pietist, saw the problem here in a book called *Holiness: The False and the True.* Only he should have called it The False and the False, for his own alternative was little better, just less obviously fallacious. He attacked the belief in "entire sanctification," "Christian perfection." This is the teaching of the Holiness denominations originating with John Wesley, the belief that by an act of faith one might unleash the sanctifying power of Christ to such a degree that the sinful inclination would be forever eliminated, at least stultified. Wesley was not about to claim this had happened to him personally, but he thought he might know one old lady to whom it had happened. Later, once the Holiness Revival blossomed within and without the borders of staid Methodism, every Holiness member and his brother were claiming to have been sanctified and fire-baptized unto holiness, "the Second Blessing."

Ironside pointed out the insidious deception involved. If one thought God had promised perfect holiness already in this life, and one claimed it, and it didn't happen (because there had been a misunderstanding, no such promise having been made), what had to happen? One could not afford to admit those sins that kept unexpectedly cropping up again and again *were* in fact sins. No, that would mean God had neglected his promise. So they must not *be* sins!

The result could be a kind of Tantric libertinism. One believes one has exorcised from one's being all sinful motivation, so what remains simply cannot be sinful! "By the same acts that cause some men to boil in hell for one hundred thousand eons, the yogi gains his eternal salvation." One might keep one's actions a secret so as not to frighten the poor "weaker brethren," but that's all. Of course most do not go this far, though I know of some personally who have: students have told me, e.g., about Nazarene wife-swapping groups! Nor is this kind of thing hypocritical. It has a peculiar and radical consistency.

But usually it doesn't go this far, and we do have classical hypocrisy, precisely as Vischer said. We rationalize away what we once would have confessed. Spite becomes sanctified as "righteous indignation," and so on. The sins themselves are sanctified, no longer the sinner. There is a self-blindedness inculcated simply because to see sharply would be to see that the promises of God had failed, or equally fatal, that by mere scriptural exegesis one could never be sure one had the promise of God after all. And then what happens to that variety of religion which centers essentially upon "claiming the promises of God"?

What was Ironside's alternative? If I'm not mistaken, he was only a single niche over on the spectrum of pietism. He would have believed in Keswick spirituality, the cultivation of the "Deeper Life," by "letting go and letting God" live the Christian life through you. It was not so much destroying the evil inclination within you but rather just playing Taoist, stepping aside to allow the power of God to do its thing. But tall claims were made for this approach, too, claims that led fundamentalists who embraced it to live in quiet self-condemnation. The Deeper Life approach is different from Christian Perfection in precisely the same way as James Frazer said religion differs from magic. Magic promised results and did not deliver them. Religion was superior only in that, while it did not improve the batting average, it made failure less embarassing since its claims were more modest.

But in the end, the result is all pretty much the same. There can be no magical sanctification. Improvement of character is always the result of hard work and always ambiguous in result. To claim sanctification by means of some therapy or miracle is an invitation to self-deception—self-deception like that of the pious inquisitor Vischer was talking about.

But there is a whole different sort of piety from this. It might be described, analyzed, mapped out as **a respect or veneration of some great tradition which one dares and rejoices to embody by becoming a link in its chain**. We can speak of a pious attachment to intellectual traditions, fraternal societies, to business concerns, to the military. One speaks appreciatively of this greater entity to which one belongs. Piety should not disallow fun-poking or criticism, and if it does, piety has become idolatry, as when a fan can brook no criticism of his idol, no suggestion that his favorite author has written both masterpieces and mediocrities. And it is evident that Vischer's ire had been roused by some who were too brittle in their idolatry.

Piety knows that the object of its veneration is so great that it does not require one's own efforts to defend or to promote it. If it needs you, it cannot be very great after all. But if you take such a patronizing and promotional stance, you become obnoxious, like those who offended Vischer. You devalue whatever it is you seek to sell like a product. It takes on the tinge of sleaze *because* you are trying to sell it, like a candidate or Amway products.

Piety is properly private. Because your veneration is precious to you, you do not expose it to the corrosive air. Because to you it is a pearl of great price, you will not eagerly cast it before the swinish leer of outsiders who perhaps are ill-prepared to appreciate it. It is you who will have made it a laughingstock by expecting others to affirm what they may not recognize as great. So much for the tastelessness of pietism.

Whence the arrogance of the thing? The hinted sense of the pietist as Grand Inquisitor in Vischer's quote? The pietist feels he has a proprietary interest in religion, and that the Higher Critic is violating his copyright. But he feels also the Olympian authority of the Word of God which he imagines himself humbly to serve. Whence this confusion of humility and arrogance? This confusion between fire and water?

Eric Hoffer explained it well in *The True Believer*. The pietist practices self-abnegation. In fact, what attracts him to a movement greater than himself in the first place is a kind of self-hatred. He sees in the recruiting call of the cause-evangelist an opportunity to lay aside the hated burden of selfhood, and to yield to what is greater. In this first stage, there is some humility: "He (or it) must increase and as for me, I must decrease." But the second moment in the process is insidious; *one assumes the mask and the mantle of that greater entity one serves*. Having hollowed out a skull cavity for it to live in inside your head, you have now installed it where your self used to be.

Or so you think. In fact you could not eliminate the self, so you have merely invested your self with the grandiose delusion of your idol's greatness. You have *become* it in your own eyes! "I said it! God believes it! That settles it!" No wonder the pietist knows how severely God disapproves of your action or opinion. It is not so much that he imagines God has told him so, though that would be bad, that would be *mad*, enough. No, he knows God's opinion because it is *his* opinion because *he* is God! How else can he be so quick with the thunderbolt? "Friend, it's not *my* opinion; it's God's opinion!" "The Gospel's not good views—it's good news!"

It is not only the religious pietist who can fall victim to this identity confusion, as you well know. A professor, a scholar, can come down like a ton of bricks because he has identified himself implicitly with the weight of learning that constitutes his field, as when one poses as an expert so as to settle a question. But in this as so many other matters, Socrates must be our guide. Socrates knew how vast a vista was wisdom, and he knew how little of it he had mastered, or allowed to master him. He did not think to pose as a living avalanche of authority. Socrates himself became an object of piety, but he tried to temper it. On his deathbed he told his disciples, "Think not of Socrates, but think of the truth." Just as Jesus warned, "Whoever believes in me, believes not in me, but in him who sent me." Here are two idols who warned against idolatry. If our piety toward them gets out of hand, out of line, we become like the pietists Vischer scorned, a man who seemingly just wanted to be left alone to do his work.

But that is just what the pietist will not let you do. For in his naiveté, in his lack of distance and perspective, he can see the rightness of no other cause than his own. Yours must be a distraction. It is not yours to choose what will occupy your hours. *He* will set your agenda as well as his own, since he cannot conceive that his cause may not be ultimate in importance. No nukes, political reform, solar energy, animal rights—his cause sets the agenda for the age. Can't you see it? He means to make you feel ashamed for not seeing it.

The pietist can use the language of mission and crusade without irony because he has not yet put away childish things. It is not that you can no longer take things seriously once you have matured. You just learn that even the salt of the earth must take things with a grain of salt. That there are no categorical imperatives, only hypothetical imperatives. Someone like Vischer, by contrast, whom I have described as pious toward the great tradition that he embodied, is perhaps all the more dedicated to that tradition, his heritage, precisely because he fears the well-meaning blundering of crusaders, those who believe the world can be sanctified as they imagine themselves to have been. The one who is pious toward the past is pious partly from pessimism about do-gooders whose ideals may be as airy and insubstantial as their estimate of themselves. The uncritical idealism is the enemy of any old order, because any old order has been seasoned and has come to terms with the realities the idealist does not see and doesn't want to see.

It may be that the opposite of pietism is cynicism, but at least one may say Socratic humility is on the latter's side. The cynic can be cynical about his cynicism, while the pietist cannot be cynical about his pietism. That, I think, is a significant clue.

4

PROTESTANT HERMENEUTICAL AXIOMATICS: A DECONSTRUCTION

THE CHALLENGE OF EXEGESIS: EXPECTING THE UNEXPECTED

What is the difference between exegesis and hermeneutics? They are two phases of biblical interpretation. The first is descriptive, the second prescriptive. Exegetes strive to reconstruct what really happened, what the original writer seems to have wanted the readers to receive. Exegesis approaches the text as a monument of culture, a window into the soul of the writer.[1] Exegetes seek to discover how the writer viewed things; what were his or her ruling assumptions? And what did they assert on the basis of their assumptions?

There is a hermeneutical or exegetical circle, a back and forth between reader and text: one's questions illumine the text, make it speak. And yet one soon meets resistance; something does not make sense. So one begins to revise one's initial assumptions about the text. Once one adjusts one's lenses in this way, the text starts making more sense. And this process will no doubt repeat several times. In fact, if it seems too easy to grasp the import of the ancient writer, one might start wondering whether one has missed something! Perhaps the greatest danger is *eisegesis*: reading into the text what one wants to find there. This is the danger of "engaged scholarship." As Kierkegaard said, your faith and its hunger for verification can cause you to lean too heavily on the saw; a more delicate touch is called for.[2] You won't be able to see how weak your scriptural evidence is if your belief preceded your evidence for it. As long as the verses you marshal are recruits fighting for the "right" cause, you think the

34

battle's won, even if none of them are armed and half of them are crippled. Most biblical apologetics partake of this weakness, leaving outsiders to question the honesty or even the sanity of believers who offer such arguments.

If one is to be honest, one must be ready to see what one doesn't want to see in the evidence. The mindset and beliefs of people in the past may seem quite alien to us, and that is why it is difficult to be sure we have read the ancient authors rightly. What their words suggest to us at first reading may have meant something quite different to them.

Albert Schweitzer[3] chronicled the long scholarly endeavor to penetrate the dogmatic screen of the Gospels, to sift through the evidence, and to delineate the outlines of the historical Jesus, the real Nazarene who lived among men and women, not the stain-glass figure of Christian theology. The result always seemed to be a Jesus tailor-made to play the figurehead for the modern, liberal agendas of the scholars who did the reconstructions. They had made Jesus over, not in the image of Christian dogma, true, but in their own images. And this was not because of any crafty scheme to employ Jesus as a poster boy for their favorite causes. No, they did their best. The problem was that they proved unable to listen for the truly *other*. All they could see or hear was what seemed plausible, what made sense, to them. This is what modern literary critics call our tendency to "naturalize" the text, to reduce the strangeness of a text to something we can more readily understand on our own terms.[4]

And so a first-century religious radical remained invisible to the questers after the historical Jesus. Schweitzer somehow managed to set aside his own criteria of verisimilitude and likely motivation, opening himself to the Other. And what he heard was the voice of a man whom we would readily call a fanatic: a proclaimer of the imminent end of the world who believed God had sentenced him to die in order to force the slowly grinding wheel of history into motion. This Jesus, Schweitzer realized, would prove an embarrassment to modern religion which had expected to find a congenial Jesus who would vindicate their own more enlightened perspective.

Or think of Vincent Bugliosi, the prosecutor in charge of the Charles Manson case. Bugliosi was certain Charlie had masterminded the series of grisly deaths, but he found it difficult establishing any credible motive. It was only once he began to suspect that Manson was operating from altogether different assumptions than he or the jury or most people would, that he began to piece the case together. He had to outline the delusional apocalyptic scenario which had prompted Manson's horrific deeds. He had staged the killings to look like a race hate crime so as to fan into flame the apocalyptic war of Helter Skelter, Armageddon. Working from conventional, familiar, sane assumptions got Bugliosi exactly nowhere. He had to be open to the Other. The problem, the challenge was well put by Mr. Spock as he explained to Captain Kirk why he had hitherto not been able to detect the source of some malignant radiation. It was unfamiliar; their sensors had not been built with this force in mind. And thus the scanner could pick up only what it had been built to scan for. How to widen the scanning capabilities? That's the task of the historical imagination.

THE CHALLENGE OF HERMENEUTICS: BRIDGING THE AGES

Hermeneutics is quite a different matter, a matter of what the ancient text means, or how it applies, now, whereas exegesis strives for the author's intent, i.e., what it meant then, to them, in their circumstances. In other words, can we draw a lesson from what the author meant, either directly or obliquely? The task of hermeneutics presupposes a distance between reader and text, ruling out, at least some of the time, direct application. So great is this challenge, so wide the gap to be covered, that one should not so blithely assume it is even possible. Islamic theologians reject the very possibility of epistles counting as Scripture, since they are directed from one human being to another. The problem is not so much that an epistolary author could not be inspired by Allah; rather, it is the particularity of the intended readership. How dare we read someone else's mail (for example, the Corinthians') and assume any of it pertains to us?

The distance may be due to cultural or philosophical differences, differences between our theological perspective and those of the ancient writers. When we demythologize what the ancients took literally, we have quite a ditch to jump, but hardly less of one when we try merely to systematize their utterances, quipped on this or that occasion. This latter is why we have such differences between Calvinism and Arminianism, for example, since both are attempts to do something the biblical authors never did: to work the various biblical statements on divine providence and grace into a coherent abstract system.

Or, it may be a set of new questions, such as medical ethics or nuclear war, arising since the scriptures were written, which set the distance hermeneutics seeks to span. When certain contemporary issues, such as abortion, are simply not mentioned in scripture, all one can do is to infer general principles from cases that are mentioned in scripture, and then speculatively apply such principles. Anti-abortionists say that the Bible condemns abortion. How is that possible when the Bible never mentions the issue? Because these folk are jumping the gun, failing to draw the vital distinction between what the text actually does say ("Thou shalt do no murder") and what they infer from it ("abortion would seem to be a sub-type of murder"). And they fail to recognize that no inference can be certain.

None of this is really new. All these challenges, pretty much, were faced by the ancient interpreters of even more ancient texts including the Torah and the *Iliad*. The techniques fashioned to do the job, including allegory, reasoning from analogous cases, etc., were already the stock in trade of the Jewish rabbis and the Stoic philosophers. I am concerned in this essay to identify some major points of tension in a particular stream of hermeneutics, namely Protestant hermeneutics. This approach represented something of a new departure in the days of Luther and Calvin, and now the approach has fallen on rough times. Once new and revolutionary, Protestant hermeneutics now seem superannuated and even obsolete. We shall see why.

PROTESTANT AXIOMATICS OF SCRIPTURE

Protestant hermeneutics are based on Martin Luther's paradigm, the first axiom of which is *Sola Scriptura*, which means that scriptural interpretation is logically prior to theology or tradition. One should get one's beliefs from scripture, and not impose one's beliefs on it, as Luther's Catholic foes did.

The second axiom asserts the normativeness of scripture's single, natural, literal sense. It must be read with the same methods one would use to decipher any other ancient writing. Thus Luther's espousal of the *grammatico-historical method*. One does exegesis of the Bible according to the historical information available on the times and according to the grammar of the Greek, Hebrew, and Aramaic languages. Just as one would never look for allegorical and kabbalistic secret meanings smuggled into Caesar's *Gallic Wars* by the Holy Spirit, neither should one so approach the Bible. Inspired though the Bible is, it is an inspired human writing, to be read by humans as humans read human writings. One needs no divine X-ray vision to discern what the scriptural authors intended to tell us. Even in the case of the Revelation of John, one does one's homework familiarizing oneself with the codes of the literary genre of apocalypses. Even puzzles are to be taken "literally," i.e., strictly according to the known rules for deciphering them. The inspiration of scripture is irrelevant during the process of exegesis. Where it becomes relevant is in the stage of hermeneutics, where we try to discern our obligation to do what scripture says.

The third axiom of Protestant hermeneutics is the *Analogy of Scripture*. This is to assume the unity and harmony of the canonical books. If a book violates this "analogy," it is excluded from the canon. Thus Luther waxed bold to relegate Hebrews, James, Jude, and Revelation to an appendix to his New Testament canon, because he felt that they did not comport with the Pauline gospel of salvation by grace through faith alone. But within the canon, the prevailing maxim shall be that "scripture interprets scripture," the "less clear by the more clear." If, say, Paul is found seeming to say in one place that people will be saved by performing the works of the Law (Romans 2:6–7, 13), we are to deem this text "less clear" than those in which he ("more clearly") says that no one will be saved by legal obedience (Romans 3::20). The apparent sense of the former may seem clear in its own right. Its supposed lack of clarity comes from its seeming failure to match up with the apparent sense of the preferred texts. "Less clear" is thus seen to mean "apparently clear in meaning, but problematical in implication." The euphemism of "clarity" (or the lack of it) is, as we shall see, important since it masks an important equivocation.

The fourth axiom of Luther's paradigm is the *Perspicuity of Scripture*. We don't need an infallible interpreter, such as the Pope, since the infallible scripture is plain in its meaning to all sane, unprejudiced, and moderately intelligent readers. That may explain why Luther was scornful of those who disagreed with him: the Pope, Ulrich Zwingli, Kaspar Schwenkfeld. He couldn't allow himself to believe they could rationally or sincerely disagree with him.

A HOUSE OF CARDS IS OUR MIGHTY FORTRESS

But, I am sorry to say, these four cardinal principles of Protestant hermeneutics contradict and devour one another, leaving biblicists with an incoherent mess. The assumption of the Analogy of Scripture is possible only insofar as we have already adopted the dogmatic presupposition of a single Divine Author of all parts of scripture ("plenary inspiration"). And then one feels one cannot read the Bible simply as any other set of texts. No one insists, for example, on harmonizing Calvin and Arminius. One does, of course, seek to iron out seeming contradictions between divergent passages in the work of a single author (St. Augustine, for example), but one does not refuse to admit as a last resort that the writer was inconsistent within a single work or may have changed his mind between one work and the next.

Even biblicists, so-called biblical literalists (though, as James Barr points out, this is a misnomer, since literal interpretation is quickly sacrificed to non-literal so long as the latter is deemed more compatible with the supposed "inerrancy" of the biblical text) will admit that scripture is filled with "apparent contradictions." Apologist Gleason Archer has even compiled an *Encyclopedia of Biblical Difficulties*, something one would hardly expect to be necessary with a perspicuous inerrant book, though the irony seems thus far to have escaped Archer and his readers. Biblicists feel they must deny that the Bible might contain "real" as opposed to "apparent" contradictions, because if it contained real ones, then biblicism ("The Bible says it; I believe it; that settles it!") would be sunk. If passage A contradicted passage B, how would poor mortals who would have no beliefs on revealed matters if we could not derive them from citing an inspired scripture, know which biblical text to believe and which to reject? Thus it seems better to hold that the contradiction is merely apparent, that the solution to the puzzle is merely elusive thus far. Somehow the seemingly clashing contents of both texts could be shown to agree if we had some extra information. In the meantime we will just effectively ignore the scripture passage that "apparently contradicts" the one which contains ideas we want to believe, that our creed or church tells us to believe. Protestants will readily stake their eternal salvation of Romans 3:20 and the doctrine of grace into which it neatly fits. What to do with Romans 2:6–7, 13? Ignore them, or, which is the same thing, pretend they say what Romans 3:20 says.

How is it possible that biblicists have not yet grasped that "apparent" contradictions are absolutely fatal to their doctrine of "biblical authority," based as it is on the "plain sense of the text"? Remember, it is none other than the plain, straightforward, apparent sense of the text that is authoritative for Protestants, that is, if we are to stick with grammatico-historical exegesis and so fend off mischievous Papistical allegorizing. That is what grammatico-historical exegesis means: the apparent meaning. Luther framed this principle precisely in order to rule out Catholic claims to have dug up some non-apparent "real" meaning of the text. And yet it is just such a stratagem to which inerrantists constantly repair with all their talk of "apparent contradictions." They are defending inerrancy in the same way medieval Catholics defended the sale of indulgences. Only in their case, the irony is all the greater since the appeal to esoteric meanings of scripture to defend desirable doctrines is an implicit repudiation of the very hermeneutic on which all their other doctrinal beliefs rest!

If one doubts the truth of this, just look at the practical results of the "apparent contradiction" or "more clear/less clear" subterfuge: is not even the biblicist left deciding whether he will accept verse A (e.g., Romans 2:6–7, 13) as normative for faith and harmonize verse B (e.g., Romans 3:20) into pretended conformity with it? Or the other way around? Is Romans 3:20 to be seized on as the true teaching of God's Word, and Romans 2:6–7, 13 subordinated to it? This is exactly the same arbitrary procedure they fear would result if they were to admit that scripture "really" contradicts itself. The sole difference is whether one wants to admit one is setting aside the passage whose plain meaning one does not like.

But is the choice arbitrary? In one sense yes, since one might equally have chosen either. In another sense, the choice is anything but arbitrary: it will be dictated by the needs of one's preferred or inherited theology. There is nothing arbitrary about that. Thus Walter Kaufmann[5] mocked that you can predict how a theologian will "gerrymander" the Bible as soon as you know what denominational label the theologian bears! And then what we are saying is that our doctrine is prior to our biblical exegesis and controls it before we ever even open the Bible. And that is the Roman Catholic view.

Moreover, the claim for the perspicuity of Scripture is demonstrably false, as witness the conflict of interpretations. Even if there were no contradictions or patent errors in scripture, the simple fact of ambiguity is enough to rule out "confident preaching of God's authoritative Word" as ridiculous and megalomaniacal.

IS THERE A "PLAIN SENSE"?

Perhaps the problem in all this is the very notion that there is such a thing as the plain sense of the text, an unadorned, objective meaning that ought to be obvious to any unprejudiced reader. What if there just is no plain meaning, whether that of a doctrine one wants to embrace or that of a contradiction one would prefer to ignore?

With Stanley Fish,[6] guru of Reader Response criticism, we must recognize that we belong to self-contained "communities of interpreters," sharing with our fellow members a set of assumptions as to what kind of thing to look for in texts, what methodology to use, and even what results we can expect. We are ultimately reading the text through a lens, feeding the text through a grinder of our own choosing. It will seem to us, secure within this "plausibility structure,"[7] that we are merely seeking the "plain sense" of the text, but it will seem so only because we naively take for granted a previously controversial reading that our community of interpreters has long ago come to take for granted. For medieval Catholics, some allegorical or anagogical reading that seems preposterous to us today seemed entirely natural, even inevitable. To them, Martin Luther's "truncated" reading of the "grammatico-historical" sense of the text seemed as crazy as it would seem to us if someone urged us to take the parables as straight historical anecdotes with no deeper meaning. Scripture is in the eye of the beholder. This subjectivity is hidden from us by the fact that both our exegetical colleagues and opponents (the only ones we are close enough to, to argue with!) hold the same basic rules and assumptions we do. Within that common frame of mind we can have variations on a theme, but other communities of interpreters are forever sealed off from us. We are playing baseball; they are playing soccer. We can't play on the same field, much less win a victory over each other.

This is what Tertullian had in mind when, in his *Prescription against Heretics*, he warned the faithful never to engage Gnostic opponents in scriptural argument. They might win! Therefore one must rule out the heretics' appeal to scripture a priori. The scriptures belong to us, not to you! Justin Martyr pursued the same course in his *Dialogue with Trypho*. He tried to demonstrate how Jesus fulfilled Old Testament prophecies—provided, of course, that one approached them from a Christian perspective! "According to your scriptures, or rather our scriptures, since they are no longer yours but ours."

THE ONLY ASSURED RESULT...

With Paul de Man,[8] one of the chief theorists of Deconstruction, we must come to accept a more modest result from our exegetical labors. No one can ever achieve an "assured result" in biblical study. We can understand a text better and better, but we can never be sure that what looks good to us now will not be overturned by subsequent scholarship, whether our own or that of others. The "truth" of the passage, however we may define it, is ever deferred, always postponed. It is a will-o'-the-wisp that enchants us, leads us on a merry chase, but one with no finish line. The truth of the text is like a North Star for exegesis: one navigates by it, but one can hardly hope ever to reach it! Only a fool thinks he has. We can never boast of having arrived at a correct, definitive "reading" of the text, but only of "misreadings" that are more or less productive of new insights into the text. The prefix "mis" serves to remind us that our exegetical suggestions, while plausible, can never be proven.

Jacques Derrida,[9] the other great Deconstructionist, poses the problem for traditional interpretation a bit differently. Derrida believes that we can often be sure enough that we have discerned what the author of a text intended to tell us, but that we may equally be able to discern within that text a "countersignature," a meaning at variance with the intended one. It will have been set loose by the very fact of the use of language itself, which always ricochets with surprising echoes unintended and uncontrollable by the author. Every utterance, every written sentence, is a stone dropped into a pool, and there is no telling how far the ripples will spread. Eventually they will collide with the banks of the pond and start to retrace their course, crossing with the ripples that are still on their way outward.

An example would be the Parable of the Sheep and the Goats in Matthew 25. Matthew presents us with two groups, one whose behavior we are to emulate, the other whose actions we are to avoid. The Sheep took every opportunity to assist the downtrodden, altogether oblivious of the fact that they were serving the incognito Son of Man. Their compassion had been spontaneous, disinterested, and so their true motives were revealed. The Goats, presented with the same opportunities, had shown as little humanitarian concern as Dives had for Lazarus. They protest upon learning that the whole thing was a sting operation, that the street bum they kicked aside was really the Son of Man. No fair!, they cry. Why, had they realized it was the Son of Man, in other words, had they known what was at stake, they would have helped quicker than you can say "asbestos!" But that's the whole point, don't you see? We can only tell what your real motives are if you don't know what's at stake! So . . . why is Matthew telling his readers what is at stake when they have the opportunity to help the downtrodden? He has not only rendered the whole scenario futile; he has also urged his readers to have the same self-seeking motives as the Goats! This cannot have been his purpose, admittedly. But he had unleashed a counter-message which utterly confuted his intended message. Which of these is "the message" of the text?

Even when texts do not present us with such paradoxes, there is the matter of whether to trust the teller or the tale. Modern literary theorists, from the New Critics on, have insisted that the author is but one more reader of the text he/she has written. The text, once down on paper, speaks for itself. Once it leaves the hand of the author, the author becomes irrelevant. Traditional scriptural hermeneutics occasionally came close to recognizing this point, as for instance when Warfield and Hodge contended that the biblical writers may have had all manner of erroneous opinions in common with their pre-scientific contemporaries, but that God had kept such things out of the text. The writers had been simple conduits for the production of texts.

POSTMORTEM HERMENEUTICS

When traditional Christian hermeneutics said God was really the author of the Bible, not so much Paul, Matthew, Isaiah, et. al., it was surprisingly close to Roland Barthes[10] when he spoke of "the death of the author," that is, his disappearance from the equation. To say that "God" is the author of Scripture is tantamount to saying that no one is the author of scripture, as when an insurance policy calls a random event of destruction "an act of God." No one caused it. Or when Origen said "God only knows who wrote the Epistle to the Hebrews," he meant "Nobody knows who wrote Hebrews." We tend to make the same mistake Odysseus tricked the Cyclops into making: "No man is killing me!"

A rabbinic tale tells how, at Javneh, when the rabbis were debating all sorts of halakhic technicalities, Rabbi Eliezer stubbornly held to his view in the teeth of united opposition from all the other sages present. He called the river outside to attest his view, hoping to silence opposition by resort to miracle. Sure enough, the river changed its course in support of his opinion. But the sages ruled out such a prodigy as irrelevant. Not to be so easily routed, Eliezer then called the tree outside to back him up, which it did by uprooting itself. When this marvel, too, was judged beside the point, Eliezer called the wall of the house of study to witness. It leaned inward, though out of respect for the other sages, it did not collapse. Again, inadmissible. Finally Eliezer called on God, whose Voice shook the rafters, pronouncing agreement with Eliezer's opinion. But even God's opinion was ruled out! Why? The chief rabbi pointed out that ever since God had caused Moses to commit the Law to writing, the prerogative of interpreting it has rested with human beings! God's is but one more opinion! God replies with mock dismay, "My children have defeated me!"

But one hardly need delve into the mysteries of Deconstruction to see how facile all the talk of Scriptural perspicuity and plain sense is; comparing several commentaries on a single text will demonstrate it readily enough. Once I read, back to back, and in their entirety, no less than seven commentaries on Romans and was startled to find major disagreements on every hand—and this among critical scholars ostensibly sharing the same methodology! There was little agreement even on points so major as whether or not Paul believed the Torah was still binding on the Christian conscience!

We can make the same point starting from Thomas S. Kuhn's work[11] on the evolution of science via the succession of paradigms rather than via discoveries of new evidence. A paradigm refers to a conceptual model, a theoretical construct applied provisionally to the same old data. One has the same set of dots before one; they haven't changed. But one tries a new way to connect the dots using fewer lines than the previous player. This is how Copernicus' paradigm of heliocentricity replaced Ptolemy's paradigm of geocentricity. A new theory gets off the ground by proposing a paradigm that would explain anomalous data that the older paradigm could not explain. If the new paradigm proves more encompassing as well as more economical (fewer variables, fewer factors involved), it gradually replaces the old one. In this way, we can trace, for example, the succession of "historical Jesus" paradigms proposed by various scholars. He was the Son of God, then a Jewish preacher of Ethical Monotheism, then a revolutionist, then an apocalyptic doomsayer, then an existentialist, a Gandhian social radical, a sort of Zen Master, a feminist, a magician. Same data, new ways of viewing it. Is one of them superior to the others? Each one does highlight elements left out or downplayed by the others, but it's hard to declare anyone the winner. It's the same way in science.

Kuhn never wanted to accept the implications, but Richard Rorty[12] and Paul Feyerabend[13] both explained why it is hard to name a definitive criterion by which to choose one paradigm over another: each way of looking at the data carries its own criteria of plausibility and is incommensurable with all the others. One's choice might be called intuitive, even aesthetic in nature, since factors like "simplicity" or "economy of explanation" may have more to do with our minds' tendency to delight in architectonic symmetry and balance than with any inherent priority these factors might have.

RUDE HANDS / ROOD SCREEN

So far I have argued that recent literary theory makes it impossible for us to claim that we have arrived at the author's intended meaning in a text, and that even if we could, we would not even be able to declare the author's meaning the authoritative meaning. But why not save ourselves the trouble of acquaintance with literary theory? Why not continue in the old ways of naively assuming that we can telepathically divine the meaning of Paul or Jesus or Jeremiah, and then thunder forth our own opinions as the Word of the Lord? We cannot take this route of escape if we are to keep hold on our Protestant membership cards, for what we would be doing is to make the old "commonsense" hermeneutics into sacred hermeneutics. We would be shielding the text of scripture behind a sacred rood-screen to protect it from profane scrutiny. But the whole point of the grammatico-historical method of Luther was precisely to lay profane hands on the sacred ark! Luther knew that the moment one makes the Bible susceptible to privileged means of interpretation, the mischief will never stop! The Bible will come to mean anything each interpreter wants it to mean! Today, for us to interpret the Bible as we would any other text, i.e., any secular text, demands that we apply to it the whole array of critical approaches in which current literary theory abounds.

IN THE BEGINNING WAS LOGOCENTRISM

The fundamental result of our taking all these developments in literary analysis seriously, as we must if we still believe the Bible is amenable to being read like any other book, is that we simply can no longer thunder forth our own exegetical results as "the Word of God." We cannot preach "with authority, not as the scribes," since we are no prophets or messiahs, but merely scribes ourselves! To ramrod home our own opinions by attributing them to God is the worst kind of manipulation and priestcraft.

Why not instead follow the lead of Socrates in our preaching? Why not abandon any appeal to authoritative names and theological pedigrees? The Bible, as in Jesus' parables, raises questions and challenges readers to come up with their own answers: "He who has ears to hear with, let him hear!" Instead of a prophet, dumping the truth like a ten-ton weight onto our hearers, why not be a Socratic midwife seeking to facilitate the drawing forth of the truth from within our hearers' own consciences and minds? That way, it will be their truth in a way a mere quiescent reception of prepackaged dogma never could be. And that way, it will hardly matter whether or not the Bible is a credible candidate for a divinely inspired and inerrant book: one will be able to recognize its truth—wherever it is true—for oneself. There is no need to appeal to external authority at all. What will be lost if we do this? What is it we are afraid of? We have shared with traditional Western philosophy what Derrida calls the Logocentric bias. The proverbs and stories of the Bible are not good enough for us. We have to abstract them, strip them down, use them as raw materials to build theological-ethical systems which we think can alone nourish us. And we seem to think that ideally every one ought to believe in the same system, to do and believe the same things. This is why we speak of "authoritative" preaching in the first place: we want to intimidate people into conformity with "the Truth." It was quite consistent with this hermeneutical/homiletical procedure when Reformed Protestant governments bloodily persecuted Catholic, Anabaptist and Socinian dissenters. Hadn't God himself dealt with Korah and his buddies pretty much the same way?

Similarly, when we invoke doctrines of inspiration and debate them vociferously, what is at stake but a fear that we will perhaps lose the secret weapon we love to use to intimidate conformity of belief? "This is the inspired Word of God; you have no option but to believe it!" Leaving aside the implicitly coercive strategy of the thing, consider the whole approach as an example of discredited "foundationalism," the notion that our most cherished intuitive beliefs ought to be defended by appeal to supposedly still more basic beliefs. Richard Rorty has exposed the absurdity of this. Do we really need to "prove" that love is better than hate? It would be horrifying to think anyone really thought they did! Can you imagine a person who was prepared to reject love if a better argument could be mounted in a debate on behalf of hate? So "open" a mind needs to be closed for repairs! Do we really think anything would be accomplished if we could demonstrate to the Nazis the untenability of their position? We can never win a theoretical debate with them, because our presuppositions and the Nazis' are utterly incommensurable. There is no common ground between us. Does that mean our confidence in our own values ought to be shaken? Hell, no! We needn't fear moral paralysis because our deepest presuppositions are not demonstrable (that's what we mean, after all, by calling them "presuppositions"!). We just have to decide what we will do about the Nazis. In Woody Allen's Manhattan there is a scene at a cocktail party where Woody's character Ike says "Has anybody read that the Nazis are gonna march in New Jersey, you know? . . . We should go down there, get some guys together, you know, get some bricks and baseball bats and really explain things to 'em." An effete martini-sipping liberal counters, "There was this devastating satirical piece on that on the Op-Ed page of the Times. It was devastating."

Another agrees, "Biting satire is always better than physical force." Ike stands his ground: "But true physical force is always better with Nazis, uh . . . because it's hard to satirize a guy with, uh, shiny boots on."[14] Exactly. We will have to clash with their beliefs, and with them. We cannot adjudicate our differences by recourse to some imaginary stock exchange of theories and opinions.

NO OTHER FOUNDATION

The same ironies crop up with the wrong-headed foundationalist attempts to secure allegiance to biblical authority by appealing to a doctrine of inspiration. When you say that we need a doctrine of inspiration to make scripture authoritative you are denigrating the contents of scripture. Do you really need some external warrant before you will take the Sermon on the Mount seriously? Does not deep speak unto deep? And if the scare-stories of Ananias and Sapphira, Dathan and Abiram, strike you as no more than superstitious priestcraft, will a claim of inspired authority make them seem less so? Any doctrine of the plenary inspiration of the Bible flattens out the whole text so that the tedious minutiae of Leviticus or Chronicles become no less important than 1 Corinthians 13 or Romans 6–8, and these latter come to be seen as no more significant than the former.

Such foundationalism leads right back again to Logocentrism: it implies that what is really central to our religious existence is a set of theoretical doctrines, as if salvation and Christian existence were one long process of cramming for a final exam. If one excavates deeply enough, one discovers that the ultimate axioms of Protestant hermeneutics are not *Sola Scriptura*, perspicuity, the grammatico-historical method, the analogy of Scripture, or even the bearing of Christ to the reader, but rather the notion that there is a single privileged doctrine or set of doctrines to which all others must be subordinated as heretical, and which all human beings must be required to parrot and to obey. It is a set of power relations at bottom. It is not so much as if Jesus should invite whoever is thirsty to come to him and drink; it is more like his counterpart requiring everyone who hungers to take the mark of the number of his name to be eligible for a ration of grain.

NOTES

1.   William Dilthey, *Pattern and Meaning in History: Thoughts on History and Society*. Trans. H.P. Rickman (NY: Harper & Row, 1962); Richard E. Palmer, *Hermeneutics: Interpretation Theory in Schleiermacher, Dilthey, Heidegger, and Gadamer*. Northwestern University Studies in Phenomenology and Existential Philosophy. (Evanson: Northwestern University Press, 1969).

2.   Van A. Harvey, *The Historian and the Believer: Tthe Morality of Historical Knowledge and Christian Belief* (NY: MacMillan, 1969), p. 124..

3.   Albert Schweitzer, *The Mystery of the Kingdom of God: The Secret of Jesus' Messiahship and Passion*. Trans. Walter Lowrie (1914; rpt. NY: Schocken Books, 1964); Schweitzer, *The Quest of the Historical Jesus: A Critical Study of its Progress from Reimarus to Wrede*. Trans. W. Montgomery (1906; rpt. NY: Macmillan, 1961).

4.   Jonathan C. Culler, *Structuralist Poetics: Structuralism, Linguistics, and the Study of Literature* (Ithaca: Cornell University Press, 1975), p. 134.

5.   Walter Kaufman, *The Faith of a Heretic* (Garden City: Doubleday Anchor, 1963), pp. 114–116.

6.   Stanley Fish, *Is There a Text in This Class? The Authority of Interpretive Communities* (Cambridge University Press, 1980).

7.   Peter L. Berger and Thomas Luckmann, *The Social Construction of Reality: A Treatise in the Sociology of Knowledge* (Garden City: Doubleday Anchor, 1967), pp. 86–87, 166–168.

8.   David Dawson, *Literary Theory*. Guides to Theological Inquiry (Minneapolis: Fortress Press, 1995), p. 44.

9.   Jacques Derrida, "Plato's Pharmacy," in Derrida, *Dissemination*. Trans. Barbara Johnson (Chicago: University of Chicago Press, 1981), pp. 61–171.

10.   Roland Barthes, "The Death of the Author," in Barthes, *Image Music Text*. Trans. Stephen Heath (NY: Noonday Press, 1977), pp. 142–148.

11.   Thomas S. Kuhn, *The Structure of Scientific Revolutions* (Chicago: University of Chicago Press, 1962).

12.   Richard Rorty, *Philosophy and the Mirror of Nature* (Princeton: Princeton University Press, 1979).

13.   Paul Feyerabend, *Against Method* (rev. ed., NY: Verso, 1988), pp. 229–230.

14.   Woody Allen and Marshall Brickman, "Manhattan," in *Four Films of Woody Allen: Annie Hall, Interiors, Manhattan, Stardust Memories* (NY: Random House, 1982), p. 203.

5

THE PSYCHOLOGY OF BIBLICISM

For many years I have studied the theology underlying biblicism, the fundamentalist belief in the absolute authority of the Bible in every aspect of life, only to conclude that it is not theological in nature at all, but rather entirely *psychological.* That is, biblicism is not, as its adherents claim and think, an implication of a set of beliefs about the Bible but rather the outgrowth of a particular frame of mind. I am not impatient with theological claims; I just do not think they are the real source or motivation of biblicism, and this becomes evident once we discover certain inconsistencies in biblicism which make nonsense of its theological claims but are quite consistent with the psychological function of biblicism. If it were a matter of theology, surely biblicists would notice the problems. But since biblicism does the job biblicists want it to do, they simply never notice the problems.

Biblicism, again, is the term for that stance toward the Bible whereby a believer intends to obey whatever the text tells him to do, and to believe whatever the text asserts. If occasionally the commands of the Bible (say, to give away all one's possessions) seem just too outrageous, biblicists may rationalize them away, but even this does not mean they are not taking them seriously; a non-biblicist would say he rejects the command of the Bible and leave it at that. And there are more liberal Christian theologies which do not entail biblicism, managing, as Reinhold Niebuhr said, to take the text seriously even if not literally. So what is it that attracts many people to biblicism?

FAITH AS SKEPTICISM

First I think we may identify the fundamentalist's, the biblicist's, desperate felt need for "a sure word from God." Why do we need God to break the silence of the ages with a revealed word, an inspired book of infallible information? Perhaps paradoxically, this need stems from a kind of *skepticism*, a lack of confidence in the ability of the human mind to discover necessary truth by reason alone. This is a very different stance from that of the old Deists who believed in a divine Creator but who did not believe in the inspiration of the Bible. Not only did the Bible appear to them a poor candidate for an inspired book, but they believed the Creator had written the only revelation book human beings needed in the world itself, nature, not scripture. And he had given us reason as the only spectacles needful to read and understand it. The biblicist, however, is flustered by *overchoice*, the condition of being faced with too many options, each with plausible arguments and spokespersons. How is he to decide between them? Suddenly, a religious claim that God has tossed confused humanity the Bible as a life-preserver sounds pretty good. The problem, of course, is that there are just as many competing revelation claims vying for our faith, and one is left without a clue as to deciding between *them*!

But whence the urgency of arriving at true and sure beliefs about all ethical and theological questions? Why not emulate the ancient Skeptics? Like fundamentalist fideists today, the Skeptics viewed the conflict of dogmas from the sidelines and despaired of joining any particular team with confidence. But their conclusion was that such answers, such knowledge, must not be either available or necessary, that one can live perfectly well in this life on the basis of common sense and mere probabilities. Why does our biblicist not adopt the same attitude? I think it is because he holds an unexamined assumption, perhaps a vestige of childhood catechism, a picture of God as some sort of punitive theology professor who stands ready to flunk you if you write the wrong answers on your theology exam. You die and appear at the Pearly Gates, and God hands you the blue book. You do your best on the Theology and Metaphysics final, but if you make enough mistakes, the floor is going to open beneath your feet, as it did beneath old Korah's, and you are going to slide down the shaft to Hell. This is a God who does not excuse honest mistakes. Again, I can understand this obnoxious God-concept only as a matter of psychology, not as the implication of any orthodox theology. What element of theology implies that God should be unfair, even peevish? To think him so is to project a childish fear of retribution which can only stifle intellectual growth. Surely it is a legacy of retrograde education, whether religious or secular.

A prime example of this fearful skepticism that needs God's word to settle issues too important for mere human minds to decide would be *abortion*. It is a difficult matter precisely because of the ambiguities of the issue. Strong cases may be made on various sides of the issue. That fact alone inclines many of us toward a pro-choice position. But some fundamentalists feel the stakes are high enough that those on the wrong side of the issue, especially abortion doctors, may be justifiably murdered. How can they be so sure they are right? Because God has told them so in the Bible. And this despite the fact that the question of abortion *never even comes up in the Bible*. The need for the Bible to adjudicate the subject produces the optical illusion that it does.

The need for a sure word from God may simply stem from the kind of intellectual laziness posited by Ludwig Feuerbach. We feel we need to know certain things but are too lazy or impatient to try to figure them out, and the belief in a divine revelation is all too convenient. Convenient both for the lazy one who wants to be spoon-fed, and for the authorities who view themselves as far more capable of finding truth than the laity. But in any case, whether it is a matter of fear or of laziness, I think we may chalk up the desire for "a sure word from God" to *a low tolerance for ambiguity*.

This is clearly seen in the advice given to pastors and students for studying the Bible. Suppose one is reading the text, seeking divine guidance for one's own life or scriptural grounding for one's beliefs (predestination or free will? Pre- or Post-Tribulation Rapture?). One will shortly discover ambiguity, individual passages that seem to point in one direction or another, or where things are just not so clear. One must then make one's best exegetical judgment call, and then go forward confident that one has achieved the truth. The biblicist awards himself a license for dogmatism, heedless of the necessary tentativeness of one's results. One intends to be dogmatic about whatever conclusions one will wind up embracing. It is just a question of which dogma one will promote.

A fear of ambiguity is the chief reason any definitive biblical canon was ever stipulated in the first place: to limit the options for textual divination. God's word and will must be sought only within certain limits. Similarly, this is why the Roman Catholic authorities sought to limit access to the Bible to properly catechized priests who could be trusted to read the text through the spectacles of church tradition. Protestants believed all Christians should be welcomed to read the Bible, over-optimistic that the central gospel truth would be clear to all readers. It wasn't, and immediately Protestants had to frame their own creeds to regulate how the Bible might be read and understood. The trend continues today as various Evangelical seminaries and denominations draft statements of how the Bible may and may not be legitimately interpreted. The goal is to get everyone to agree with the traditional interpretation of the sponsoring group. "Heresy," after all, simply means "choice," the idea being that it is effrontery to choose one's own beliefs rather than submit meekly to spoon-feeding.

WHAT A TANGLED WEB WE WEAVE
WHEN WE PRACTICE TO BELIEVE

I mentioned above that there are liberal theologies of biblical authority that do not entail biblicism. Such theologies often accommodate the possibility that the Bible writers may have contradicted each other. A more liberal theologian might observe that Paul and James disagree over whether faith is sufficient to save one's soul, or whether faith must be realized through works. Such a theologian would consider neither Paul nor James mouthpieces of revelation, both as possible sources of religious wisdom. The theologian's task would be not to *submit to* either Paul's or James' teaching, but to *draw upon* both in the process of forming his own (tentative) beliefs. The fundamentalist theologian, by contrast, dismisses the liberal's form of faith as mere speculation, worthless in the face of the ultimate question of salvation. With one's eternal destiny at stake, one must *know*. And thus one needs revelation, not mere speculations whether ancient (James' and Paul's, if that's all they are) or modern (one's own). Since he wants revelation, that is what he is determined to find in the ancient text.

The fundamentalist cannot even recognize that Paul and James contradict one another, since if he did, this would disqualify either or both as mouthpieces of revelation. One might be accepted as a true prophet, the other rejected as a counterfeit, but then who is to decide, and how? Martin Luther had no hesitation in relegating James to the status of a mere appendix to scripture, but most are not so bold. A statement is authoritative for the fundamentalist simply because it appears somewhere in the canon of scripture, all canonical texts being equally authoritative. This is what the slogan "plenary inspiration" means. Unlike in liberal theology, no parts of the Bible are deemed superior or inferior to others. The biblicist, remember, wants to be able just to open the Bible and find his answer. If it is up to him and his meager human abilities to weigh and choose, he is back to square one. He does not want to have to make decisions like this! That's the whole point!

But he cannot escape the horns of dilemmas like this. Fundamentalists follow Martin Luther in wanting to interpret the text of scripture *literally*, or according to the "plain sense," what it apparently means by straightforward exegesis, such as one would apply to any ancient text. The Bible is inspired, but this only means that its message, once determined by exegesis, must be heeded. Inspiration does not entitle us to read the Bible in some esoteric way, as medieval Catholics did, discerning all manner of secret meanings between the lines. If the Bible may be taken to mean just about anything, then the Bible becomes a Rorschach blot. Again, as a literalist, the biblicist wants to banish ambiguity. Reading the text in a careful and "literal" way, however, sooner or later discloses "apparent contradictions" like those between Paul and James. And at this point the biblicist abandons literalism, falling back to a less-than-literal reading. Suddenly one may and must read between the lines after all. An exception to the straightforward reading is allowed when otherwise the two texts would negate each other's authority and inspiration, a collapse that would take the whole canon with it!

But the cure is worse than the disease! Whatever a "real contradiction" might be, "apparent contradictions" are quite sufficient to vitiate a doctrine of biblical authority that is based on the supposedly "apparent" reading of the text. And it is not just a technicality. For the poor biblicists finds himself situated like the proverbial donkey between the two haystacks: he must decide whether it is Paul or James who is to be taken literally, and which is to be read in a looser way as if he agreed with the other. Though the phrase used is that one must "interpret the less clear texts by the more clear texts," the biblicist is really interpreting the text he doesn't like as if it said the same thing as the one he does like. In short, he is in precisely the same position as the liberal theologian, choosing between biblical voices; he just doesn't realize it.

How can he continue in such self-deception? Simply because his choice is an automatic one, determined in advance by his particular church's tradition of interpretation. If he were a Catholic, he would read Paul as agreeing with James. As a Protestant, he reads James as echoing Paul once you "really understand" him. The biblicist is submitting to authority, all right, but it is not, as he imagines, the authority of the text but rather that of his church. And this, too, is fatal, since the first principle of the biblicist is *Sola Scriptura*: "Scripture alone!"

It is such gross, vitiating contradictions that reveal the origin of biblicism to be essentially nontheological. If it had been theological in origin, it would have more consistency. To call on a related field of supernaturalist belief, we might compare biblicism to astrology. A survey of horoscope readers in Britain revealed that most of them admitted the newspaper predictions proved accurate less than half the time. Why then did they continue to read the horoscope? If it were a matter of theoretical consistency, the utter failure of astrology would have been quickly evident. But it was not a matter of theory. It was a matter of psychology: the astrology believers really sought, not knowledge of the future, but rather peace of mind for the night, permission to sleep well in the confidence of being forewarned and thus forearmed for the morrow. When the morrow came and the prediction, probably forgotten, turned out not to prepare them for events, it hardly mattered. They were competent to deal with the day's surprises, but the night before they felt they needed an edge, and reading their horoscope allowed them to imagine they had it. Even so with the biblicist. What he wants from the Bible is not so much a coherent system for divining infallible revelations, but only the permission to dogmatize, whether the goal is to quiet his own fears or to push others around.

A MIGHTY FORTRESS IS OUR MENTALITY

Once one has adopted the belief that the Bible must function as the final authority in all matters, some strange results follow. Above, I gave abortion as an example of how the desire for a sure word of revelation leads some biblicists to imagine that the Bible speaks to issues of which it is in fact innocent. To do this is what I call *hermeneutical ventriloquism*. The biblicist may chant "The Bible said it! I believe it! That settles it!" But in practice this often amounts to "I said it! The Bible believes it! That settles it!" One does the scripture the dubious favor of attributing to it one's own beliefs. The (psycho)logical process goes like this: "My opinion is true. The Bible teaches the truth. Therefore the Bible must teach my opinion." One suspects that the dogmatist has simply become so accustomed to dogmatizing that appealing to the Bible is just his way of asserting the truth of his opinion, wherever he got it. Saying "The Bible says" is tantamount to saying, "Verily I say unto thee . . ."

One's imaginary possession of the word of God, or the mind of God, allows the biblicist to wield what I call the Prophetic Ramrod, an attitude of invulnerable narrow-mindedness: "Friend, there is your view, and then there is *God's* view."

Such dogmatism may even rub off onto areas where the biblicist feels no especial need to quote the Bible or knows he cannot, areas such as party politics or even selling merchandise. Whether one is "witnessing" to the glories of Christian salvation, Amway products, or Mary Kay Cosmetics, one uses the same methods (as Southern Baptist salesman and evangelist Zig Ziglar freely admits in his book *Secrets of Closing the Sale*).

THE SLIDING SCALE OF BIBLICAL INERRANCY

Another anomaly resulting from the psychological, not theological, basis of biblicism is the shifting opinion of biblicists over the years as to what the allegedly infallible teaching of the Bible is when it comes to the world of nature. There was a time when readers of the Bible could see quite well that it "taught" (or presupposed) a flat earth that floated on water, covered by a solid firmament (dome) that kept out another ocean above. The earth was orbited by the sun and supported by pillars. And every Bible reader understood this. In the name of the infallible Bible, religious authorities opposed the progress of science. Today, most fundamentalists reject evolution because it contradicts the Bible. But only a tiny minority still believe the earth is flat. A slightly larger minority believe that the sun orbits the earth. Most fundamentalists believe that the earth is round and that it orbits the sun. And they do not even realize that the biblical picture of the earth contradicts these notions. Their religious upbringing has told them that the Bible contradicts science only at the point of evolution. As for the rest, they have even been told that the ancient writers of the Bible miraculously foreknew what it took modern science centuries to learn, that the earth is round, that it orbits the sun, etc. These assertions are read into the Bible by forced and implausible readings of various passages out of context, akin to attempts to show that the Bible writers knew about flying saucers. The true teaching of the Bible on these matters, they say, could not be understood until modern science allowed us to understand the relevant texts correctly! This is very close to (but also very far from) a frank admission of the game of catch-up being played here.

But what makes the difference between whether one recognizes contradictions between the Bible and science or one pretends the Bible anticipated modern science? It is simply peer pressure, massive and permeating public opinion. Ancient biblicists lived in a peer group (a "plausibility structure," as Peter Berger would call it) that believed in a flat earth orbited by the sun, created in a week. It would have been hard to believe anything radically different. As the plausibility structure shifted, so that most people in the culture no longer took the ancient world-picture seriously, it ceased to be an option for biblicists to retain the biblical cosmology. They couldn't withstand the cognitive peer pressure. And today the great majority, including biblicists, believe in a round, sun-orbiting earth, but it is not so obvious to the great majority that all life forms gradually evolved from a common ancestor. One still has breathing room on that point; one can still afford to recognize what the Bible says. One can still, for the time being, reject evolution and not seem a freak. The fundamentalist dreads the time when universal belief might turn to accept evolution, and so they seek to defer that day by means of public debates, censoring biology textbooks, etc. Their effort is not to persuade the intelligensia (scientists) of the truth of anti-evolutionism, but rather to appeal to the gallery in the manner of a political campaign,. They are looking for votes in order to retain an amenable plausibility structure. It is all psychological, not theological, since what the Bible says or does not say about the natural world is utterly beside the point. The day will eventually come when biblicists will reinterpret Genesis to teach evolution and will claim that God had revealed it to the ancient scriptural writers ages before scientists supposedly discovered it. And these new scriptural "insights" will have come not from exegesis but solely from social peer pressure.

If one wishes to get anywhere reasoning with fundamentalists and biblicists, I suggest one try to determine the emotional issues that attach believers to their beliefs. The beliefs themselves are, I think, a function of certain psychological needs that would be better met in other ways. But until those psychological needs are identified and met in other ways, we will have no way of getting believers to budge from their beliefs, and we might not even have the right to do so.

6

A MIGHTY FORTRESS IS OUR MENTALITY
(DO OUR DOCTRINES GIVE US
PERMISSION TO THINK?)

Many of us with a background in fundamentalist Christianity can attest that often this form of faith is very closed-minded. How likely is it, for instance, that someone representing an opposing viewpoint would be welcomed to share it from a fundamentalist pulpit? "If you asked me what Jerry Falwell could do to really flesh out the kind of love and fellowship and mercy he *talks* about—well, very simply, he could invite a person like Troy Perry to speak on his show. He could say, 'We totally disagree with Mr. Perry and the gay church, but we feel that he claims to be a Christian and has something to say, and we should in the spirit of dialogue let him say it.'"[1] This is not very likely to happen. Recently I attended a Baptist church where the vitriolic anti-Mormon propaganda film *The God-Makers* was shown. Not only was no Mormon invited to respond, but when a Mormon in the audience asked to make a statement, he was not allowed. I have seen the staff of a Christian book store get in trouble for stocking books by liberal theologians like Hans Küng. And it is common to hear how conservative seminaries do not assign books by liberal theologians. Instead, the seminarians "must hear positions stated— secondhand by an instructor who is quick to offer his 'Christian' critique on the heels of every description."[2]

Evangelical students sometimes complain that liberal seminary professors are just as narrow because they never assign books by conservatives. I suspect that the situation is a bit different in this case because these professors are often ex-conservatives themselves, and they would see it as a waste of time (and of students' money) to assign what are really books of apologetics for an anti-critical position they see as discredited. Yet I do see some fairness in this charge: the critical stance of religious liberals does stem from a definite set of (usually unspoken) theological commitments. Let's take a look at where both fundamentalists and liberals stand on certain basic issues. Then we may be able to understand their different approaches to thinking and open-mindedness.

THE DOCTRINE OF FAITH

First, religious liberals have to a greater or lesser extent abandoned the traditional view of faith as assent to certain revealed or creedal propositions. Instead they have adopted Paul Tillich's understanding of faith as "concern." For example, as Van A. Harvey forcefully makes clear in *The Historian and the Believer*, a different ethic informs the liberal Bible critic's studies than the one that makes the believer say as a matter of conscience: "The Bible said it! I believe it! That settles it!" Even when the two wind up giving assent to the same proposition, say, that Jesus lived in Nazareth, they do so in very different ways. The liberal sees enough evidence to believe it, while no amount of evidence could make the fundamentalist *not* believe it.

Liberal Christians believe in Truth, but they never have more than qualified and tentative confidence that a particular set of beliefs may be identified with it. Ideally, they are ready to follow biblical criticism, comparative religion research, and philosophical inquiry wherever they lead, and let the traditional articles of faith fall where they may. Fundamentalists, too, believe that faith and truth will always finally agree, but they wind up straitjacketing and harmonizing facts into apparent conformity with dogma. Francis Schaeffer assured his readers that they never had to fear finding the facts to be in conflict with fundamentalist doctrine: "The truth of Christianity is that it is true to what is there. You can go to the end of the world and you never need be afraid, like the ancients, that you will fall off the end and the dragons will eat you up. You can carry out your intellectual discussion to the end of the game, because Christianity is . . . true to what is there, and you will never fall off the end of the world!"[3]

Fundamentalists, then, sacrifice the truth (i.e., an open-ended reading of the facts); liberals sacrifice "the faith once for all delivered to the saints"

(Jude 3). Now if open-mindedness inherently entails such skeptical scrutiny, such doubt in the interests of truth, can we really imagine an open-minded fundamentalist? No, because for fundamentalism, faith requires a believer to be a "true believer." Liberals can only afford to be open-minded because of their Tillichian concept of faith as concern for the *questions* rather than as assent to a given set of *answers*.

Conservative theologian Thomas F. Torrance (certainly not a fundamentalist, but rather what I consider to be a Barthian fideist) argues in his book *Theological Science* that liberals ever since Schleiermacher have approached theology more as a quest to find what we do *not* know than as the study of what we do know from revelation. If revelation has been given and we do not accept it and start from there, all our searching will be in vain. God's truth is already under our noses. Yet it would seem that religious liberalism proceeds squarely from the assumption that such revelation has *not* been given. If liberals accepted the claim of traditional Christianity that God has revealed himself normatively in the Bible, they would not regard the honest, inductive *search for* the truth to be worthwhile or needful. So religious open-mindedness assumes that one holds, or better, that one does *not* hold, a certain view of revelation. The fundamentalist, by contrast, honestly believes the truth has been revealed and that he *has* it, thanks to God's grace. Why go searching for it?

All this implies that liberal Christians believe that the quested-for truth will be the kind of thing that our much-prized reason can discover. It will not, they feel sure, be something one must accept by a leap of faith, something that cannot be revealed by flesh and blood, but only by the Father in heaven (Matthew 16:17). So to pursue the open-minded search for truth is already to have made a fairly major theological choice: reason, not revelation.

THE DOCTRINE OF HUMANITY

The belief in an open-minded search for the truth implies a decidedly optimistic doctrine of human capability. Liberals encourage the search for truth, obviously, because they believe the searcher can find it. They have a higher estimate of what most people are capable of than Plato and Aristotle did, to say nothing of John Calvin. Men and women by using their minds should be able to find the truth and to tell it apart from its rivals. They most certainly do *not* believe in "total depravity": the doctrine that sin taints or warps every part of the human person just enough that no one may discover God without divine grace. Liberals seem to believe that human beings have adequate brains and good will to free themselves from preferences and prejudices and to discover religious truth.

Yet most of us would admit we *might* make a mistake and fail to discover the truth. Even so, liberals feel quite confident of hearing "Well done, thou good and faithful servant" one day; even if they do not find the truth, can God ask more than that they should have honestly sought for it? Thomas Henry Huxley said "In matters of the intellect, follow your reason as far as it will take you, without regard to any other consideration [and] do not pretend that conclusions are certain which are not demonstrated or demonstrable. That I take to be the agnostic faith, which if a man keep whole and undefiled, he shall not be ashamed to look the universe in the face, whatever the future may have in store for him."[4] Religious liberals say "Amen to that." But doesn't this imply *more* than a commitment to intellectual honesty? Does it not also imply a very definite soteriology? They are advocating a kind of "salvation by works" scheme. Courageous doubters will be saved because the plan of salvation is not the cross of Christ, but rather sincerity in searching.

THE DOCTRINE OF THE ADVERSARY

Often fundamentalists discourage the presentation of other viewpoints because they do not believe it is actually a question of an autonomous hearer freely weighing and choosing between options. The real situation as the fundamentalist sees it is pretty much like the familiar cartoon showing a person wavering between the whispered promptings of a miniature devil on one shoulder and a tiny angel on the other. Just so, Paul chalks up the faith of the Corinthian Christians to the supernatural conviction of the Holy Spirit: "my speech and my message were not in plausible words of human wisdom, but in demonstration of the Spirit and of power, that your faith might not rest in the wisdom of men but in the power of God" (1 Corinthians 2:4–5). Likewise, the unbelief of outsiders Paul links directly to Satan: "The god of this age has blinded the minds of the unbelievers, to keep them from seeing the light of the gospel" (2 Corinthians 4:4). Mark, too, sees at least some unbelief this way: "Satan immediately comes and takes away the word which is sown in them" (Mark 4:15).

Reasoning has little or nothing to do with it, which Paul (1 Corinthians 2:4–5) regards as a good thing (presumably since rational argument can only result in tentative and provisional opinions, not in the certainty of the Spirit). Instead, the *will* is all-important. "If any man's will is to do his [God's] will, he shall know whether the teaching is from God or whether I am speaking on my own authority" (John 7:17). The fundamentalist sees the choice between beliefs as a tug-of-war between God and Satan for the individual soul. The situation of the individual, the hearer of the gospel, is *not* one of intellectual challenge, but one of moral persuasion; his job is simply to resist the temptation of Satan and yield to God instead. The choice is entirely *moral, not intellectual.*

This is why fundamentalists are so impatient with the skeptic's objections; they are thought to be a mere smokescreen thrown out by a guilty sinner who only wants to avoid the issue of moral repentance. "Unbelief always has a moral cause—unwillingness to do the will of God in some point. The difficulty is not with our faculties, nor with the evidences, but with our moral state."[5] If you were willing to come clean morally, you would accept the fundamentalist belief: it's that simple.

It is because they see things in this frame of reference that fundamentalists do not encourage or permit the expression of alternate views. "Satan might sow seeds of doubt," one hears again and again. Once I was warned by a fundamentalist not to read Hugh J. Schonfield's *The Passover Plot* because the book was "poison."

Religious liberals, by contrast, believe that a decision between alternative beliefs is essentially a rational one, and should be approached that way. They do not believe in a personal devil or at least that Satan pays such attention to each of us. Religious liberals seem to believe optimistically that the truth they encourage people freely to seek will not be obscured by error or turn out to be the belief with less evidence seeming to support it. They believe you ought to believe the position for which there is most evidence. In other words, they say that a responsible belief will never be a matter of believing against the weight of the evidence, as harmonizing inerrantists do, since that would involve a sacrifice of the intellect. Liberals feel sure that "the truth will out."

Sure, in exceptional cases, the evidence *might*, at the moment, seem to point in the wrong direction, but fundamentalists make the exception into the rule; they never decide inductively from the evidence. They assume that inherited dogma reveals the truth, and that if the evidence seems not to support it now, one day, when we get to heaven and can see the whole picture, it will.

CONCLUSION

Open-mindedness, then, is not simply an attitude; it is a doctrine, or at least the result of prior theological choices. If this is so, if certain beliefs are more productive of open-mindedness, more consistent with free inquiry than others, how should we make our choices between them? There seem to be two options. First, we might try to argue and weigh the merits of both the fundamentalist and the liberal positions *theologically*, and *then* accept narrow- or broad-mindedness as consistency requires. Are there better reasons for accepting or rejecting a belief in Satan, revelation, etc.? Second, in the process of evaluating the two theologies, we might weigh among their merits the very fact of whether they produce tolerance or intolerance, just as we would probably reject any theology which entailed hatred or cruelty. Are beliefs prior to values, or are values prior to beliefs? In such a choice between presuppositions, probably only intuition can finally decide.

NOTES

1.   "An Interview with Richard Quebedeaux," *Faith and Thought* Vol. 1, No.2, Summer 1983, p. 37.

2.   Dennis MacDonald, John Topliff, Jim Wallis, Bob Sabath, Dwight McKee, and Pamela MacDonald, "The New Left Student Movement and the Christian Liberal Arts College," in Mark Tuttle (ed.), *About School* (Houghton, NY: Lanthorn Publications, 1972), p. 109.

3.   Francis A. Schaeffer, *He is There and He is Not Silent* (Wheaton, IL: Tyndale House, 1972), p. 17.

4.   Thomas Henry Huxley, *Science and the Christian Tradition* (New York: Appleton and Company, 1900), p. 246.

5.   Thomas Cook, *New Testament Holiness* (Fort Washington, PA: Christian Literature Crusade, n. d.), p. 119.

7

ON HAVING YOUR HEAD UP
YOUR ASSUMPTIONS

When one hears the word *apologetics*—a word that denotes the rational defense of the faith—one usually thinks of people like Josh McDowell and William Lane Craig, who urge the cogency of "the evidence for the resurrection" and for the infallibility of the Bible. But there is a growing legion of apologists who blatantly reject such an (at least ostensibly) inductive approach. They are called "presuppositionalists." As far as I know, "presuppositional apologetics" is the brainchild of Cornelius Van Til, a stalwart of Westminster Theological Seminary, a school that was formed when fundamentalist faculty fled Princeton Theological Seminary in the 1920s.

Van Til was ahead of his time. The rest of us began catching up only in the1970s and 1980s when we began reading Thomas S. Kuhn (*The Structure of Scientific Revolutions*) and realized how much our perception of the "facts" is shaped by paradigms, the conceptual models we use to interpret them. Van Til had already been advising apologists not to seek common ground with unbelievers, just to proclaim Christ and summon them to jump ship and come on over! Since Christ is the Universal Logos, the Christian worldview would be seen as *ipso facto* logical once it was embraced. Until one did, it would make no sense; whether one embraced it or not was a moral decision. Recently, more and more debates between theists and atheists have been contests between presuppositionalists and nonbelievers who mainly just can't believe what they're hearing!

Though I was an evangelical and even in a small way an apologist, I have never seen the sense of the presuppositionalist argument. I have read it from Van Til, Francis A. Schaeffer, and Alvin Plantinga, but it never captured me. Here's my problem. It seems to use a probabilistic argument to vindicate a stance that ostensibly repudiates probabilistic argument. It says we must despair of attaining certain knowledge through our own reason. Certainty, we are told, is possible only if we posit the existence of a God in whose certain knowledge we share. Schaeffer compares presuppositionalism to someone looking through an old house for the missing piece of a jigsaw puzzle. Months later he discovers what appears to be the piece in an old trunk in the attic. It wasn't with the other pieces in the box, so he can't be sure it belongs to the same puzzle, but its shape does fit the remaining gap perfectly, and it completes the puzzle's picture perfectly, too! Wouldn't a reasonable person conclude that he had found the missing piece? And if the Christian Gospel fits so well the epistemological need of the human mind, supplying the needful certainty, mustn't we accept it as the truth?

But this is itself a probabilistic argument, the sort of exercise in reason and evidence that presuppositionalism thinks to refute. It is an argument among many other arguments about epistemology, or how one can have real knowledge. It is no less a human striving for an epistemological guarantee than those theories it hopes to have stultified. And then it cannot evade, as it seems to want to do, the need to *justify* its belief in an infallible God who guarantees knowledge. It must try to convince us that such a God exists. If so, our problem might be solved. But whether such a God does exist is just the point at issue. If you're going to beg the question, at least don't be proud of it!

If you really mean you will cut the knot by presupposing that God exists and provides a guarantee of knowledge and leave it at that, how can you complain if I eliminate the middleman, or middle *god*, and simply presuppose that human reason can achieve certainty? I have no need for the God hypothesis if I presuppose that we do in fact know. What is sauce for the Christian goose is surely sauce for the naturalist gander.

But let me turn the tables: if you say belief in God guarantees certain knowledge, I ask *how*? By sheer illuminism? Do you intuitively know what God is saying? You can't be that naïve! Every pietist can remember times thinking he or she knew God's will, and it blew up in his or her face. Or is infallible knowledge found in Scripture? Then we will be left in the lurch as soon as we ask a question that Scripture, an ancient book, does not deal with. Even the presuppositionalist will be left, like everybody else, with fallible guesswork. Besides, remember the ambiguity of the Bible on many points: what certainty is possible there?

Worse yet, the Bible itself contains instances of God making false revelations, a collection of texts strangely never mentioned in those surveys of biblical teachings about inspiration. Remember when Micaiah told the king of Israel that God had sent a lying spirit into the mouths of his prophets to trick and humiliate him?

> Then a spirit came forward and stood before Jehovah, saying, "I will entice him." And Jehovah said to him, "By what means?" And he said, "I will go forth and will be a lying spirit in the mouths of all his prophets." And he said, "You are to entice him, and you shall succeed! Go forth and do so!" Now, therefore, behold: Jehovah has put a lying spirit in the mouth of all these, your prophets. (1 Kings 22:21–23)

Remember when Ezekiel said God had once commanded infant sacrifice to lead his people astray: "Moreover, I gave them statutes that were not good and ordinances by which they could not have life; and I defiled them in their very gifts in making them offer by fire all their first-born, that I might horrify them" (Ezekiel 20:25–26). Remember when Paul said that God would send the rebellious a lie to believe since they did not prefer the truth: "Therefore God sends upon them a strong delusion, to make them believe what is false" (2 Thessalonians 2:11–12). I would say that, if we take these cases seriously (and I know that no theologian does), God does not guarantee true knowledge.

But in fact I think the presuppositionalist argument is a kind of shell game that depends parasitically on the very doctrine it pretends to vindicate. It is like asking, "What can wash away my sin?" and answering, "Nothing but the blood of Jesus." But the doctrine of Original Sin was posited for the very purpose of justifying the death of Jesus. So if you ask the Christian question, it is no surprise that only the Christian answer will fit! Presuppositionalism compares to arguing that "Jesus must have truly died, since he then rose from the dead. How could he rise if he had not died?" The deck is stacked! In the same way, who says we either *need* or *have* certain knowledge? Only the dogmatist requires dogmatic certainty. No one else will miss it.

Many of us find the advice of the ancient Skeptics useful: you can live without certainty on matters where no certainty seems available. Just because you feel the need for certitude doesn't mean you have the right to posit that you have it, any more than my felt need for money justifies me in robbing a bank if there is no other way to get it. And don't tell me that I contradict myself by dogmatically claiming that we can have no knowledge. I make no such claim at all. I merely say I do not see that certain knowledge is available. I make no claim on what knowledge is or ever will be possible. If you are a dogmatist, you may tend to assume that everyone's position is held dogmatically. Some are, some aren't.

Any historian knows that certainty about the past is never possible; we deal only in shifting probabilities. Any literary interpreter knows that we can never be sure we have definitively captured the author's intention in a text. Any scientist knows that future discoveries may alter today's best working hypotheses, and that those hypotheses must be cast away as soon as a better one enters the arena. The "final truth" is like the North Star: it is an ideal by which we navigate; it is not a destination we imagine we can ever reach. Thinking at any point that we have certain knowledge only tends to choke off the progress of research.

Sometimes presuppositionalists sound like they mean that logic is self-evidently true, that there is a manifest logos-structure in the universe, but that we must somehow account for it and explain where it came from, or else we will have no right to it. And they account for it by saying God must have created it. That would be another form of the hackneyed argument from design, which Hume long ago refuted. And you don't argue for your presuppositions. That's what makes them presuppositions.

Presuppositionalists sometimes seem to be saying that a denial of God as the author of logic would vitiate logic; that a denial of God ought to undermine our confidence in logic. But this argument results in a fatal backfire. It implies that logic is merely nominal in character. It would seem valid and count as valid only because the Creator made it *seem* so. And if he wanted, he could reverse things tomorrow such that henceforth A should be the same as Non-A. This is divine voluntarism, and it undermines logic as surely as it undermines ethics, making both into arbitrary products of God's whim. Otherwise the presuppositionalist would have to admit that God commands morality and logic because he himself acknowledges an objective truth they possess prior to his endorsement. If logic is valid only insofar as God says it is, then it is not valid at all, but only the ad hoc "policy" dictated by a superhuman entity.

8

DAMNABLE SYLLOGISM: THE (PSYCHO-)LOGIC OF THE ATONEMENT

THE ESSENCE OF CHRISTIANITY

What is Christianity all about? Or, as at least two important books (by Adolf von Harnack and Ludwig Feuerbach) from around the turn of the century put it, what is the "essence of Christianity"? For this is what we want to know, e.g., when we ask in the abstract how Christianity is to be estimated alongside the other world religions. Is it just one more can of soup in a row of others? It might be so even if this can has a label reading "Hinds," while that one says "Campbell." Often such redundant products are even made by the same company! To a great degree, I think the analogy is not a bad one. On the one hand, there are theological differences within each faith that are easily as great as those separating one faith from another. So no religion has a monolithic unity of identity. But on the other hand, all of them sooner or later, here or there, turn out to be facing the same agenda of issues and to have evolved a similar smorgasbord of responses to those issues.

So we must ask what makes Christianity unique, or more modestly, what is distinctive about it in the sense that every religion is unique or distinct unto itself. Jacques Derrida (*Limited, Inc.*) contends that there is no "proper" use of any piece of language. There is no inherent "real" meaning that governs "correct" use. There is only convention. Dictionary writers and grammarians just agree that a certain cross-section of current usage will count as "proper English," "the King's English." But every "straight" use of it invites "twisted" use.

Without "isn't" it would be no fun to say "ain't." Everything invites a parody of itself, a distortion of itself. The straight line doesn't rule out flexibility; rather, it gives you something to be flexible *with*.

This implies that any definition of what Christianity "really is" or "is supposed to be" is going to be merely *descriptive*, not *prescriptive*. Any textbook orthodoxy will be useful only as an "ideal type," a conceptual yardstick to use in measuring the varying proportions of real live Christian groups. Their variations from the norm do not count against them. They are not "heresy" in the sense of "thoughtcrime." To the contrary, these differences reveal what is distinctive about a particular Christian sect or thinker. If they are to some extent "not true to type," unorthodox, so what? That just helps to chart their position on the theological map. It doesn't mean they're charting a course to Hell, or out of the True Church. Maybe the Moonies or the Mormons or Matthew Fox are getting pretty far from the essential Christian norm. That may mean they are in the process of evolution into something else, just as Christianity eventually reached the point where it could no longer be counted a Jewish sect. Maybe you think they should call themselves something else than Christian. Eventually they'll probably agree with you. Till then, why be in such a rush to segregate the wheat from the tares?

THE ESSENCE OF THE ESSENCE OF CHRISTIANITY

What is, then, the essence of Christianity? Before we separate the form from the content, we have to make an even finer-tuned distinction. We have to use a heuristic device that is sharper than any two-edged sword, dividing between joints and marrow, soul and spirit, and, as Seymour Chatman says (*Story and Discourse*), between "the *content* of the content" and "the *form* of the content." I think that what constitutes the essential content of Christianity is a central doctrine, and a theological doctrine is a different *kind* of thing from, say, a central principle or a central moral value. It matters a great deal whether you think the essence of Christianity is love, or you think it is the doctrine of the atonement. Everything is going to be different from there on in, depending on that starting point.

And I am going to argue that the essence of Christianity is *not* love, but is in fact the doctrine of the atonement. That does not mean that the atonement is supposed to be "better" than love or more important than love. It's just that love is the common possession of all the religions. It is not what distinguishes them from each other. Contrary to what the Johannine Jesus says, "all will [*not*] know that you are [his] disciples [merely] because you have love toward one another." That wouldn't tell them you weren't Jews, Muslims, Hindus, Humanists, etc.

If you are thinking there is something wrong here, you are thinking what Kant and the Eighteenth-Century Rational Religionists thought: it is the distinctives of religion that lead to religious wars, not what they have in common, certainly not love. Might it not be better to shear away those distinctives, since they threaten to get in the way of love?

As I understand it, the Christian doctrine of the atonement means more or less this. Human beings, thanks to the Fall of Adam, are fatally tainted with sin, in a fundamental state of moral impotence and alienation from God. The self is the center of interest, where God should be. And if God were central, things would fall naturally into place. Loving and serving God, we would thrive like a heliotropic plant that always bows in the direction of the sunlight. Such was our nature till it jumped the track when Adam sinned and fathered a race and a social system of sinners. We are born in sin like a fish born in water. Thus it would take radical surgery to lift us out of the briny deeps of sin and make us breathe air on the surface. We can no more reform ourselves by good intents and efforts than a fish can simply decide to live on land from now on. God would have been well within his rights to wash his hands of us, but instead he went the second mile and provided the radical surgery, the means of re-creation, rebirth. This he did by the atonement of Jesus Christ. At the very least this means that Jesus was altogether righteous and thus could not have deserved the punishment of death or indeed any punishment at all. But he died a punitive death, on the Roman cross, to take the punishment for the sins of the human race. And though his atoning work is said to be all-sufficient, we are not out of the woods till we consciously embrace his sacrifice on our behalf. We have to admit we are sinners and accept a salvation we need and could never have earned. Those who do not consciously embrace the gospel of salvation will not receive its benefits.

IF JESUS IS THE ANSWER, WHAT IS THE QUESTION?

This salvation, this solution, raises more problems than it solves.

One: What about the future? Once converted, are you on your own with the sins you may commit before you die and get past the finish line? Many early Christians lived in fear and postponed baptism till their deathbed just to play it safe.

Two: If the change conversion makes is more than a clean slate ("Go and sin no more, lest something worse befall you" John 5:14), if it is rebirth as a new creature who walks in the Spirit, why do we still find pretty much the same old temptations and defeats awaiting us after the initial period of neophyte enthusiasm?

Three: Why should your response to the atonement, or even your knowledge of it, make any difference? If Christ died to save you, mustn't it have worked?

To make salvation depend on your believing in the atonement, i.e., in the doctrine of the atonement, aren't we simply saying you are saved by *cognitive* works? Maybe not *doing* the right thing, but by *believing* the right thing. This is the inevitable result once we say morally noble non-believers are not saved. The options would seem to be:

1. *You are saved by good works, regardless of your beliefs.* This means God's grace overlooks error in belief, but not immoral actions.

2. *You are saved by orthodox beliefs, regardless of your works.* This means God's grace overlooks immoral actions but not errors in belief. He is a strict theology professor, and he doesn't curve grades. But neither does he care how wild you party, as long as you study for the exam.

3. *Everyone is saved by the grace of God, regardless of their beliefs or deeds.*

4. The traditional popular Christian view, that you are saved by *a combination of faith and works* (a diversified portfolio), *each being necessary but neither being sufficient by itself. But in this case, grace has little to do with it.*

It seems to me that Christian theology has usually gone with number two. You are saved by right belief. When all is said and done, a "sinner" seems to mean simply "not a Christian believer," since the latter is the dangerous and depraved state from which one must be extricated. That is not to say that immoral behavior is ignored. No, specific sins are roundly condemned. But the crucial point is that *conversion does not necessarily change this.* If you're lucky, it may, but stories of such dramatic night-and-day turnabouts are tall tales that float around the evangelical community like water-cooler chatter about someone on TV who won the Lottery. Most lives are mediocre and stay that way, despite all the "Dieting with Jesus" books.

What conversion does change is your beliefs, or the intensity of them, or your membership in a particular religious group. So belief, being "in with the in-crowd" of the 144,000, is what matters. You can still commit sins and yet be a Christian, as the bumper sticker assures a surprised world: "Christians aren't perfect, just forgiven." And *why* are they, and *not you*, forgiven? Because they are Christians. Not because Christ has died for them. If that were all there was to it, why, then you, Mr. Satanist, you, Ms. Secular Humanist, would be forgiven, too! But there are no bumper stickers proclaiming *these* glad tidings.

No, *they* are forgiven because, unlike you, they *believe* Christ died for them. It all comes down to passing that exam. Thus the old joke is no joke: Junior sees his grampa reading the Bible and religious tracts and he asks mom why. She says, "He's cramming for his finals!" He'd *better*!

WHAT A TANGLED WEB WE WEAVE
WHEN WE PRACTISE TO BELIEVE

You see, Christianity did not bring into the world an answer to an ancient longing, a long-delayed salve for a festering wound. No, *it created the problem to be able to peddle the solution.* You only think you have the problem the Christian gospel will solve if you already accept the Christian bill of goods. Karl Barth put it euphemistically by saying that we are so blinded by sin that we do not even know the right question to ask till we hear the answer. But I think Dietrich Bonhoeffer was more to the point when he said Christianity survives by circling like a vulture, trying to make the healthy believe they're sick so they will buy the patent medicine we have to sell. Like asbestos in your basement: the stuff's only toxic once the environmental experts get there to remove it and start stirring up the dust of death.

How did the doctrine first emerge? Here is one plausible scenario. Jesus of Nazareth is put to death for anti-Roman sedition. His followers denied he deserved a criminal death; he was innocent of all charges. (Was he? That's another can of worms.) His disciples faced two options for understanding what had happened. Either he was a sinner abandoned by God to a richly deserved fate, which is what Jesus' enemies thought, or he did not deserve his fate. They believed the latter. But then a related problem had to be addressed: *how come*

God let him die? He wasn't being punished for any sins of his own. But death *is* a punishment for sin, so he must have died for *some* sins. It must have been the sins of *others*.

This was nothing new. Jewish martyrs' deaths were typically explained this way. At this stage of the game there was no central doctrine of an atonement. It was simply a rationalization for the otherwise apparent failure of divine providence to safeguard Jesus. The earliest Jewish Jesus sectarians probably did not view him as a savior in the now-traditional Christian sense at all. *Nor were they called Christians.* (The word "Christian" appears only three times in the New Testament, and in late writings, Acts and 1 Peter, and it is always a term applied by outsiders.) This is an important point, implying as it does that *Christianity as such did not exist till the atonement doctrine existed.* Thus the atonement is what constitutes a religion as Christian.

The atonement doctrine may well have emerged (as Sam K. Williams argues in *Jesus' Death as Saving Event*) as a piece of Hellenistic Jewish missionary theology. Gentile "God-fearers" admired Jewish theology and ethics, but they remained hangers-on at the margins of the synagogue, not full, circumcised proselytes, because they did not relish embracing the whole mass of Jewish dietary and ceremonial customs. Some of them began to join communities of Jews who expected the return of Jesus as the Messiah, and a new problem arose. Jews looked to the Jerusalem temple sacrifices to atone for their sins. Gentiles were beyond the pale, unclean before God, outside the Levitical system of sacrificial atonement. How could God accept them as full members of the household of faith? In other words, how could they now receive full admission to the synagogues of Jews who revered Jesus? We can see the controversy over this point in Paul's Epistle to the Galatians: do Gentile believers in Jesus have to become full proselytes to Judaism and keep the Torah regulations? Many Jewish Jesus sectarians assumed so. Remember, they weren't trying to start a new Jesus religion. That came later.

A big step in that direction was the theological answer to this question that said Gentiles did *not* have to keep the rituals of the Torah, because the death of Jesus had cleansed Gentile unholiness, like the atoning deaths of sacrificial animals had for the Jews. God had accepted Jesus' faithful martyr death as an atonement on the Gentiles' behalf. The Epistle to the Ephesians and 1 Peter both make this point clearly. Christ's death has included Gentiles in the Jewish fold. His death has torn down the Berlin Wall that separated Jew from Gentile.

What was it Gentiles needed to be saved *from*? Ritual uncleanness, being "unwashed heathen." Traditionally Jewish thought held that God required of Gentiles only the rudimentary commandments of Noah in Genesis 9, an elementary slate of decency laws. Non-Jews were not required to keep the 613 commandments of the Torah. Those were for Jews alone. Gentiles weren't damned, unless they were immoral pagans, whose idol-worship led them into immorality. Righteous Gentiles would be saved all right, but in the meantime, they just weren't part of the House of Israel. Even so, the question Paul and others faced was not whether Gentile God-fearers would be *damned*. The issue was whether they were entitled to full membership in the Household of God. And the death of Jesus provided for their adoption as sons and daughters, as Jews already were by birth. This early version of the atonement doctrine was still quite a different thing than it has since become.

The big change came once the Jesus sect had spread further in time and space beyond its Jewish origin. Since Jewish ritual taboos were dropped, the distinction between sin as ritual uncleanness and sin as moral guilt was lost. To say that Jesus died "for the world" first meant "for the *rest* of the world outside Israel," but now it came to mean "for the whole human race, *including* Jews." The original Jewish Jesus sect did not necessarily think their fellow Jews were damned for not believing in Jesus, any more than Rabbi Akiba would have damned Jews who didn't agree that Simon bar Kochba was the Messiah in 132 CE. But now Jesus was understood as the Savior from moral guilt and from divine damnation. So everyone had to jump on the bandwagon!

EPIDEMIC OF SALVATION

Here is the logic as I see it: Look, we've got an explanation for the death of Jesus that says he can't have died for sins of his own, so it must have been for someone else's. This means these others must have *needed* him to die for them. So their sin must have been something more serious than the Jewish concept of "spot sins" that could be dealt with by "spot forgiveness" here and there. Otherwise, why go to the trouble to send a divine savior? Again, Galatians: if things are still as they were under Judaism, then what was the point of Christ dying? It must have been necessary, so let's posit a condition serious enough to require it! That's original sin, total depravity, something going way beyond the *Yetzer Harah* (evil imagination) that Judaism ascribes to human nature.

Ironically, redemption theology only begins to make sense once you drop the expectation that it makes sense! That is, you only begin to see what's really going on once you recognize that it is not theoretically coherent. You can stop looking for the logic of the thing and start looking for the "psycho-logic" that went into it. It is not an inference inductively arrived at. It is an after-the-fact rationalization. You stop looking for the reasons that account for it, for there are none. You seek instead for what the atonement is *rationalizing*. E.P. Sanders recognizes this. He observes that Paul "thought backwards, from solution to plight, and . . . his thinking in this, as in many respects, was governed by the over-riding conviction that salvation is through Christ. Since Christ came to save all, all needed salvation . . . . Paul did not begin by analyzing the human situation" (*Paul, the Law, and the Jewish People*, 68).

How can the Christian be sure *every*one needs Christ's atonement? This is what we are asking when we tell the pushy evangelist that his faith is fine for *him*, but that we prefer another way. Why do I have to go your way? The answer, the real, psychological answer, is that "It *has* to be the way for everybody without exception. If it's only for *some* people, I won't know if I am one of the ones it *will* work for!"

Sometimes, like Paul, who claimed to have been the chief of sinners, an evangelist will say, "If it worked for me, it can work for anybody." But what this really means is, "Since it will work for everybody, then I can be sure, deductively, that it will work for me." The revival chorus celebrates "All sufficient grace for even me." I must have certainty! So for me to be sure the gospel will redeem *me*, I have to believe that *you* need it, too. Hence I cannot be satisfied thinking you might not need it. If I admit that something else might do the trick for you, I have to suspect that something else might work better for me, too. And since the much-vaunted claims that "Christ changed my life" are usually more statements of faith than accurate descriptions of experience, this suspicion would be fatal. I might then have to recognize that Christ is not living up to the advertising rhetoric and get back on the road looking for another panacea. And I'm sick of that.

A good but partial analogy might be the disingenuousness with which certain AIDS activists warn us that heterosexuals are every bit as much at risk as homosexuals are. The assumption is that straights will not get serious about stamping out AIDS if they don't think *everyone* needs a cure or vaccine for it.

It's another version of the problem that plagues Calvinists. God predestines the elect to be saved; there's no way they can fumble the ball. So the belief in predestination should be a source of great reassurance, right? Calvin thought so. But he was wrong. His successors realized that since one could never be sure one was in fact one of the elect, *since not everybody was*, there was more reason to worry than ever before! This is pretty much the same anxiety that the Christian evangelist is trying to fend off by insisting that you need his gospel, too, whether you like it or not. If it's not for everyone without exception, it may not be for him either. And the fundamentalist wants nothing so much as security.

Once unleashed, the doctrine of the atonement runs amok like a computer virus, corrupting every file. Once the question arises as to how sin could first have entered the picture in Eden, how the Fall of Adam was even possible in the first place, God himself gets implicated. (And it *is him*self, not "herself" half the time, because I am willing to argue that the maleness of God is a structural necessity in traditional Christian theology, the kind we are discussing here.) The logic will sound familiar to us by now, though no less pernicious. And Calvinists did not hesitate to embrace it. God, being all-knowing and all-powerful, cannot, in the nature of the case, have merely waited to see whether Adam would obey or disobey him. No, God must actually have *caused* the Fall of Adam. Oh, don't worry, Francis Turretin reassures us, God didn't force Adam's hand. He just pulled the plug of sustaining grace at the crucial moment so that Adam lacked the wherewithal to resist Satan's temptation. (As if that gets God off the hook! At least it shows the uneasy conscience of the Calvinist in the matter.) Why would the Almighty pull such a stunt? Well . . . if it's not broke you can't fix it, and God had this little plan of salvation in his pocket, see?

This doesn't sound kosher to you? Despite their protests that it all makes perfect sense, theologians know how it sounds to any fair-minded person. "You will say to me, then, 'Why does he still find fault? For who can resist his will?' But who are you, a mere mortal, to answer back to God? Will what is molded say to its molder, 'Why have you made me thus'?" (Romans 9:19–20). In other words, *Sit down and shut up!* But we are *not* answering back to God; we are answering back to fellow mortals who seem to think they are God. Mortals who think it lies in their power to condemn you to Hell for not believing in the doctrine of the atonement.

APOLOGETICS MEANS NEVER HAVING TO SAY YOU'RE SORRY

Once things assume such nightmarishly surreal proportions, wouldn't you think someone would conclude their theory had, like Bugs Bunny, made a wrong turn at Albuquerque? How much more could the atonement doctrine find itself reduced to absurdity? By now, merely to explain it is to refute it. Perhaps it is no surprise, given the male monopoly on theology, that theologians would show the male propensity, when hopelessly lost, to just keep going and not ask directions. To stop and double back now would be too devastating an admission of error. It is all a matter of cognitive dissonance reduction. If you're hell-bent on hanging on to the paradigm of classical Christianity, there is no expedient you won't seize upon to patch the rags.

Wilfred Cantwell Smith hits the nail on the head:

> Actually the only basis on which their position can and does rest is a logical inference. It seems to them a theoretical implication of what they themselves consider to be true, that other people's faith *must* be illusory. Personally, I think that this is to put far too much weight on logical implication. There have been innumerable illustrations of man's capacity for starting from some cogent theoretical position and then inferring from it logically something else that at the time seems to him persuasive but that in fact turns out on practical examination not to hold. It is far too sweeping to condemn the great majority of mankind to lives of utter meaninglessness and perhaps to Hell, simply on the basis of what seems to some individuals the force of logic . . . . The damnation of my neighbor is too weighty a matter to rest on a syllogism. (*The Faith of Other Men*, 122–123)

But such hobgoblin consistency is just what we might expect, seeing that the whole thing *began* as a cognitive dissonance reduction maneuver. In the wake of the execution of Jesus, somehow virtue had to be made of necessity. The atonement doctrine was the result. Otherwise, "Christ died to no purpose" (Galatians 2:21). And we can't have that. We can't brook genuine tragedy. It must have a happy ending. Forgive me for paraphrasing Paul: "I have been crucified with Christ; it is no longer I who live, but Christ lives in me; and the life I now live in the flesh I live in denial."

The history of the doctrine of the atonement is a long series of proposals for lending some sense to the thing. One grotesque analogy follows another, but, recalling what the Epistle to the Hebrews said of the Levitical sacrifices, if any one of them had possessed any merit, the rest wouldn't have been necessary!

It is not merely a question of cross-cultural equivalencies, finding the appropriate counterpart in our cultural frame of reference. The problem is that of a drastic discontinuity of values between the biblical culture and our own, something far more serious than the ancients believing heaven was literally above us, while we imagine it as, I suppose, another dimension. No, the whole atonement transaction presupposes the ancient confusion of criminal law with tort law, as if the sins of the world merely required a fine which a generous friend could pay off for us. Once one sees the logical difference between the two, as we have long ago drawn the distinction between astronomy and astrology, we should see that the atonement doctrine really has *nothing at all to do with justice as we define it.* The closest analogy in our justice system might be a friend posting bail for a criminal pending trial. This is a buying of someone's freedom by paying the price he cannot pay for himself. But I doubt that this is really adequate. And nothing else is.

If we bemoan the unreasonableness of Christian spokesmen who insist on belief in the cross, we should not be surprised at it. How can one hold fast to such a doctrine *except* unreasonably? If they could coherently explain it to anyone's satisfaction, you can be sure they would.

ARE YOU LONELY TONIGHT?

There is a terrible irony when modern theologians claim that, against critiques like mine, some sense *can* be made of the atonement. We are not talking anymore about a savior of sick mankind. Now we are talking about whether we can save the ailing doctrine of the atonement itself. It is like the Ottoman Empire in its declining days, "the Sick Man of Europe." It is no longer saving *us*; *we* must save *it.* But I say, why bother? The patient's brain-dead; why bankrupt the family by paying for the life-support contraption? Pull the plug!

But can the centrality of Jesus Christ be maintained without the doctrine of the atonement? If he is not central in this way, what is left? Harry Emerson Fosdick held that it is "the personality of Jesus" (as if we knew anything about it) that is "the soul of Christianity." But this is to make Christianity into sentimental fan-worship, a maudlin personality cult like the Elvis Cult. Or suppose we hold, as Tillich did, that we value Jesus only insofar as that which is Jesus in him yields to that which is Christ in him, so that he becomes a perfect window through which we can behold God. If Jesus in this way tells us anything about God we did not know before, then it is something his individual personhood has contributed, and we are back to worshiping him. To say that "God is like Jesus" is really to say we worship Jesus as a god. Ritschl admitted it when he redefined the Incarnation as the belief that "Jesus has the value of God for us."

But, as I said at the start, the essence of Christianity, as of anything else, is a variable, a moving target. The center of gravity may change as the movement evolves into new shapes. I think that, measured by the most successful forms of globe-circling Christian denominations, Christianity is consolidating itself into a differernt sort of religion that does not depend upon the atonement doctrine, though that doctrine is usually (residually) cherished by the Christians I am thinking of. I believe that we are witnessing the transformation of Christianity into a devotional cult where the criterion of salvation is emotional committment to a chosen savior and the projective psychology of a personal relationship with him. The analogy with the Elvis cult is unflattering, though telling. But a more charitable comparison would be to the Hindu-Buddhist cults of *Bhakti* in which the devotee chooses (or inherits) a divine savior (Ram, Krishna, Kali, Avalokiteshvara, Amida, Siva, Chaitanya), usually believed to have been an ancient mortal avatar of a God. And one dedicates every breathing moment to the personal savior as a living sacrifice of praise, seeking not mundane reward (karma) but rather the saving grace of the Bhagavad.

Though the Gospel of John is quite amenable to such devotional reading, in the process becoming a Christian counterpart to the Bhagavad Gita, I am persuaded that such Christianity never dawned till the Pietist Movement of the Eighteenth Century. That is when belief- and sacrament-centered Christianity (both based on the atonement doctrine) began to share ground with, then to give ground to, devotional, *bhakti* Christianity. This is when we began to hear from the mouths of the most vocal Christians that one could believe as earnestly as one chose in the Christian creed yet not be a real Christian without the "heart-warming" experience of true grace. "Have you accepted Jesus Christ as your personal savior?"

Such is the shibboleth of Pietism. One can be a Pietist and a believer in atonement theology. The two go well together, as they do in the religion of Avalokiteshvara, the Bodhisattva of compassion who suffers in hell for his devotees, among other favors. But the mere fact that an individual entity is available to do such a thing shows that the focus has shifted from the balance of karma or the technique of self-salvation through Yoga, to a person-centered cult, a personality cult. Some sparks of the same mystic fire have ignited some quarters in Hassidic Judaism, when the personified Sabbath is pictured as giving the damned a periodic day of respite. Yes, evangelical Pietists can believe in the atonement, but I say it has become theologically secondary.

We have witnessed a cameo of this larger transformation of Roman Catholicism in the United States in the form of the Catholic Charismatic

Movement as of 1967, when a group of educators, priests, and nuns, all read Pentecostal David Wilkerson's autobiographical *The Cross and the Switchblade* and sought initiation into the Pentecostal experience. They and their burgeoning movement remained within the Catholic framework, soothing the occasional jitters of the hierarchy. Their influence has since thoroughly permeated the Catholic Church in the United States, so that Catholic laity are urged to undertake a personal relationship with Christ in terms reminiscent of Baptist revivalism. Personal savior Pietism has become the most popular form of Christianity on earth, just as it has dominated Buddhism in the form of Pure Land Buddhism, founded upon the saving grace of Amida (Amitabha) Buddha, appropriated by faith by his devotees who henceforth live a life of goodness as gratitude for salvation. While some may understandably call the dominance of Pure Land Buddhism a Westernizing of Buddhism, it shows no real sign of having been influenced by Christianity. It seems rather to have asked similar questions and supplied similar answers in parallel, like the emergence of homologous structures among different animal specieis (wings on flies, birds, pterodactyls, and bats). And I would rather switch the terms around and suggest that we are witnessing the shift in religious evolution to where Christianity will best be understood theologically, not by comparison to Judaism, but rather in comparison with Buddhism and Hinduism.

9

A MESS OF MIRACLES

In my opinion, miracles are much more trouble than they're worth. Often used as a line of defense on behalf of religion, they are actually just giving your enemy more targets to shoot at.

Even if a miracle actually happened, if a contemporary could have videotaped it, still, without benefit of time travel, today's historian could never render the judgment that it "probably" happened (the best verdict the historian can ever render). The rarity of such an event (reported or actual) means there will be no historical analogies at hand with which to compare it and render it likely. What sort of mark does a freak phenomenon leave behind? How do you verify such a thing? What signs do you look for? If we read that Samson slaughtered 1, 000 men single-handedly (Judges 15:15), we cannot consider it "probably authentic" because, while there may be fictional or legendary parallels to it, there are no known historical examples. If there were, it might look different. Say, if we had other cases that showed us how it had been done or might be done.

Then there is the nagging fact that the miracles of the gospels were "done in a corner," unlike the Technicolor wonders of Exodus and Elijah. The more spectacular gospel miracles are set in private. The Transfiguration (Mark 9:2–4) was seen by only three people who were told to keep it under their turbans (Mark 9:9). No one but the twelve disciples knew about the multiplication of loaves and fish (Mark 6:35–44; 8:1–9), not the crowd. Only the twelve were on the scene when Jesus stilled the storm (Mark 4:35–41) and walked on the water

(Mark 6:45–52). Only the steward at the Cana wedding feast understood what had happened, besides the disciples (John 2:1–11). The risen Jesus appeared to a grand total of two people on the Emmaus road (Luke 24:13–35), to disciples on lonely beaches (John 21:1–14) and behind locked doors (John 20:19–29). (The 500 brethren appear only in 1 Corinthians 15:6, a sure sign the story did not yet exist when the gospels were written.) We have to ask reasonably whether all this is clever excuse- making for why no one knew about it at the time. (The question of exorcisms and healings, performed before many crowds, is different. Such scenes are common today and were in the ancient world; no one would have denied that such things happened. They don't prove anything today, and they didn't then.)

Theologians tell us that the miracles function as signs to create faith, but this is a vicious circle. If we are just supposed to believe something for its own sake, why are proofs offered? Is it supposed to be faith, or not? And if miracles are deemed needful, why are they ambiguous and indefinite, in need of proof themselves? Since they become the object of their own apologetics, they become objects of faith in their own right, obstacles rendering the original object of faith secondary. Tillich calls this "idolatrous faith." The resurrection is supposed to aid and abet faith in Jesus, but then we need evidence for the resurrection, so we must believe in the resurrection of Jesus, and not just in Jesus himself. An irony. It's like bringing in the Shroud of Turin as proof, then having to defend it! So now it's Jesus, the resurrection, and the shroud! The line of defense just keeps growing!

Also, the very idea of historically verifying miracles is utterly ironic because an event that can be comprehended by the criteria used to verify it cannot transcend those criteria. They will explain it adequately. If they don't, if there is an inexplicable element left over that science cannot explain, to that extent the miracle has not after all been verified. By contrast, K.A. Kitchen, in his book *Ancient Orient and Old Testament* (as James Barr points out in his great book *Fundamentalism*), defends the historical nature of the Egyptian plagues in Exodus by showing that most of them occur naturally in the wake of the periodic flooding of the Nile. So why should the historian have any trouble accepting them? (Or, more to the point, why not accept the unity of the Exodus narrative, chapters 7–12, which contains the whole series, instead of divvying it up between J and E, each of which mentioned only a few plagues?). The Plagues have been rendered historically likely precisely to the extent that we need no longer consider them miraculous! Same with Mathew's star: if it really turned out to be a nova or a planetary conjunction, then is Matthew right? If so, it was no miracle after all. Apologists do not see that they are playing the old game of the eighteenth-century rationalist theologians. Where did the Swoon Theory of the crucifixion come from? It is a piece of apologetics! You see, the historian can see his way to accept the Easter stories if he decides there was no silly miracle connecting one gospel scene (the cross) with the other (the appearances of Jesus). Both scenes can be accepted if we simply omit the supernatural causation! Voila! The resurrection narratives are true, even though the resurrection itself isn't! That's where they're headed and they don't see it.

And the silliest apologetics arguments are those pointing to archaeological verification of the Bible (e.g., Sodom did exist) as if it confirmed a miracle story involving the place (fire and brimstone rained down on it—though this one is often explained on purely scientific grounds and rendered no longer miraculous, too!). If a village called Nain existed, does this mean Jesus raised a dead person there? We know Oral Roberts University exists. What we don't know is whether an 800 feet high Jesus appeared to Oral there.

Another common approach to defending the miracle stories of the Bible is to blur the line between the supernatural and the natural. What seemed miraculous might turn out to be then-unknown science. The biblical authors just didn't know how to explain what was going on in terms that would satisfy modern science. Suppose we knew that Jesus was virginally conceived by means of advanced science. What are we saying? If it wasn't supernaturalism, was it space aliens? If Jesus did things that seemed miraculous to his contemporaries but it was actually scientific, how'd he know how to do it? Was he a time-traveler from the future? Like Dr. McCoy in the barbaric 20th-century hospital in *Star Trek IV*?

Philosopher D.Z. Phillips has pointed out something else relevant to this point. He asks just how mind-blowing a dining hall would have to be for a Viking to conclude it was Valhalla. Old Thorlief, knocked out (or killed?) on the battlefield, awakens surrounded by tall, buxom redheads treating his wounds. They lead him into a banqueting hall, lined with shields and filled with warriors quaffing jacks of mead, munching joints of beef. Where should he conclude he is? Valhalla? It's pretty impressive all right, but can it live up to his lifelong fantasies of the posthumous Hall of Heroes? No matter what he saw, couldn't it always be imagined as just a bit snazzier?

I think, too, of an old *Penthouse* cartoon: two guys are sitting on a splitting

Naugahide couch in a shabby room with cracked plaster and a single naked light bulb hanging from the ceiling. They are wearing starchy sheets with wire haloes over their heads. On the wall, a tilted plaque reads "Heaven." One guy says to the other, "Somehow I always thought it would be classier than this." Suppose, as he once tried to do, Pat Robertson managed to videotape the descent of Christ to the Mount of Olives and televised it. Wouldn't even the most pious believer have to wonder whether he were the victim of an elaborate joke? "Wait a minute . . . how can I be sure that's really the Second Coming?" What would it take?

Phillips says all this implies people are not really believing in literal realities even when they imagine that they are! What would it take to measure up to what they secretly imagine? Anything at all? Nothing could match it because really there is no literal referent! Ask a fundamentalist, what does he think it looked like for Jesus to multiply the loaves? Did they stretch like sponges? Ask him if the divine Christ, treading the dusty roads of Palestine, remembered the good old days when he created the planet Pluto.

Ask him what he expects to happen and not to happen to him because a miracle- working God is watching over him. What concrete difference does it make? Does he expect the angelic cavalry to march over the hill to get him out of a tight spot? Has it ever happened? Why not? Doesn't his pious rhetoric suggest it? Or is he just a Stoic, willing to take whatever Fate happens to dish out to him? He doesn't really believe alleged miracles of the past provide any guide for what he may expect in his own experience. What does he really have in mind, besides a worn-out slogan?

In the end, I think people's "beliefs" are not really assertions and affirmations about supposed events. I suspect they are slogans, and that if you repeat the right ones, you're in the group, in with the in-crowd. The whole thing's more a matter of social psychology than of metaphysical belief. I guess I'm no longer in the club. If I were, believe me, it'd be a miracle.

10

THE MARGINALITY OF THE CROSS

Is it possible that the significance of the cross in the New Testament has been overrated? Can it be that, at least in significant portions of the New Testament, we have become used to reading familiar texts through the even more familiar lens of Western atonement theologies? It is hard sometimes to remember that doctrines have grown from the seeds of individual verses and that, by themselves, those verses have a more modest meaning. I grant that in most of the Pauline epistles and 1 Peter we find a great, even a central, focus on the redemption wrought through the crucifixion death of Jesus. But I wonder if another look at the gospels will support a similar evaluation of the cruciality of the cross there. I suspect not. It will be a question of what significance the cross has, for the sheer amount of space all the gospels devote to the Passion certainly means the event was important. But are the gospels based on a Pauline-type (or later orthodox) belief in world atonement? Not exactly. For my contention will be that the gospels place the significance of the cross in theological contexts largely alien to subsequent Christian theology.

MARK: "RIM CRATER OF REDEMPTION"

Theodore J. Weeden, in one of those truly ground-breaking books in New Testament scholarship, *Mark: Traditions in Conflict*,[1] sets forth the case that Mark has taken over a then-familiar pattern of Jesus-faith that cast Jesus in the role of a divine man (*theios aner*), an inspired superman or demigod.[2]

There are many such characters in the religious literature of the time, including Empedocles, Pythagoras, Apollonius of Tyana, even Moses as the Hellenistic Jews Josephus and Philo of Alexandria depict him. Connected to such a conception of Christ would have been a charismatic, triumphalistic "enthusiasm" such as that discerned in first-century Corinth by Ernst Käsemann[3] and others. For them the apocalyptic glory of the Kingdom of God was already present in the miraculous powers at work in Jesus and in Christians as they practiced supernatural arts of healing and prophecy. In the fashion of later messianic movements like that of Jacob Frank in the seventeenth century,[4] such Christians may have been libertines, regarding the prohibitions of the Torah as obsolete in an age of perfection when nothing could any longer count as sin. Martyrdom would take such Christians by surprise, and Gnostic Christians considered themselves fully entitled to engage in dissimulation (or as it is called today, "heavenly deception")[5] to avoid suffering to which they viewed themselves as superior and thus exempt in Christ.[6]

Weeden acknowledged that Mark's Jesus is still a superman, walking on water, silencing demons, feeding the multitudes with heavenly supplies. But Weeden sees Mark as periodically trying to bring the hot air balloon of such hero-cult faith safely down to earth or, to change the metaphor, to recall Icarus from his high-flying proximity to the sun before it was too late. Weeden's Mark took seriously the martyrdom facing Christians and feared, like the writer to the Hebrews, that the close approach of martyrdom would shatter superficial faith, puncture the balloon. He fears for the fair-weather believers he builds into the interpretation of the Parable of the Sower (or, as some call it, of the Soils, Mark 4:16–17). And so Weeden's Mark pauses the gospel train to glory periodically to warn the reader that the way of discipleship to Jesus is the way of suffering, the way of the cross.

The most important such pressing of the brakes occurs in the Caesarea Philippi scene of Peter's confession (Mark 8:27–38). No sooner does Peter confess his faith in Jesus as the Christ than Jesus tells him the Son of Man must soon be martyred, though he will also rise from the dead. There follows the summons to the crowd (really, to Mark's readers, since no one on the scene could have made the connection)[7] that if you are to follow Jesus, you must take up your own cross and follow him to your own Golgotha.

The Markan apocalypse (chapter 13) goes into some detail outlining the persecutions Christian readers may expect if they are faithful (verses 9–13). The storm clouds have gathered in Mark's day, and he is trying to prepare immature Christians for the storm, lest they become disillusioned by it, like a child who repudiates faith in God when his prayers for a pony go unanswered.[8] To borrow a term from Reinhold Niebuhr, Weeden's Mark was trying to sketch a Christology of "Christian Realism." But it is important to note that even on Weeden's reading, the heightened import of the cross has nothing really to do with soteriology. Rather, the cross is a model for dedicated discipleship in a time of martyrdom.

In a sense, Weeden comes close to positing not a mere change of emphasis in Mark's retelling of the gospel tale, but to making Mark the inventor of the Passion Narrative. This is because he argues[9] in great and, to me, convincing detail that, of the New Testament evangelists, Mark and John evidence such striking parallels with Josephus' account of the arrest, interrogation, flogging, and eventual death of the Jerusalem prophet Jesus ben-Ananias (*Wars of the Jews* 6.5.3) that they simply must have known the story and even borrowed it for Jesus. Mark and John must have known of previous preaching of "Christ crucified" (such as we read in the Pauline epistles, albeit—and this is significant—with absolutely no narrative or socio-political context). But when it came time to tell a story, Mark and John borrowed one that lay ready to hand, that of "another Jesus" (2 Corinthians 11:4).

The pre-Markan version of Jesus as a divine hero would have contained some form of a trial and martyrdom, and the presence of such plot elements in no way infringes on the nature of the narrative as that of a triumphant superman who cannot be kept down. Indeed, the trial and execution of Jesus would make sense (I think most sense) as the darkness before the dawn. Just as Apollonius easily escapes the ire of Domitian (Philostratus, *Life of Apollonius of Tyana* 8.8), so does Jesus finally elude the grasp of Pontius Pilate. Whether Jesus was originally shown surviving the cross, as several data in the gospels imply (see my *Deconstructing Jesus*)[10] or as rising from genuine death hardly matters. Even if truly dead, he is dead for only a day and a half. The Passion Narrative then, does not in itself imply a focus on the saving death of Jesus Christ. It is rather that predictable portion of a heroic saga in which the initial glory of the hero is set aside by a temporary reversal of fortune so that his final victory does not seem to come too cheap and easily.

It seems to me that we are in the presence of any sort of atonement talk only at the Last Supper, Mark 14:24, "This is my blood of the [new?] covenant, which is poured out for many" and its twin text, Mark 10:45, "For the Son of Man also came not to be served but to serve, and to give his life as a ransom for many." What we have here, as Loisy pointed out, is a piece of cult liturgy, not historical memory.[11] But what is the intended scope of this sacrifice? Without reviewing the whole history of the tradition, it is sufficient here to note that the language of "giving one's life as a ransom for many" is martyrdom language familiar from Hellenistic Judaism and expresses the hope that the sufferings of the persecuted righteous may avail in the eyes of God to expiate the sins of those unfaithful Jews whose laxity has caused God to send the persecution (2 Maccabees 7:38, "Through me and my brothers, may there be an end to the wrath of the Almighty that has justly fallen on our whole nation." Also 4 Maccabees 6:28–29, "Be merciful to your people, and let our punishment suffice for them. Make my blood their purification, and take my life in exchange for theirs."). To find here a statement that Jesus means to die for the human race as a whole, and in future ages, is gratuitous. The scope of the language, which is all we have to go on, is more restricted and modest.

"Blood of the covenant" represents a midrashic attempt to understand the death of Jesus as a sacrifice performed to seal or renew a covenant between God and the Jewish people, as in Exodus 24:8. Such a theology is spelled out in great detail in the Epistle to the Hebrews. Matthew uses similar language, derived from Mark, and the whole structure of his gospel justifies it, as we will see in the next section. But in Mark, it falls like a bolt from the blue. It makes no more sense in the narrative context than does the fleeing away naked of the young man in the Garden (Mark 14:51–52). The formula seems to have been carried along by Mark since he found it present in the bit of liturgy known to him from his congregation's sacraments. But he does not bother working it into the plot or even into the teaching of Jesus as he presents it elsewhere.

Is the cross as a saving deed pivotal for Mark? Even important? Perhaps not. At most, to borrow Albert Schweitzer's metaphor for the marginality of Justification by Faith in Pauline theology,[12] the cross in Mark is at best a "rim-crater" on the literary lunar surface.

MATTHEW: SANGUINARY SEAL

Matthew's gospel, a wide-ranging expansion of Mark's, provides a theological context, if only by suggestion, in which Mark's eucharistic utterance makes sense. His Jesus elaborates: "This is my blood of the [new?] covenant, which is poured out for many for forgiveness of sins" (Matthew 26:28). We should love to know the precise significance of the added phrase "for forgiveness of sins."

Does it imply something deeper, a la Paul and the Epistle to the Hebrews, about the expunging of the moral failures and flaws of the contrite heart, in contrast to the apparently purely ritual expiation of ritual trespasses entailed in the Mosaic sacrifice system? If the sacrifice of the blood of Jesus is taken to inaugurate a *new* covenant, as in several manuscripts of both Matthew and Mark, would this added moral and/or psychological dimension be the relevant novelty? It might be that the purification of Gentile sinfulness (Galatians 2:15) is in view here. As Sam K. Williams argued in *Jesus' Death as Saving Event*,[13] the death of Jesus may first have taken on sacrificial coloring in the minds of Hellenistic Jewish Christians as a means whereby God might make the newly converted Gentiles (reeking of ham sandwiches and shrimp cocktails) acceptable to himself, something Jewish believers did not need, having already grown up in the covenant with its purifying taboos and sacrifices. Such a question must have engaged Matthew's attention, given his own identity as a Hellenized (trilingual) Jew committed to the niceties of Torah, probably resident in Antioch, the hub of the Gentile Mission.

The echo we hear in Mark/Matthew of the Mosaic saying, "Behold the blood of the covenant which Yahve has made with you in accordance with all these commandments" (Exodus 24:8) makes ample sense in Matthew because of the Matthean "new Moses" theme. As is well known, Matthew likes to depict Jesus issuing revelation atop a mountain, whence he delivers the Sermon on the Mount (Q apparently gave no location, since Luke has a Sermon on the Plain) and issues the Great Commission. He is transfigured like Moses on the mountain top, a scene borrowed from Mark, but brought into closer conformity to its Mosaic prototype by having Jesus' face (not just his clothing) glow like the sun (compare Mark 9:3; Matthew 17:2; Exodus 34:29). And if Moses was the mediator of the original Pentateuch, Matthew deems it scarcely less fitting for Jesus to be the messenger of a new one. This is why he divides (somewhat arbitrarily) the teachings of Jesus into five great sections: the Sermon on the Mount (chapters 5–7), the Mission Charge (10), the Parables (12), the Manual of Discipline (18–19), and the Denunciation of the Pharisees/Olivet Discourse (23–25). Given its inconsistently topical organization, we may feel there ought to have been a Hexateuch, dividing the last section into two, but the fact that Matthew joined the last two topics in such a forced manner only shows how determined he was for the thing to come out to five. It is to these five "books" of the teaching of Jesus that we must look for the content intended in the Great Commission: "Make disciples of all nations, teaching them to observe everything I have commanded you" (28:19–20). Furthermore, the wording of the Commission at this point again recalls that of Moses' phrase "in accordance with all these commandments" (Exodus 24:8).

In view of these Mosaic parallels, especially to Exodus 24:8, surely we are to understand Jesus' eucharistic saying in Matthew as a counterpart to the Exodus prototype, "Behold the blood of the covenant." The parallel may go even further as we will shortly see, but for the present let us note that the general trend of the parallel is to appropriate Jeremiah's theme of the post-Exilic New Covenant (Jeremiah 31:31–34), whence also the addition "for forgiveness of sins" also probably comes: "for I will forgive their iniquity, and their sin I will remember no more" (Jeremiah 31:34). Thus it is a matter of indifference, at least in Matthew, whether the original text had Jesus speak of the covenant or of the *new* covenant. The point is the same.

A final Matthean parallel to the scene of Exodus 24:8 must claim our attention. To what, precisely, was Moses directing the attention of the Israelites on that fateful day when he bade them "Behold the blood of the covenant"? Back up just a little, if you please: "Then he took the book of the covenant and read it in the hearing of the people, and they said, 'All that Yahve has spoken we will do, and we will be obedient.' So Moses took the blood and sprinkled it on the people, and said, 'Behold the blood of the covenant, which Yahve has made with you in accordance with all these commandments" (Exodus 24:7–8). These words seem to possess a familiar ring, and yet what a surprise to realize where their counterparts occur! "Once Pilate realized he was getting nowhere, only that a riot was brewing, he took water and washed his hands in plain view, saying, 'I am innocent of this man's blood! See to it yourselves!' And all the people said, 'His blood be on us and all our children!'" (Matthew 27:24–25).

On any traditional reading, Matthew is signing the death-warrant of future generations of "Christ-killing" Jews. They have invited divine reprisal, albeit unwittingly, as if a sincere but mistaken person should exclaim, "And may God strike me dead if I'm wrong!" Persecutors of Jews in the name of Jesus Christ have too often read these words and satisfied their consciences, saying, "Well, they asked for it!" But is this Matthew's intent?

Admittedly, Matthew regarded the fall of Jerusalem as judgment for the generation that rejected Jesus' call to share the banqueting table of his Father. Matthew has interpolated such an unmistakable lesson (Matthew 22:6–7) into the middle of the Great Supper parable which he had from Q (Mathew 22:2–5, 8–10; Luke 14:16–24). If he means to have the Jewish mob before Pilate represent the people as a whole, then the reference to "all our children" at least need denote no more than the very next generation, an adjustment required to link the fall of Jerusalem in 70 CE with the death of Jesus a generation before.

But one dares to wonder, in light of the parallel to Exodus 24:7–8, whether what Matthew intends here is the embrace by the Jewish people, perhaps despite themselves, of the covenant sacrifice of Jesus, about to transpire. We would then have an exact parallel to John 11:47–53, with its Balaam-like prophecy of the saving death of Jesus: "'it is expedient for you that one man die for the people, and that the whole nation not perish.' Now he did not say this on his own initiative, but being high priest that year, he prophesied that Jesus was going to die for the nation, and not for the nation only, but that he might gather together into one the children of God who are scattered abroad" (John 11:50–52).

If this should prove to be the real intention of Matthew, the implications would be far-reaching indeed. But for our purposes, the point is that the passage would complete the parallel between Exodus 24:7–8 and various portions of Matthew, implying strongly that the evangelist intended the death of Jesus as a saving event in the particular sense that it inaugurated a new covenant of faithful observance of the Torah and the commandments of Jesus, the new Moses.

We are far here from any sort of Paulinism, much less any traditional orthodox soteriology. One might invoke the theology of the Epistle to the Hebrews, which is usually located in the Paulinist orbit: does it not similarly suppose that Christ brought a new covenant, sealed in his blood? And is not the result apparently the wholesale dispensing with the ritual regulations of the Torah? Not at all. (Our task here is to expound the teaching of the gospels, not the epistles; the relevant issue is whether Hebrews casts any light on Matthew.) The sympathies of Hebrews would seem to lie more in the direction of the Dead Sea Scrolls community, given (among other things) the mention of repeated baptisms (Hebrews 10:22) and the esoteric doctrine of Melchizedek (chapter 7). It is not evident that the writer to the Hebrews envisioned believers as forsaking ritual observance. All his talk about the superannuation and obsolescence of the temple sacrifice system is better understood as a kind of theodicy for the fall of the temple in 70 CE.[14] The end of the sacrifices need not have entailed suspension of other laws, as the Javneh deliberations of Rabbinic Judaism make perfectly clear. But absolutely no doubt can remain about Matthew: he certainly believed exhaustive legal observance was incumbent upon every disciple.

Matthew 5:17–19 even condemns Pauline Christians for so much as relaxing commandments, and the least important ones at that. Remember, too, that Matthew 23:23 congratulates the Pharisees for tithing garden herbs, though he faults them for neglecting weightier issues (unlike the Q original, preserved for us only in Marcion's text, where Luke 11:42 lacks "without neglecting the others").

Is the cross central to this plan of salvation? Hardly. One senses that Matthew would have been quite satisfied with a Jesus who died at a ripe old age, like his brother Simon bar-Cleophas, like Johannon ben-Zakkai, and like Moses, at 120 years. Matthew can make a place for the cross, as inaugurating the New Covenant, but this is just because he finds the fact of Jesus' death unavoidable. The Dead Sea Scrolls sect lived the life of the New Covenant, too, but they did it without any doctrine of human sacrifice. (Indeed, Robert Eisenman suggests[15] that the Markan/Matthean "new covenant in my blood" is a pun on and derivative from the Qumran term "new covenant of Damascus," since the Hebrew for "blood" is *dam*, while "cup" is *chos*. Paul and others, initially part of the Dead Sea Scrolls community and partakers of their communal "messianic" meals, Eisenman postulates, carried the idea of the supper (and even the original Hebrew phraseology for it) with them when they apostatized from the Torah-zealous movement and preached a law-free gospel to Gentiles instead. The "Covenant of Damascus" thus became the "covenant of the blood cup," assimilating the rite to the Mystery Cult sacraments with which the Gentile converts were already familiar. Thus the connection with the death of a divine savior, Jesus, would represent a secondary understanding of the ritual.

LUKE: MISSION AND OMISSION

The Third Evangelist's antipathy for cross-based soteriology is well known, if not entirely understood. It is not that he denies the reality of the crucifixion in the manner of Christian docetists, Basilides, or the Koran (4:156–159). No, it is just that, for Luke, the cross is important in a secondary sense. While not a sufficient condition for salvation as it is for Paul, it is a necessary condition. That is, while the cross is not the thing that saves believers, it forms a necessary hurdle for him who would be Christ. This is the thrust of the scripture survey the Unknown Christ imparts to his Emmaus disciples on the road: "Was it not required of the Christ to suffer these trials, and only then to enter into his splendor?" (Luke 24: 26). They had entertained the vain hope (as they came to view it) that Jesus might be the one to "redeem" (i.e., to liberate) Israel. But, they concluded, Jesus' terrible fate disqualified him. Back to the drawing board. Next time maybe Menachem the Zealot. But, no. Jesus tells them they had it all wrong: the crucifixion was predicted. It was on the true messiah's agenda. Thus any candidate who shunned the cross could never qualify! Thus the crucified Jesus deserves a second look.

It is a brilliant *tour de force*, albeit a manifest case of transforming necessity into virtue. At any rate, we are not surprised to read this much. What may surprise us is the utter lack, here or anywhere else in Luke-Acts, of any mention of the saving virtue of the cross. When Jesus teleports back to Jerusalem (thoughtlessly leaving the Emmaus pair to hoof it under their own steam), he reasons similarly with the eleven: "Scripture stipulates that the Christ must needs suffer and, on the third day following, return from the dead, and that [a message of] repentance and forgiveness should be preached in [association with] his name to all nations, radiating outward from Jerusalem" (Luke 24:46–47). What is "missing" from this scenario? Any link between the death of Jesus and the efficacy of repentance for forgiveness. True, if Jesus had not died, repentance would not be preached in his name. If Christ had not died, our faith should be in vain. But there is not a word of his death enabling or effecting our salvation.

The same tendency can be seen in the apostolic speeches (all Luke's work, if that even needs to be asserted anymore). In Peter's Pentecost sermon we learn of a startling reversal: "this Jesus, delivered by the fixed plan and foreknowledge of God, you crucified and killed by the hands of unwashed pagans. But God raised him up" (Acts 2:23–24a). Whence salvation? That is another matter. It stems from Jesus' exaltation to heaven: "having received from the Father the promise [of Joel] that he would dispense the Holy Spirit, he has poured out [the signs] that you see and hear" (Acts 2:33a). "Repent and be baptized, each one of you, in the name of Jesus Christ for the forgiveness of your sins; and you will receive the gift of the Holy Spirit" (Acts 2:38). Again, one looks in vain for any link between the death of Jesus (itself no mistake, but a predestined milestone) and the salvation of believers. We read only that Jesus is the name which makes baptism effective and entitles one to the reception of the Spirit.

Peter proclaims both the death of Jesus (with its dramatic reversal and foreordination, 3:13–15, 18–19) and the salvation available through his name (Acts 3:16), but the one remains unconnected with the other save as successive events in the same story. The same situation obtains in Acts 5:30-31: Jews killed Jesus, God raised him up, he gives repentance and forgiveness to Israel, no connection. The import of Philip's coaching of the Ethiopian eunuch had naught to do with the salvation wrought by the old rugged cross; rather, the point again is that the Christ had to suffer as (Deutero-)Isaiah had laid down (Acts 8:34: "Sir, of whom does the prophet predicate these things? Himself? Or someone else?") To Cornelius Peter explains how God reversed the seeming triumph of Jesus' foes (Acts 10:39–40) and how "every one who believes in him receives forgiveness of sins through his name" (10:43), but he does not intimate that the death makes that forgiveness possible. Acts 13:27–30 has Paul reiterate the secret plan for Jesus' death and the unwitting cooperation of Jesus' enemies, an act of murder that God reversed. And he goes on to say that (13:38–39) forgiveness and freedom are to be had through him. Not through his death, though.

The single possible exception to the otherwise consistent trend is Acts 20:28, a reference to "the church of God which he obtained with his own blood" or, as other manuscripts have it, "the church of the Lord [or, "of the Lord and God"], which he obtained with his own blood" (or, as others read, "with the blood of his own [Son])."[16] Textual uncertainty of this kind often marks interpolation, even scribal harmonization of different interpolations. It appears that someone has sought to import into Luke's text some of the "butcher shop religion" (Harry Emerson Fosdick) that Luke sought so fastidiously to avoid.

Evangelistic tracts often diagram the gospel, representing the sinner on one lip of a great chasm with heaven on the far side and hell yawning in between. He is enabled to cross over only when, in the next frame, the horizontal beam of Jesus' cross forms a bridge over the abyss. Such a diagram does not fit Luke's understanding of salvation, where the cross is not the bridge. A Lukan tract would show a series of huge block letters spelling out the name "Jesus" as a bridge across the ravine.

We saw that Matthew retained the two scant Markan references to Jesus' coming death as a ransom for many, supplying a more elaborate theological context, that of the new covenant and its sealing in sacrificial blood. Luke does just the opposite: he cuts them both! Where Mark had Jesus say, "the Son of Man came not to be served but to serve, and to give his life as a ransom for many" (10:45), Luke has, "which is the greater personage, the one who reclines at table? Or the one who serves? Surely, it is the one who reclines, no? And yet I conduct myself among you as one who serves" (Luke 22:27). Conspicuously absent are both the Son of Man references (given the context, a simple mark of self-abnegating humility anyway) and the business about him dying, much less as a ransom.

Some suggest that Luke preferred a parallel tradition (another version of the saying) to Mark's, others that Luke just rewrote Mark. The only difference between the two opinions is that the former opens the possibility that Mark had added either or both the ransom and the Son of Man phrases to a prior, simpler tradition, represented by Luke, to which Luke had independent access. Only it is hard to see why Mark would have changed it, since at least the ransom notion is so comparatively unimportant for him, as we have seen. In either case, Luke, who knew Mark, did not want to carry over Mark's reference to Jesus' death as a ransom.

The same tendency is at work in Luke's treatment of the Last Supper, where Luke has trimmed, really truncated, Mark's Words of Institution. Mark had, "And as they were eating, he took bread and blessed and broke it and gave it to them, saying, 'Take it—this is my body.' And he took a cup, and when he had given thanks, he gave it to them, and they all drank of it. And he said to them, 'This is my blood of the [new?] covenant, which is poured out for many. Amen: I tell you, I shall not drink again of the fruit of the vine until that day when I drink it anew in the kingdom of God.'" (Mark 14:22–25). Luke's version looks rather different: "'I have earnestly desired to eat this Passover with you before I suffer; for I tell you I will not eat it [again?] until it is fulfilled in the kingdom of God.' And he took a cup, and when he had given thanks he said, 'Take this, and divide it among yourselves; for I tell you that henceforth I shall not drink of the fruit of the vine until that day when I drink it anew in the kingdom of God.' And he took bread, and when he had given thanks he broke it and gave it to them, saying, 'This is my body'" (Luke 22:15–19a). This must be the original text, contra the efforts of Joachim Jeremias [17] and others who prefer those manuscripts that continue thusly: "'which is given for you. Do this in remembrance of me.' And the same with the cup after supper, saying, 'This cup which is poured out for you is the new covenant in my blood'" (22:19b–20). The Lukan original is abrupt enough, but the attempt to bring it closer to Mark, Matthew, and 1 Corinthians 11:24–26 is so clumsy that the interpolator does not even mind adding a second eucharistic cup just to fit everything in!

We see, then, that Luke has taken the knife to Mark's text again, aiming to remove any impression that the bread and wine have anything to do with a redemptive sacrifice.

On our topic, as with some others, the Gospel of John seems conflicted, pointing in two directions. It would be no surprise if the cause were simply the evangelist's own lack of closure, a failure to think systematically. But, given the patterns that seem to form, it appears more likely to me that our present text of John is the result of a late harmonization of the recensions cherished and redacted by two competing Johannine factions: the Gnosticizing group condemned in 1 and 2 John and the Catholicizing group who condemned them as false offshoots. My guess is that each had its version of the gospel, and that later scribes, perhaps oblivious of the obsolete debate, decided to combine readings from both versions, thinking in that way not to risk losing any of the precious text. It seems to me that the vast majority of Johannine salvation texts understand Jesus as the Gnostic Revealer come to earth to break the silence of eternity, which not even the imposter Moses was able to penetrate (John 1:17; 10:8). He gives authority to become God's children only to those who believe in him and his word. Without his light, one walks forever in darkness. Without his water, one thirsts with the thirst of Tantalus. Without his resurrection, one remains among the hordes of living dead.

On the other hand, there are a few passages which seem to approximate something like Pauline soteriology, though without spelling it out. Let us briefly survey them. First, John the Baptist speaks with the voice of the evangelist when he calls Jesus "the Lamb of God who takes away the sin of the world" (John 1:29). That imagery, though succinct, certainly seems to posit Jesus dying as an atoning sacrifice. Raymond E. Brown posited an earlier meaning of the phrase, though, one which had no sacrificial slant. Brown thought the evangelist might be employing a traditional saying of John the Baptist which prophesied the advent of a warrior messiah along the lines of the messianic Ram of 1 Enoch 90:38. For such a one to "take away the sins of the world" need denote no more than his conquering the reign of sin by vanquishing the wicked.[18] Brown does not think that the evangelist had this in mind, but rather that he was reinterpreting such a traditional Johannine oracle in the framework of Christian soteriology. I think Brown's guess is probably correct; still, while we are reopening the question of precisely what sort of soteriology John's Gospel may feature, perhaps we ought to hold open the possibility that John the evangelist intended the meaning Brown ascribes only to John the Baptist. The well-known "realized eschatology" of the Fourth Gospel need not militate against this possibility, since the evangelist would simply be understood as applying one more traditional messianic designation, albeit in a demythologized way.

And though the echo is fainter, we catch a Pauline note in John 3:16, that "God… gave his only-begotten Son" so we might "have eternal life." And yet the Son is not said to be "delivered up" or "handed over" to *death*. The Father's gift of the Son might simply refer to his sending him as a revelation.

Twice the Johannine Jesus speaks of "being lifted up," presumably on the cross. "As Moses lifted up the serpent in the wilderness, so must the Son of Man be lifted up, that whoever believes in him may have eternal life" (John 3:14–15). "'I, when I am lifted up from the earth, will draw all men to myself.' He said this to specify the mode of his death" (John 12:32–33). Interestingly, without the narrator's comment, we might very well understand the "lifting up from earth" to refer to the ascension (John 6:62; 20:17), as in a larger sense it does seem to do, as if the cross is a stairway to heaven, the means or the beginning of the ascension (John 17:1–5, where the impending arrest is said to mark Jesus' return to his Father's side in heavenly glory). In any case, this elevation of Jesus like Moses' apotropaic caduceus in Numbers 21:9 serves to make Jesus visible, figuratively, to the crowds who only need believe in him to be saved. There is nothing here of a blood sacrifice.

Thrice Jesus speaks of laying down or giving up his life or flesh for the sake of others. "The bread which I shall give for the life of the world is my flesh" (John 6:51). This verse occurs in the midst of a sacramental section added by the Ecclesiastical (or Catholicizing) Redactor, as Loisy and Bultmann clearly saw.[19]

"I lay down my life for the sheep" (John 10:15b). Here is a reference, reminiscent of both Calvinism and Gnosticism, whereby Jesus' saving death avails only for his predestined elect, no one else, though the sentence may merely be telescoping intention with result: Jesus dies to save, and those who heed him are saved by that death.

"This is my commandment: that you love one another as I have loved you. No one has greater love than this, that he should lay down his life for his friends" (John 15:12–13). And yet Paul could think of a greater: "Why, it is rare for one to die for a righteous man, though it is conceivable that someone might. But God shows his love for us in that while we were still sinners, Christ died for us" (Romans 5:7–8). That is not necessarily what the Johannine Jesus is doing. His "friends" implies they are already identified as his in some important manner, suggesting the Gnosticism which this gospel is otherwise so frequently redolent.

We see, then, that the first passage, part of a Catholicizing interpolation, may be discounted, and the second and third seem to tend in a Gnostic direction in that the focus is on the elect, who in a sense are already saved by nature. We may be seeing the first steps from a Gnostic soteriology of receiving the word of the extra-cosmic Revealer, toward a more Catholic notion of the sacrifice of the Redeemer of the cosmos. Whether this transformation is occurring in the mind of the evangelist or in the process of textual interpolation and harmonization is impossible to say.

CONCLUSION

Why do we find merely the hints and intimations of a doctrine of salvation by the crucifixion of Jesus in the gospels? There is nothing in them like the exposition of Paul on the subject. Granted, the very character of the gospels as narratives is going to limit the amount of exposition on any topic, but there remains much teaching in their pages, and that teaching bears little resemblance to that of the Pauline epistles. But perhaps the question of genre does hold the key. As Helmut Koester suggested some years ago, [20] the very nature of a hero biography or hagiography implies a certain kind of faith among those by and for whom it is written. Among such Christians there was a great interest in Jesus as a hero to admire and to emulate. The gospels are largely aretalogies (though Mark, followed by Matthew, Luke, and John, decided to combine that narrative form with the teaching materials which, circulating at first by themselves in non-narrative collections like Q and the Gospel of Thomas, presupposed a more disembodied faith in a sage and his words, a "talking head"). In the epistles, by contrast, the plot and action are replaced by the flow and development of argument. Ideas and doctrines take the place of characters and locales. And I suggest that the conception of Jesus' death as a saving event fits more naturally into the epistles' world of ideas than into the gospels' world of events. So the death of Jesus winds up meaning something very different in the one genre than in the other. Salvation by the cross seems to be central to the epistles, but marginal in the gospels.

I do not mean to say that it *only seems*, in reading the gospels, that there is a lighter emphasis being placed upon the redemption of the cross, whereas in fact the evangelists must also have believed in something like Pauline soteriology. No, to the contrary, we have absolutely no right to assume that all early Christians held unanimously to the same creed. That is the fantasy of apologetical harmonists. We have no right to ascribe any belief to the writer of a document that is not set forth in its pages. Granted, one might yet believe something even if one had no occasion to write it down, but in the case of "gospels," accounts of the Good News of Salvation, we must assume the writers were putting down in black and white what they thought essential to that salvific message. So if a gospel lacks one version of soteriology, we can rightly infer that its author did not believe in it. If the historical fact was otherwise, we have no way of knowing it. Certainly wishful thinking is no adequate reason. No, I mean rather to say that various versions of Christian soteriology evolved in the course of early Christian preaching, exhorting, and evangelism, along the lines of different media, oral and written. And we may discern how, during that propagation, genre considerations led to very different theologies of salvation. A "Gospel Christian" held a different sort of faith than an "Epistle Christian" did. Not all whose faith was nourished by admonitory epistles necessarily read much in the way of cross-soteriology (good luck finding it in James, Jude, or the Thessalonians!).

Beyond the question of implicit genre trajectories, we have to account for the fact that the developed gospels we possess in the canon are by no means shy of Christological teaching, implicit and explicit. So had their authors wished to propagate something like Pauline soteriology, there was nothing stopping them. Why didn't they do it? All we can say (though it may be enough) is that the evangelists' rather different depictions of the death of Jesus and its importance show no anxiety about departing from a Pauline norm, implying that there was no such norm to reject or modify. Luke's treatment seems to be as close to this as we come, since admittedly it does seem to avoid, and not merely to be innocent of, relevant Markan materials. Whether or not Mark intended such texts as Luke bypasses to be hints of a cross-soteriology we cannot say, but Luke apparently took them as such and rejected them. Even here what we are seeing is a period of Christianity in theological flux. The Pauline option, which seems to undergird eventual Western Catholic soteriology, is but one voice in the early Christian canon, and it had its work cut out for it shouldering aside Gnostic, *theios aner*, nomistic covenant sealing, and other understandings of the cross. Once we know this, our own theologies, even if we fancy ourselves still to be Biblicists in some manner, must partake of the same freedom of interpretation. Theological experimentation on the cross has never really ceased, as witness the theories of Francis Turretin, Hosea Ballou, Karl Barth, Donald M. Baillie, Charles Fillmore, and the Reverend Sun Myung Moon. And there is no reason that they should.

NOTES

1. Theodore J. Weeden, *Mark: Traditions in Conflict* (Philadelphia: Fortress Press, 1971), Chapter II, "The Christological Conflict," pp. 52–69.

2. Gail Anne Paterson, "The Divine Man in Hellenistic Popular Religion." A Ph.D. dissertation for Drew University, 1983. Ann Arbor: University Microfilms, 1996. Clyde Weber Votaw, *The Gospels and Contemporary Biographies in the Greco-Roman World*. Facet Books Biblical Series 27 (Philadelphia: Fortress Press, 1970). Charles H. Talbert, *What Is a Gospel? The Genre of the Canonical Gospels* (Philadelphia: Fortress Press, 1977).

3. Ernst Käsemann, *New Testament Questions of Today*. Trans. W.J. Montague (Philadelphia: Fortress Press, 1979), Chapter V, "On the Subject of Primitive Christian Apocalyptic," section 2, pp. 124–127ff.

4. Gershom G. Scholem, *Major Trends in Jewish Mysticism* (NY: Schocken Books, 1973), Eighth Lecture: "Sabbatianism and Mystical Heresy," pp. 287–324. Scholem, *The Messianic Idea in Judaism and Other Essays on Jewish Spirituality* (NY: Schocken Books, 1971). Lecture Four: "Redemption Through Sin." Trans. Hillel Halkin. Pp. 78–141. Arthur Mandel, *The Militant Messiah, or The Flight from the Ghetto: The Story of Jacob Frank and the Frankist Movement* (Atlantic Highlands, NJ: Humanities Press,1979).

5. Frederick Sontag, *Sun Myung Moon and the Unification Church* (NY: Abingdon Press, 1977), pp. 184–187.

6. Elaine Pagels, *The Gnostic Gospels* (NY: Random House, 1979), Chapter IV, "The Passion of Christ and Persecution of Christians," pp. 70-101. Sami Nasib Makarem explains the same practice of holy dissimulation among the Druze sect in *The Druze Faith* (Delmar, NY: Caravan Books, 1974), pp. 100–101.

7. Robert M. Fowler, *Let the Reader Understand: Reader-Response Criticism and the Gospel of Mark* (Minneapolis: Fortress Press, 1991), pp. 76–77.

8. Gordon W. Allport, *The Individual and his Religion* (NY: Macmillan, 1950, 1974): "The child who finds his personal advantage not immediately and satisfactorily served by his prayers may discard his conceptions and terminate once and for all his religious quest. Sometimes the issue comes to a head only later in life, in conjunction with acute personal need. 'Prayer does not stop bullets,' was the refrain of many [WW2] veterans; 'they perforate both devout and infidel.' … A faith centered in self-advantage

is bound to break up" (p. 120).

9.   Theodore J. Weeden, "Two Jesuses," a paper delivered to the Jesus Seminar of the Westar Institute, Fall, 2003.

10.   Robert M. Price, *Deconstructing Jesus* (Amherst: Prometheus Books, 2000), pp. 221–224.

11.   Alfred Loisy, *The Birth of the Christian Religion*. Trans. L.P. Jacks (London: George Allen & Unwin LTD, 1948), p.249.

12.   Albert Schweitzer, *The Mysticism of Paul the Apostle*. Trans. William Montgomery (NY: Seabury Press, 1968), p. 225. Montgomery renders the phrase "subsidiary crater," which loses Schweitzer's typically striking visual imagery.

13.   Sam K. Williams, *Jesus' Death as Saving Event: The Background and Origin of a Concept.* Harvard Dissertations in Religion 2 (Missoula: Scholars Press, 1975).

14.   John C. O'Neill, *The Theology of Acts in its Historical Setting* (London: SPCK, 1961), pp. 83–93.

15.   Robert Eisenman, "Qumran's 'New Covenant in the Land of Damascus' and the New Testament's 'Cup of the New Covenant in (His) Blood'" *Journal of Higher Criticism* 10/1 (Spring 2003), pp. 121–136.

16.   Bart D. Ehrman, *The Orthodox Corruption of Scripture: The Effect of Early Christological Controversies on the Text of the New Testament* (NY: Oxford University Press, 1993), pp. 87–88. Ehrman holds for "the church of God which he obtained with the blood of his own [Son]," but I think the original was simply, "the church of God."

17.   Joachim Jeremias, *The Eucharistic Words of Jesus*. Trans. Arnold Ehrhardt (Oxford: Basil Blackwell, 1955), pp. 87–106.

18.   Raymond E. Brown, "John the Baptist in the Gospel of John," in Brown, *New Testament Essays* (Garden City: Doubleday Image, 1968), pp. 179–181.

19.   Loisy, *Birth of the Christian Religion*, p. 243. Rudolf Bultmann, *The Gospel of John: A Commentary*. Trans. G.W. Beasley-Murray, R.W.N. Hoare, and J.K. Riches (Philadelphia: Westminster Press, 1975), p. 219.

20.   Helmut Koester, "GNOMAI DIAPHOROI: The Origin and Nature of Diversification in the History of Early Christianity," in James M. Robinson and Helmut Koester, *Trajectories through Early Christianity* ({Philadelphia: Fortress Press, 1971), pp. 151–153.

11

NOTHING BESPEAKS THE DIVINE INSPIRATION OF THE BIBLE

The old joke has it that the wide-eyed fundamentalist, who needs little to convince him but the sound of his own voice (or his pastor's), affirms "The Bible is the Word of God!" and, when asked why anyone ought to believe that, replies, "Because the Bible says so!" And why should we believe *that*? He answers, "Because it's God's word!" This is not a caricature. It is no over-simplification; it is only a simplification, a clarification, a clearing away of the lush growth of apologetical obfuscation. The apologetical argumentation for an inspired Bible is an elaborate and frantic juggling exercise, trying to keep a large series of balls in the air at the same time and calling it a solar system.

RIGHT OUT OF THE GATE

The claim for divine inspiration of the Bible quickly betrays itself and all who employ it because of a crucial conceptual contradiction, a Catch-22. One invests the text with infallible authority, claiming merely to "recognize" that authority, for one reason: so that all teachings of that text may be credited as true without cavil or confirmation. Thus does the weary brain find surcease. Agnosticism turns magically into fideism. But the believer brings to the text a prior definition both of what kind of thing an inspired scripture is and of what doctrines it may and may not teach (since the believer is a member of an established communion, not a religious founder in most cases). Behold how

101

he is already violating his own procedure. First, he prescribes the properties of his text on the basis of an inherited theology he has not himself fashioned,[1] whereas the logic of his appeal to scripture is to allow divine truth revealed there to provide his beliefs. He has begun with the cart leading the horse. And, though he thinks he is allowing the text to determine his views, he is doing the very opposite as soon as he finds the need to harmonize any verse of the Bible with any other verse or with any prior belief taught in his church. In fact, his theology determines what the Bible may and may not mean. It is a mischievous doctrine that leaves the reader who realizes it (though apparently none does) in the position of the soliloquist of Romans Chapter 7: he does he very thing he says he hates. Here is precisely the circularity of the ostensible joke told above: a thing is to be believed because the Bible says it, the Bible being infallible. And that claim is to be credited because the book is by definition infallible scripture. And that we know only because it tells us so. The circle of deductive faith knows nothing of any inductive appeal to evidence.

In this system, if we may call it one, scripture texts have ultimately an ornamental value and function. The doctrines and the matching verses arise together for the believer, one merely the illustration for the other. One thinks of the Arian objection to Nicene Christology which posited an eternal coexistence of Father and Son. Arians pointed out that this would make Jehovah and Jesus a pair of brothers, not Father and Son. And in the same way, Biblicists seem to imagine that their beliefs come from Bible verses, but in fact, both enter the believer's world simultaneously with no real derivation or causation. So no Biblicist is actually undergoing the temporal process of deriving doctrine from texts. The believer is engaged in a no-win shell game. While he considers the doctrine of the Trinity, for instance, he believes it to be well-founded because of the set of proof texts he has inherited. When he thinks of a hand full of texts making triple references to Jesus, God, and the Spirit, he construes their "real" meaning by reference to the doctrine that allegedly provides the key to them. Sadly, he fails to see that each pole of his contemplation cancels the other out rather than upholding it, since the items in question cannot be derived each from the other simultaneously. Neither can they document one another at the same time, because each must be in need of support at the moment it is ostensibly supporting the other. Both stand for a split second in the air, as if two aerialists should fly forth, expecting to meet the open arms of the other, anchored to some perch—and both crash to the ground.

"WHAT DO YOU SAY OF YOURSELF?
WHAT SHALL WE TELL THOSE WHO SENT US?"

Is it true that an entity called "The Bible" makes a blanket claim for its own inspiration and infallibility? It is needful to deconstruct this seeming monolith of scripture. Plainly, believers and theologians alike are completely begging the question of canonicity and of theological epistemology. They ought to pause for at least forty years in the wilderness to consider how the (largely unknown and unnamed) ancient Jewish scribes and Christian bishops decided on the contents of the Bible, what criteria they employed (most of them utterly indefensible today), and whether their choices ought to bind us. But notoriously the standard replies at this point betray the impatience of the mind that is already made up and does not like to linger among the facts. There is an eagerness to jump from one peak to another without traversing the valleys between. I think of the heretical kosher butcher in Isaac Beshevis Singer's *Satan in Goray*: without much of a second look, he says, "It's clean! It's clean!"[2] How does the Protestant apologist feel entitled to embrace, only in a single case, the Catholic epistemology of believing in an infallible Magisterium ("The Spirit guided the Church to choose these particular books.") or the Neo-Orthodox epistemology of an experientially self-authenticating text? Never mind, good enough: "It's clean! It's clean!"

Only if we already know that these and no other books constitute a uniative whole of consistent teaching can we be so sure that anything said of/by part of that whole applies to the rest. "What I am writing to you is a command of the Lord" (1 Cor. 14:37). Does that somehow secure the inspiration and authority of 2 Chronicles?

When Old Testament prophets preface their thunderings with the ascription, "Thus says Jehovah!" does this claim infallible inspiration for the written text some listener subsequently wrote down? How accurately?

When the Biblicist appeals to Jesus Christ as authenticating the Old Testament (whatever books it contained in his day) and pre-authenticating the New by promising the Twelve that the Paraclete Spirit would remind them of all his teachings and would convey new ones to them,[3] he ignores the fact that Paul and Luke were not present. Worse yet, he is quoting Dorothy Gale as to the reality of *The Wizard of Oz*. Jesus is , for all anyone can prove, simply a character in the very story the authenticity of which is at issue. Apologists seem to jump out of the magic (vicious) circle right at this point, when they marshal arguments that Jesus was an infallible oracle of truth and that the scriptures have accurately recorded his teaching.[4] But all of that is special pleading, working dubiously but inexorably to the pre-set conclusion: we are determined to believe what the text says, and, once we know what it says, that is what we are going to believe. So a Jesus who is himself a function of the text ("Scripture's Christ" as they revealingly call him!) is the supposed warrant for believing the text. And this despite the fact that his "quoted" guarantees do not even encompass most of the scriptural texts. It is apparent the believer and the apologist alike have a destination in mind, and they want to get there as soon as possible, even if that means veering off the road of intricate argument and cutting across open country.

THE ENEMY IS US

Much of the inerrancy debate among evangelicals has centered on how much relative weight is to be assigned the "phenomena of scripture" versus the "claims of scripture," since the two apparently contradict one another. It is a question, some quip, of what scripture *says* versus what it *does*. Neo-Evangelicals like Dewey M. Beegle[5] held that it was a mockery to get all fired up about Holy Scripture and then give short shrift to what that scripture actually says. Why privilege *one's (tradition's) reading* of the relatively few verses that speak of inspiration and its predicates at the expense of the far greater number of verses that do or do not bear out those claims or our understanding of them? Essentially, what the rock-ribbed Biblicists insisted on was to construct, from their best inferences, a concept of what a scripture must be like (e.g., "inerrant, because God cannot lie") and then to harmonize ill-fitting data elsewhere in the Bible.[6] That means reverting to a less plausible reading of this or that verse when a straightforward reading would make them seem to contradict one another or contradict a cherished doctrine. In other words, harmonizing contradictions. It means accepting resolutions that would never commend themselves exegetically if one were not trying to get out of a tight spot.

On the other side, Neo-Evangelicals sought to construct their theological model of scripture "from below;" accommodating "scriptural authority" to the sort of moves scripture texts actually made, according to the straightforward readings. Thus their inexorable retreat from an inerrant text to a Bible infallible only in matters of faith and practice, to a scripture infallible as to its central, saving message, etc, eventually to a repository of museum exhibits of man's attempts to discover the divine. The inevitable destination is Harry Emerson Fosdick's[7] estimate of the Bible as the product and repository of "progressive revelation," the overside being god's self-disclosure, the underside being human religious experience, the medium of God's self-disclosure. The limits of that revelation are set by the degree of spiritual and intellectual enlightenment possessed by Jews and Christians at the time.

It was a question of whether one would engage in the hermeneutical circle as Bultmann, dependent on his colleague Martin Heidegger, described it.[8] One approaches scripture with certain questions in mind, together with some "preunderstanding" of the resources of the book he is opening. As one reads ever more deeply, he not only begins to find the text answering for itself but also demanding revision of his initial assumptions about what sort of an entity the text is. Chastened, the reader approaches the text again, this time with a better idea of the voice he is listening for. Eventually one may even realize he has been approaching the text with the wrong questions. This he realizes as soon as the right ones occur to him in the light of the proffered answers, which his interaction has at last enabled him to see. I think it is safe to say that, despite their pious protestations of willingness to bow humbly before the teaching of scripture, fundamentalist "Bible-believers" have always been unwilling to listen to scripture, except insofar as they re-read there certain individual verses familiar to them from sermonic brow-beating. "Thank you sir! May I have another!" But this was simply an echo chamber, not a spectacle of, as the Plymouth Rock Pilgrims had it, new light breaking forth from the pages of holy writ.

Both sides faced a mortal dilemma. Neo-Evangelicals were left with a claim to "revelation" with no predictive value of what one was likely to find in the text, a theology of inspiration that effectively meant no more than mute providence. The Bible is what it is, and that must be good. On the other hand, the fundamentalist has a Bible that is merely a ventriloquist dummy for prior theology. The fundamentalist cannot bring himself to recognize what the holy text actually says for fear that it will pop his bubble. The Neo-Evangelical or Liberal fearlessly scrutinizes the text, but it all looks quite strange, and he finds that he must proof text it to make it appear relevant to his favorite religious and political hobbyhorses. We can conclude from these ironies at least that a claim for inspiration, weak or strong, does not make the Bible any better than it is. Nor does it really have a voice of its own.

IT IS WHAT IT IS, AND IT ISN'T INSPIRED

If we ask the Liberal or the Neo-Evangelical whether the Bible appears to live up to the claim made for it as an inspired book, the answer will be "Yes, of course," for it will be a tautology. Whatever it looks like, warts and all, that must be the way God wanted it, so yes, it's God's "inspired" book. If one asks what difference inspiration makes, it will probably boil down to the sense of honor paid the book in worship, and the fact that it is still called the "Holy" Bible. The inspiration claim fits with whatever may turn out to be true of the Bible and is not inconsistent with any state of affairs. In short, it is meaningless.[9] In detail, this means that one cannot expect an inspired book to contain only historical fact, since there is no telling whether God likes myth and legend. He might, and if you think you know better, why, you don't *need* any Bible! There is no reason to exclude the possibility that inspired writers might contradict one another, since both might partake of "progressive revelation," and we cannot know which is closer to the truth. For the same reason we cannot expect the Bible to give us only good and noble commands, since the ancient prophets might have been hearing God's word through their culture-bound conventions, or in other words, reducing God's word *to* culture-bound conventions.

So the question of whether the Bible looks like an inspired book only has content insofar as we adopt the fundamentalist's abstract pre-definition.[10] If we grant him the right to stipulate what a scripture must be, we will at least have some criterion by which to judge, as opposed to the Liberal/Neo-Evangelical "Yeah, whatever" alternative.

Traditionally, Christians (and others, including Stoics, Kabbalists, and Hindus) understood that one of the predicates of an inspired book was that it possessed and conveyed meaning on many levels. In other words, one might employ allegory, gematria, etc., to plumb the imagined depths of the text. The Protestant Reformers rejected this aspect of inspiration and of an inspired text, because it resulted in such a plenitude of meaning as to make the text mean anything and everything at once. Who is to tell what is a legitimate reading of inspired scripture? Of course, the Roman Catholic answer was "our inspired interpreter." But if you had an inspired, infallible interpreter, why not just skip the middleman and rely directly on the oracle himself? And that the Protestants could not brook. The Pope was the Antichrist. There had to be an alternative: the Bible.

And yet Protestants did retain allegorical interpretations of Old Testament texts, because that was the only way to retain the interpretation of them as predictions of Jesus. Harmonization of contradictions is another form of allegorization, since it amounts to preferring a less obvious reading over a more straightforward, "literal" reading. But the critical reader finds such readings of the Bible to be nothing but special pleading. When he sees the Biblicist engaging in it, he sees how little the actual book called the Bible fits the textbook definition of "scripture." It shouldn't have to come to this. Martin Luther believed scripture was and must be "perspicacious," clear in meaning to any reader. But it is not, and not only because of contradictions. Many, many, many times its teaching is ambiguous. The bugle plays an uncertain note, and we know not whether to prepare for battle (1 Cor. 14:8). We need allege no error, no mistake, no contradiction: we just cannot tell what the writer means. God cannot lie, all right, but can't he at least make himself understood?[11]

If the Bible were the inspired Word of God, would it not speak equally, like a shining beacon, to all historical periods and cultures? Would fancy footwork like hermeneutics be necessary? Some will say I am asking for a fairyland Bible. But I say, no, it is the grandiose claims of fundamentalists about the Bible that imply such a Tinkerbible. Don't blame me. To put it another way, if one offers the excuse that God wants us to exercise our wits and practice our judgment by wrestling with questions of cross-cultural hermeneutics, is that not to admit that we are finally to rely on our wits and judgment? What does scripture add to that? This becomes inescapably obvious when those who crow about their precious guidance from God in scripture, faced with some intractable dilemma of bio-ethics, confess themselves baffled. The Bible does not deal with it; thus they're on the same footing with the rest of us heathens and humanists. Why can't they admit we're all in the same boat, and that no one has any epistemological advantage?

Speaking of morals, I have already alluded to the stumbling block of the Bible's advocacy of barbarism, the best behavior of ancient savages and warlords. Nonbelievers take this as evidence that the God of the Bible is simply a projection of the mores and morals of his worshippers, who invented him in the first place and who go right on reinventing him. The believer argues instead that God was never at liberty to reveal everything all in one lump sum, since the socially-conditioned mind of man would have rebelled. Hence God's cautious policy of gradualism, like mild sanctions against South Africa in the 70s. But isn't the human mind supposedly always at enmity with God? When are we to imagine God figured he might stand to readjust the human race's moral thermostat? And why didn't he adjust it among Jews and Christians till many centuries after Greek philosophers discovered, e.g., the abhorrent character of slavery? No, sorry, but the minute one evokes doctrines of progressive revelation, one has given up the game. One is developing a doctrine of *non-revelation*, for Pete's sake. It is theodicy: explaining with a nervous chuckle how it is that the infallible paragon of moral action not only allows but commands genocide and baby-sacrifice. No explanation will absolve the Bible of barbarism (which is no surprise to find in *Beowulf* or *The Iliad*, but in the inspired Word of God?) as long as we recognize it as such.[12] And if we do not recognize it, if we do not feel we must make sense of it, if we pretend there is not a problem, then we are implicitly condoning barbarism ourselves. In fact, anyone who believes a morally perfect God could condemn anyone to Hell, eternal torture, essentially for not holding the "correct" religious beliefs, is learning to make himself a miniature monster in the image of his tribal totem Jehovah.

Would we expect an inspired scripture to be factually inerrant? I suppose we would, since the chief value of believing in such a book is that, whatever it says, I can trust it implicitly. If I have to start scrutinizing it for myself, well, then who needs the Bible? If the ball's back in my court, I'm back where I was in the first place: wishing I had some Book to save me the trouble of thinking for myself. Oh, I know, we can start pleading for critics not to impose artificial modern standards of accuracy on the old book.[13] But that's the very cultural relativism that lets Bultmann's nose under the tent! The whole idea of inerrancy (isn't it?) is to remove such possibilities, because we are supposed to be dealing with a book *not* subject to the ambiguities of worldly existence. Keep going in this direction, and you wind up saying it is inerrant when the gospels say Jesus rose from the dead, even though he didn't, because it was a mythic metaphor for authentic existence.

INSPIRED AND INFALLIBLE CONTRADICTIONS?

Lest someone accuse me of skipping specifics because in fact there are no errors or contradictions, I will venture to set before you a collection of some of the most pronounced instances. If you've already read Wellhausen, Ingersoll, Strauss, Wheless,[14] and others, feel free to skip this section.

Genesis 1 has Elohim create plants (vv. 11–12), then various animal species (vv. 20–25), and finally men and women (vv. 26–27), apparently several, as with the animals, all at the same time. But Genesis 2 has a different order of creation: first a male human (v. 7), then plants (the Garden of Eden, vv. 8–9), then the animals (vv. 18–20) in case any might prove to be suitable company for him, and finally a female human (21–23). Please note, in the Eden story, God does not merely *show* Adam the animals but *creates them on the spot,* from the dust of the ground, even as Adam himself was created. Nor does it say "God *had* made all the creatures from the dust of the ground," as if at some earlier time. It is quite clear that his creating them immediately preceded his showing them to the man.

Who was Mrs. Cain (Gen. 4:17a)? Cain's sister? Did God suspend the incest taboo as well as any ill genetic effects? But why bother with such nonsense? For the rest of the Cain stories make it quite clear that he is not usually pictured as the first human born into an otherwise empty world. For whom did he build the city (v. 17b)? Who is he afraid is going to kill him (4:14)? His mother? These stories all presuppose Cain lives at a later time when the earth is populated. The editor of Genesis has simply patched together disparate legends about Cain, whether or not they presuppose a consistent time line. Did you ever watch *Xena: Warrior Princess*? Ever notice how the writers place Xena all over the ancient world? In one episode, she is with Galen the physician, who lived in the second century CE, while in another she is helping to defend Troy in remote antiquity! In another, she pals around with Goliath, about 1000 BCE! It's the same way with Cain.

Genesis 4:2 depicts Abel as the first shepherd, Cain the first farmer. But verse 20 makes Jabal the first nomadic herdsman, while in Genesis 9:20 Noah is the first tiller of the soil. (You can't just say it means Noah was the first tiller of the soil *after the* Flood, because his being the inventor-vintner implicitly exonerates his drunkenness as naïve ignorance: since no one had ever grown grapes before, he didn't know what would happen if you made wine out of them!) Besides this, Jabal is spoken of as "the father of all who dwell in tents and have livestock" in the reader's day, implying unbroken continuity with no flood interrupting between Jabal and the readers.

Did the Flood last 150 days in all (Gen. 7:24)? Or only 61 (40 days of rain plus three weeks of drainage, as in 8:6–12)? Did Noah bring aboard a *single* pair of *all* animal species (6:19–20) or *seven pairs* of kosher animals with *one* pair of nonkosher ones (7:2–3)? Actually, the differences are important markers that two older Flood stories have been combined here, one from the Yahwist ("J") Source, the other from the Priestly Code ("P"). *The J versions was*: Gen. 6:5–8; 7:1–5, 7–10, 12, 16b–17, 22–23; 8:2b–3a, 6–12, 13b, 20–22; 9:18–19. In it, the Flood is caused by rain, and the waters increased for 40 days, taking another three weeks to dry up, a total of 61 days. Noah observes kosher laws, taking aboard a single pair of unclean animal species, seven pairs of kosher species. The *P version includes:* Gen. 6:9–22; 7:6, 11, 13–16a, 18–21, 24; 8:1–2a, 3–5, 13a, 14–19; 9:1–17, 28–29. This time, the waters deepen for 150 days and recede gradually, the whole flood lasting one year, 11 days. The Priestly author knew kosher laws began much later, so he has Noah, a vegetarian, bring only a single pair of animals. And the Flood results from the gushing up of the subterranean sources of the *Tehom*, the world ocean. Personally, I prefer an approach to the Bible that actually provides reasonable solutions to its puzzles. Source criticism, as opposed to harmonization, does just that, in case after case.

Genesis 37:28 says Joseph was pulled out of the pit by Midianites, who sold him to Ishmaelites, who in turn sold him into Egyptian slavery. But 37:36 says the Midianites sold him as a slave themselves once *they* got into Egypt. It won't work to say that the second verse is just summarizing the events of the first, eliminating the middle man for brevity's sake, because verse 36 specifically locates the Midianites as in Egypt when *they* sold Joseph into slavery. Our editor just did not want to leave out any material. He had two versions, one of them fragmentary, and decided to include everything.

When did people start calling God Yahweh (Jehovah, YHWH)? Was it in Enosh's day (Gen. 4:26), before the Flood? Or was it only once Yahweh appeared to Moses at the bush (Exod. 6:2–3)? Some desperate harmonizers will come back with pious nonsense such as "Well, er, you see, they hadn't known the *theological fullness* of the divine name until God revealed himself to Moses! Yeah, *that's* the ticket!" I'm not even sure I know what that's supposed to mean, but in any case, such hair-splitting subtleties have to be shoe-horned into the text—and you know it! "You just can't [lie] for Jesus."[15]

How many times did the Egyptian cattle die (Exod. 9:6, 18–26; 12:29)? But, you might suggest, maybe there were exceptions each time, and it was they who died the next time around. Sorry, there were indeed exceptions each time: the cattle owned by the Israelites! God spared theirs—and only theirs! If he had also spared some/any Egyptian cows, that would have introduced an ambiguity that would have totally undermined the lesson being taught to Pharaoh. Again, I am not saying that a biblical writer made stupid mistakes. No, just the opposite: there were already three different versions of the Plagues story, and our later editor didn't feel at liberty to leave any of it out.

When did Saul first meet David? When he recruited him as a musician to ease his possession spells (1 Sam. 16:14–23)? Or after the battle with Goliath (17:55–58)? Again, it's no "mistake." Two sources have been spliced together.

Who killed Goliath of Gath? David (1 Sam. 17:48–51), or Elhanan (2 Sam. 21:19)? Or do you think maybe there were two giants from Gath in Philistia who had the same huge armor and gigantic stature? And were both named Goliath?!?

Which of the genealogies (Matt. 1:1–17; Lk. 3:23–38) of Jesus is correct? Neither is Mary's. Both explicitly trace his descent through Joseph. And Mark 12:35–37 contradicts both, since in it Jesus denies the Messiah will be descended from David. It amazes me that people can try to evade the force of the argument in Mark 12:35–37, as if Jesus were implying that, *though he is also David's son* the messiah must be something greater, namely God's son. Listen, that's just rewriting the passage into what you *wish* it had said! The logic is clear: David would never call his own son his Lord, even if that son were the messiah, just as he would never have called Solomon his Lord, nor would Solomon have called his son Rehoboam "my Lord." That would have violated court rhetoric.

Where did Mary and Joseph live before Jesus was born? Bethlehem (Matthew) or Nazareth (Luke)? Take a close look at both nativity stories. In Luke they dwell in Nazareth, and it is only a special circumstance that takes the couple to Bethlehem where, in the providence of God, Jesus is born. In Matthew they originally live in Bethlehem, where Jesus is born in their home, where the Magi visit them. Then they flee to Egypt, and upon their subsequent return home, they flee again, this time to Nazareth where Archelaeus will never find them.

What did the heavenly voice say to Jesus at his baptism: "This is my beloved Son" (Matt. 3:17)? Or "You are my beloved Son" (Mk. 1:11; Lk. 3:22)? Did he somehow say both at once, and different people heard it differently? Careful! That is getting mighty close to saying there *was* no heavenly voice, that people were hallucinating.

Which did Satan do last: take Jesus to the temple pinnacle (Lk. 4:9) or to a high mountain (Matt. 4:8)? Isn't it much more natural to admit that either Matthew or Luke changed the order of their shared original (the Q source) to make for a more climactic ending? I mean, what else can you say? That Satan repeated the temptation, and that Matthew and Luke each chose one instance of each temptation and ignored the other? Say this sort of stuff, and you're just asking not to be taken seriously. You're letting everybody know that you'll say any nutty thing you have to in order to stick to the party line. Do you think people can't see that?

Did Jesus list the signs which would signal the Kingdom was near (Mark 13:28–30)? Or did he say there would be no advance warning (Luke 17:20-21)? "Oh, maybe we'll just have to wait till we get to heaven for the explanation of that one (or any of the others)!"[16] Too bad that Bible contradictions and ambiguities will be cleared up only once it is all moot, when you don't really even *need* a Bible, since the perfect will have come, and you will know as you are known! It is down here, in the grimy, sinful, confusing world that you ostensibly need the guidance of the Bible, and if one passage cancels the other out, it is useless to you. Call it an "apparent" contradiction if it makes you feel any better: either way, the text is doing you no good in the here and now. You'll just have to think for yourself—not a bad idea! Why didn't you just do that to start with?

Did Jesus say his disciples would no longer fast (Mk. 2:21–22), that they would suspend fasting temporarily (Mk. 2:18–20)? Or that they ought to fast, just not like the hypocrites (Matt. 6:16–18)? Look at the metaphors in Mark: they point in very different directions, implying different positions on the issue.

Did Jesus allow *no* excuse for divorce (Mk. 10:2–9; Lk. 16:18) or *one* excuse (Matt. 5:31–32; 19:3–9)? Clearly, Matthew saw the difficulties an absolute ban on divorce was causing, so he emended the gospel text so as to restore the escape-clause of Deuteronomy. Does this mean Matthew was "lying" about what Jesus said? Of course not! It just means he regarded the text as a new law for Christians, and that law needed to be amended.

Was it only Jesus who walked on water, as in Mark 6:45–52 and John 6:15–21? Or did Peter, too, walk on the waves, as in Matthew 14:22–33? Did the others just forget about Peter? Ran out of ink? No, of course it is a sermonic, edifying addition, to urge readers to keep their faith fixed on Jesus during troubled times, a point the added material makes beautifully.

Did Jesus heal one Gerasene demoniac (Mk. 5:1–20; Lk. 8:26–39), or two (Matt. 8:28–34)? And don't tell me it was two but that two evangelists picked their favorite demoniac to mention without actually denying the presence of another! What sense would that make? But it does fit in with Matthew's editorial tendency to double single items in his sources, such as the pair of blind men modeled on Mark's Bartimaeus story and the doubling of the donkeys Jesus rides into Jerusalem. Did Jesus ride one beast into Jerusalem (Mk. 11:1–10; Lk. 19:28–38; John 12:12–15)? Or two, somehow, at the same time (Matt. 21:1–9)?

When did Jesus cleanse the temple? At the start of his ministry, as in John

2:13–17? Or was it at the end, as in all three other gospels (Mk. 11:15–19; Lk. 19:45–48; Matt. 21:12–13)? Since it sealed his doom, he couldn't have done it twice.

Whom and in what order did Peter answer when he denied Jesus three times (Mk. 14:66, 69, 70; Matt. 26:69, 71, 73; Lk. 22:56, 58, 59; John 18:17, 25, 26?) And don't tell me he denied him six or eight times, just to get them all in. The text says three.

Was Jesus crucified at noon (John 19:14) or 9 a.m. (Mk. 15:25)?

Was Jesus crucified on Passover (John 19:14, 31) or on the day after (in the other gospels the Last Supper is already a Passover seder)? No doubt John changed it to make a theological, symbolic point: Jesus died as the new Passover lamb. It isn't some kind of stupid mistake; nobody's charging that. No, it's a purposeful change to a literary text. The reason Evangelicals don't like to admit that sort of thing is that they are afraid they won't know where to draw the line between fiction and history in the gospels. But just because something may make things more complicated for you doesn't mean it's not true.

Did the women at the tomb behold Jesus himself (Matt. 28:9) or only the two men (Luke 24:1–8)? Did most women see nothing (John 20:2), leaving Mary to see Jesus by herself (20:11–17)?

The sudden appearance of Jesus amidst the disciples in Luke 24:36–43/ John 20:19–23 appears to be the initial resurrection appearance. But so does the appearance on the Sea of Tiberias in John 21:1–13, with v. 14 being an editorial harmonization. Which one was first?

Did the Risen Jesus appear only in the environs of Jerusalem (Luke 24:13, 49) or only in Galilee (Mk. 16:7 and Matt. 28:7, 10, 16)? Did the angel tell the women "Remember how he said he would meet you in Galilee?" (Mk. 16:7)? Or "Remember how, when he was in Galilee, he told you the son of man must rise," etc. (Lk. 24:6)?

Did the women flee the tomb and tell no one what they had seen (Mk. 16:8) or did they tell the disciples after all (Matt. 28:8; Lk. 24:10; John 20:18)? The Longer Ending of Mark (16:9–20) is lacking in the earliest manuscripts. This contradiction is very, very important because it means Matthew, Luke, and John didn't like Mark's ending and changed it. Everything they have happen after the empty tomb story is *predicated on changing Mark's ending. This has to mean whatever they added is fiction.*

Did Jesus ascend to heaven Easter evening (Luke 24:13, 33, 36, 50–52) or forty days later (Acts 1:3, 9)? Any writer who can vary the story like this is simply not interested in "getting the facts straight," whether we might wish he had been or not.

Did Paul's companions hear the voice of Jesus without seeing anyone or anything (9:7)? Or did they see the light but not hear the voice (22:9)? Is it a goof? It might be. But it may simply be a case of Luke varying the details so the story remains fresh for the audience, who is hearing it for the third time!

Critical scholars of the Bible do not gleefully pounce on contradictions in order to debunk the Bible. Rather, close scrutiny zeroes in on inconsistencies as clues for differentiating underlying source documents and different authors, earlier and later versions of stories and doctrines, etc. It is all part of an appreciative effort to understand the Bible. The problem is that inerrancy belief prevents us from going deeper into the roots of the Bible. It reinforces an over-simple Sunday School view of the Bible, and that is the only view of the Bible that needs to fear and hate critical scrutiny. It is time to "put away childish things."

HINDSIGHT PROPHECY

An extreme example of trying to make the Bible into a magical book that could not have been written by mere human beings is the flood of books on the so-called Bible code. The claim was that, if you set the computer to mark every seventh, seventeenth, seven hundredth, or whatever letter in the Hebrew test, the resulting string might yield hitherto hidden messages about either ancient, biblical events or modern ones, including today's headlines. Some statisticians debunk this as a selection fallacy. Others, equally adept as far as my poor brain can judge, protest that, no, the thing really works. But suppose it does. What sort of image of God does it imply? Why would he mess with trickery like this? Why not show he is there, or that the Bible is his inspired Word, through some direct means, obvious to all, one that would do anyone any good? Why not include clear predictions of future events, so we might be able to avoid tragedies instead of rejoicing in them as proofs of the Bible?

So-called Messianic prophecy is constantly trotted out as proof both of Jesus' messiahship and of the inspiration of the Bible. There they were, hundreds of Old Testament passages, waiting to be fulfilled by the right man. And along came Jesus of Nazareth to do just that! This must attest the inspiration of the Bible, no? I lack the space to do so here, but let me refer readers to my book *The Paperback Apocalypse*,[17] in which I examine the whole gamut at least of the important supposed messianic prophecies and demonstrate that not a single one of them, in its original context, has anything to do with the sense made of it by New Testament reinterpretation. You see, the New Testament writers evidently felt they could take individual verses of scripture out of context in order to fathom deeper references, just as we find in the Dead Sea Scrolls. Ancient Christians like Matthew did not even mean that Jesus fulfilled predictions that were already recognized as such, like young Arthur pulling the sword Excalibur out of the stone. No, the idea was that esoteric exegesis could allow one to recognize certain predictions *as predictions* only after their fulfillment had occurred, unnoticed in the moment of fulfillment. You had to already believe in Jesus as messiah before the trick worked; that's the whole idea. It's retrospective, almost like a perspective puzzle. The whole endeavor is based on a way of using scripture that Protestants in principle repudiate, ostensibly preferring the grammatico-historical method of the Reformers. The early Christians were not charlatans when they claimed Jesus fulfilled prophecy; they were just playing the game by different rules than we think appropriate.[18] My point is simply, all these maneuvers, these devices, look like games people (human beings) play, to make things seem to sparkle with divine inspiration. Just special effects, evidence of little more than cleverness.

One would not imagine a God-inspired book to be held captive to ancient ignorance of the natural world. Biblicists affirm that the Bible does indeed anticipate modern science. The Bible, we are told, spoke of nuclear catastrophe, automobiles, penicillin, a spherical earth, supernovas, the Big Bang, and what not. Every one of these claims is a matter of comical text-twisting. I refer readers to a paper written by myself and Reggie Finley on Freethoughtmedia.com, "Heaven and Its Wonders, and Earth: The World the Bible Writers Thought They Lived In."[19]

Beyond this, there are two fatal flaws in this sort of apologetics. First, once again, we must ask why modern Bible readers were able to "recognize" these verses as speaking of scientific truths only so late in the game? What good is a prophecy or an advanced scientific revelation if no one is able to understand it as such or appreciate it until *after* normal mortals discover it on their own? And second, if these things were really known in Israelite antiquity, why and how did such knowledge vanish without a trace? Why did it take so long for everyone, including Israelites, to grasp and utilize the knowledge? The answer is: it was not knowledge at all. It is ventriloquism by moderns.

Theoretically, God could have revealed all manner of medical and technological advances that would have made human life less miserable and given people more occasion to ponder the meaning of their lives. But obviously he didn't.

Approach the Bible, I mean the phenomena of scripture, from any angle you want, without trying to make it look like what it is not, and you will find nothing at all that demands, even suggests, an authorship transcending human genius. Much of it does not even reach that high. And when we argue that the mediocre, worse yet, the barbaric and the illogical, are God's truth, then we reduce God to an idol and elevate an ancient artifact to godhood.

NOTES

1.   Rudolf Bultmann, *Jesus Christ and Mythology* (NY: Scribner's, 1958), pp. 54–55: "It is an illusion to hold that any exegesis can be independent of secular conceptions. Every interpreter is inescapably dependent on conceptions which he has inherited from a tradition, consciously or unconsciously, and every tradition is dependent on some philosophy or other."

2.   Isaac Beshevis Singer, *Satan in Goray* (NY: Fawcett Crest, 1955), 156, 163.

3.   John Warwick Montgomery, "The Suicide of Christian Theology and a Modest Proposal for its Resurrection." In Montgomery, *The Suicide of Christian Theology* (Minneapolis: Bethany Fellowship, 1970), pp. 39–40.

4.   Ibid., pp. 38–39.

5.   Dewey M. Beegle, *The Inspiration of Scripture* (Philadelphia: Westminster Press, 1963), Chapter 4, "Inerrancy and the Phenomena of Scripture," pp. 41–69.

6.   Clark H. Pinnock, *Biblical Revelation: The Foundation of Christian Theology* (Chicago: Moody Press, 1971), Chapter 5, "The Phenomena of Scripture," pp. 175–207.

7.   Harry Emerson Fosdick, *The Modern Use of the Bible* (NY: Macmillan, 1961), p. 30.

8.   Rudolf Bultmann, "Is Exegesis without Presuppositions Possible?" In Schbert M. Ogden, ed. & trans., *Existence & Faith: Shorter Writings of Rudolf Bultmann*. A Living Age Book (NY: Meridian Books/World Publishing, 1960), pp. 289–296. Also, Bultmann, *Jesus Christ and Mythology*, pp. 49, 54.

9.   Montgomery, *Suicide*, section "The Analytical Meaninglessness of a 'Non-Inerrant Scripture," pp. 334–342.

10. Pinnock, p. 75: "Inerrancy is the standpoint for a Christian to adopt in his examination of Scripture. This *Gestalt* is inductively derived and provides the

framework for understanding what kind of book the Bible is."

11. Ibid., p. 100: "But as to the Christocentric and Redemptive focus of Scripture, there can be no doubt; and those who claim obscurity do so to evade the clear teaching of Scripture." Not only does Pinnock thus proclaim himself a mind-reader, he has also back-pedaled: for him it is not every page of Scripture but only the broadest salvific theme (and good luck finding anything about a personal relationship with Jesus in Obadiah!).

12. Robert G. Ingersoll, *Some Mistakes of Moses* (Buffalo: Prometheus Books, 1986), pp. viii–ix: "Too great praise challenges attention, and often brings to light a thousand faults that otherwise the general eye would never see. Were we allowed to read the Bible as we do all other books, we would admire its beauties, treasure its worthy thoughts, and account for all its absurd, grotesque and cruel things, by saying that its authors lived in rude, barbaric times. But we are told that it was written by inspired men; that it contains the will of God; that it is perfect, pure, and true in all its parts; the source and standard of all moral and religious truth... These claims are so at variance with every known recorded fact, so palpably absurd, that every free, unbiased soul is forced to raise the standard of revolt."

13. Everett F. Harrison, "Criteria of Biblical Inerrancy." In Frank E. Gaebelein, ed., *Christianity Today* (NY: Pyramid Books, 1968), pp. 86–90.

14. Julius Wellhausen, *Prolegomena to the History of Ancient Israel*. Trans. Menzies and Black (NY: Meridian Books/World Publishing, 1957); David Friedrich Strauss, *The Life of Jesus Critically Examined*. Trans. George Eliot. Lives of Jesus Series (Philadelphia: Fortress Press, 1972); Joseph Wheless, *Is It God's Word?An Exposition of the Fables and Mythology of the Bible and of the Impostures of Theology* (NY: Alfred A. Knopf, 1926).

15. James Taylor, "Lo and Behold," *Sweet Baby James* (Burbank: Warner Brothers Records, 1970).

16. Pinnock, p. 92: "It is a subject to raise when heaven's school begins its classes." Also p. 107.

17. Robert M. Price, *The Paperback Apocalypse: How the Christian Church Was Left Behind* (Amherst: Prometheus Books, 2007). See also David Berger and Michael Wyschogrod, *Jews and 'Jewish Christianity'* (NY: Ktav Publishing House, 1978), Chapter 4, "'Proofs' of Christianity in the Hebrew Bible," pp. 34–51.

18. Richard N. Longenecker, *Biblical Exegesis in the Apostolic Period* (Grand Rapids: Eerdmans, 1975). Himself an Evangelical, Longenecker repudiates the possibility of treating the Bible in the ancient manner today. In those far-off days, such exegesis may have been truly led by the Holy Spirit, Longenecker gladly allows, but who is to judge valid *pesher* interpretations these days, when we (Protestants) are bereft

of an infallible Teacher of Righteousness?

19.   See also J. Edward Wright, *The Early History of Heaven* (NY: Oxford University Press, 2000). The fatal flaw (besides bad exegesis) of the apologists' attempt to make the ancient texts speak of a round earth, etc., is that, if the biblical references (e.g., to a curved *vault over* the earth) are to be taken instead to denote nature as we understand it (e.g., as denoting an earth globe), then so must the usages of the same words and descriptions in other ancient writings, and this would produce the illusion that *everybody* in the ancient world was really talking about a spherical earth, not a solid firmament, etc. And if they did know all this, why did it all come as such a surprise to Galileo, Copernicus and the rest? When and how did everyone lose sight of the "real" meanings of the Bible and veer off into flat earths, Antipodean races, subterranean oceans, etc.? Why and how were things discovered all over *again* as they must have been? Thus Creationist apologetics reveal themselves as the cousin of modern myths of the Ancient Sea Kings, Atlantean super-science, etc.

PART TWO: WORLD RELIGIONS

12

KOSHER PIGS AND JEWS FOR JESUS

Who are "Jews for Jesus"? *Why* are Jews for Jesus? How can there *be* Jews for Jesus? Isn't that kind of like "Christians for Muhammad"? Capitalists for Marx? According to most folks' dictionaries, such a group shouldn't exist. But it does. Jews for Jesus have been around for nearly a quarter of a century. And all that time they have stuck in the craws of just about all Jews and a good many Christians. And Jesus? He is unavailable for comment.

Jews for Jesus, on the other hand, are more than available for comment. In fact, they tend to be available for comment whether you want them to be or not! Like Hare Krishnas, they may be found leafleting on the streets, spreading their gospel in a manner nostalgically reminiscent of New Left Radicals left over from the 60s, which some of them are. But unlike the Krishnas, they have a sense of humor. Aimed at non-Christian Jews, their pamphlets, called "broadsides," bear titles like "Kosher Pigs," confronting the issue of their contradictory identity head-on. Here's the deal: Jews for Jesus, started by a Jew-turned-Presbyterian named Martin Rosen in 1973, claim that Christianity is true Judaism, that Christian Jews are "completed Jews." The idea is that Jesus was a Jew, in fact the predicted messiah (anointed one) of Judaism, that his first followers were Jews, and that he never said anything about starting a new religion called Christianity. Obviously, they admit, most Jewish contemporaries of Jesus never jumped on the bandwagon, while many Gentiles did. Not surprisingly, the name of Jesus soon became associated with Gentiles and non-Jewish culture. Today very, very few Jews believe in Jesus as the messiah. But, Jews for Jesus say, that doesn't take away the essentially Jewish character of the gospel message about Jesus. It's just a historical irony, just like the fact that Buddhism started among Hindus in India but now exists mostly among Japanese, Chinese, Vietnamese, Koreans, etc., but hardly at all in India. Does that mean Buddhism shouldn't be considered an Indian religion? Hardly.

DECONSTRUCTIONIST JUDAISM?

Jews for Jesus, then, claim that they're being more Jewish than most Jews, who haven't got with God's program since they don't believe in Messiah Jesus. The splinter group of the Lubavitcher Hasidim who are waiting for the late Rebbe Menachem Mendel Schneerson to return from the dead as the Messiah feel pretty much the same way. They know they are very much in the minority, and they hope their fellow Jews will catch up with them sooner or later.

But it's a pretty safe bet that if you're a Jew but not a member of either the Schneerson sect or Jews for Jesus, you probably don't tend to view the two groups in the same light at all. Chances are, you think of the Schneerson sect the way most people view the Elvis cult: they're just going a bit overboard, though harmless enough. But Jews for Jesus? Most Jews have little patience with them, tend to see them as dangerous phonies. Why?

In many ways it is a question of who owns the copyright on the word "Jew." Who gets to decide who qualifies? Suppose you are a Reform Jew who takes a dim view of Jews for Jesus. Just remember that Orthodox rabbis think pretty much the same thing about you! Remember when the Falashas, the so-called "Black Jews" of Ethiopia, applied for admission to the State of Israel a few years ago? They got the nod. Should the rule be, "If you think you're a Jew, then you're a Jew?" I don't know. Whoever has the copyright, it's not me, that's for sure.

But why do most Jews think Jews for Jesus don't qualify? Jews see so-called Jews for Jesus as nothing but sneaky Christian evangelists masquerading as Jews. Basically Jews for Jesus seem to be inviting young Jews to leave the Jewish faith. But, unlike traditional Christian missionaries aiming at Jews, Jews for Jesus try to make the transition appear easier by denying it is a matter of converting at all—which, however, it is. "You'll still be Jewish!" But will you?

And then there's the matter of Jews for Jesus as an organization, as distinct from the wider movement of "Hebrew Christians" or "Messianic Jews." Jews for Jesus, Rosen's organization, sees itself overtly as a missionary organization and proclaims itself avowedly a group of evangelical Christians. They aim to persuade individual Jews to embrace faith in Jesus Christ, but after that, Jews for Jesus merely recommends the newly "completed Jew" join a local fellowship, whether a fundamentalist church or a "Messianic synagogue." It doesn't matter to them which. Jews for Jesus does not organize or sponsor local congregations. They are the type of organization that has a staff, but not members. More like United Jewish Appeal than the Lubavitchers. So asking about "Jews for Jesus" is not quite the same thing as talking about Jewish believers in Jesus or Jewish Christians.

SILK PURSE, SOW'S EAR

To really understand the gripe most Jews have with Jews for Jesus you need to look at the big historical picture. Sure, Jesus was a Jew; most Jews today are happy to admit that. Many see him as a liberal Pharisee, even as a reforming prophet. And Christianity began as a sect of messianic Jews. Everybody admits that. But today's Jews for Jesus are not like those early "Jewish Christians" (who called themselves Nazoreans and Ebionites). The ancient Jewish believers in Jesus were pious nationalistic Jews whose beliefs would not look much like anything we would recognize as Christianity today. They would look a lot more like the Essenes of the Dead Sea Scrolls. (For a good historical treatment, see Robert Eisenman, *James the Brother of Jesus*. Viking Penguin 1997.)

The apostle Paul and other Greek-speaking Jews and Gentiles rapidly transformed Christianity into something like the pagan Mystery Religions of the Greco-Roman world, and eventually our Roman Catholic and Eastern Orthodox Churches were the result. (As for Protestantism, it split off from Catholicism 500 years ago.) During all these centuries Christians kept the Jewish scripture as their own "Old Testament," and they developed ways of reading it as if it were written to Christians, not Jews. For instance, most of the "Old Testament" was reinterpreted, grossly out of context, as predictions of the coming of Jesus, his crucifixion, resurrection, etc. All the promises of God for his people were treated as if they were aimed at Christians, with Jews ejected from the picture for failing to believe in Jesus. The Christian view of Jews was all one big rationale for why Jews were no longer God's chosen people now that (Gentile) Christians had taken their place. In the process just about everything got redefined—including the notion of the messiah, which now came to denote the incarnation of God himself.

Where do Jews for Jesus fit into this picture? Their movement grows not out of Judaism but out of late 20th century Protestant fundamentalism. What happened was that some Jews who had converted to Christianity in effect decided that Protestant fundamentalism, as long as it wore a yarmulke and ate matzoh, counted as the real Judaism. As long as you lit your menorah, it would be Jewish to believe Jesus was God and had died for your sins. But would it be? The whole thing appears to be symbolized in one fact: the founder of Jews for Jesus changed his name from Martin Rosen to Moishe Rosen, obviously, so he would appear to be more Jewish. And that's all the Jews for Jesus Bible-quoting amounts to: Christianity pretending to be Jewish.

You can even look at it as a case of the Stockholm Syndrome, where prisoners come to identify with their captors, as some Jews did with their Nazi prison guards in the concentration camps. Jews take great pride in maintaining their community against all the attempts to eradicate them, including Christian evangelism which, if successful, would have to result in total assimilation, the cultural and religious disappearance of Judaism. Jews for Jesus seem to have, so to speak, joined the enemy and learned to play the enemy's game. Jews for Jesus are Jews, true, but they have thrown in the towel and internalized the ideology of Christianity, a set of explanations for why God has abandoned Jews in favor of Christians. At least from a historical standpoint, then, Jews for Jesus is at heart a Christian movement, not a Jewish one. The Judaism of the thing seems purely cosmetic. You can't make a Jewish silk purse out of a Christian sow's ear, I guess.

SEMANTICS AND SEMITICS

I have spoken with "Moishe" Rosen and even attended a Protestant seminary (Gordon-Conwell Theological Seminary, 1976–1977) along with Jews for Jesus members. There was no question in anyone's mind that these people were, like me at the time, evangelical Christians. There was essentially no difference between them and many other friends of mine who didn't mind saying straight out that they had converted from Judaism but were now Christians. It was all a matter of semantics, but not of Semitics. That they were Christians was not up for dispute; whether they were Jews was. Even today, they are careful to include Gentile Christian missionary leaders on their board of directors, one suspects, in order to make it clear to Christian supporters that Jews for Jesus are indeed good Christians, not some "Judaizing" sect of half-Jewish/half-Christian heretics.

There is no reason to question the sincerity of Rosen, his organization, or any other self-styled "Messianic Jews." The question is whether their position makes any sense. There's no sense in accusing them of being phonies; the relevant question is, are they *confused*? Let's compare Jewish Christians with Jewish Buddhists, and you'll see what I mean. *Jewish Buddhists*? That's right, there are a number of Jews (I have never seen any statistics) who practice both Judaism and Zen meditation. They see no problem because Zen, though Buddhist in origin, transcends its roots, and it is a technique people use to induce a new state of awareness. Nothing in this even overlaps Judaism, much less contradicts it. In Asia, for the same reason, you can find plenty of Confucianist Buddhists and Taoist Buddhists. The two religions don't have enough to do with each other to be contradictory, so if you have sufficient time and energy, you can practice both. But can you be a Jewish Christian in the same way? It gets tricky because Judaism and Christianity do have a considerable overlap, and while much of it is compatible, like the ethics of both faiths, some of the beliefs clash pretty severely.

About twenty years ago I happened to check out a congregation of Messianic Jews who met, ironically, in a Lutheran church in Long Island. This group had begun some years before as an evangelistic outreach to Jews by a number of converted Jews in the Lutheran congregation. They had adopted the "completed Jew" pose, but eventually they started taking it more seriously than they had probably expected to. By the time I met them, they were strict, almost Hasidic, Torah-keepers. Their worship looked nothing like any Christian service I had ever attended, and I was fascinated to hear their discussions of theology. They had begun to reinterpret Jesus in categories from the Book of Enoch and the Kabbalah. Okay, these people were Jewish Christians. They deserved the name. It wasn't long before the Lutheran Church got fed up with them, and the two parted ways. My guess, however, is that Jews for Jesus wouldn't have liked them any better, because underneath the yarmulke, Jews for Jesus is one more Protestant fundamentalist missionary effort aimed at Jews.

HEBREWS AND HYBRIDS

The Messianic synagogue I visited was genuinely syncretistic, combining elements of belief from two religions. By contrast, I have suggested that Jews for Jesus is pushing Christian beliefs as the right kind for Jews to hold. Its beliefs about Jews, Jesus, Gentiles, and salvation are Christian, not Jewish, in origin. Are these elements of Christianity compatible with Judaism, as Jews for Jesus claim? Like I claimed Zen and Judaism are? Maybe *so*.

In one sense you could look at Jews for Jesus as kind of like Reconstructionist Jews (though I suspect neither would relish the comparison!). Both seem to think that what makes you Jewish is *being a member of the Jewish culture (or subculture), not particular religious beliefs.* Thus it is not rare to find Torah-reading atheists in Reconstructionist synagogues. And if atheism is compatible with Judaism, why couldn't Christianity be compatible with Judaism, too? If, that is, Judaism is Jewish culture. Jews for Jesus happily celebrate Passover, for instance, yarmulkes and all, though they will give you a play-by-play description of how each part of the seder stands for Jesus or the Trinity, etc. They are combining elements of *Jewish culture*, including lifestyle and liturgy, with elements of *Christian belief*, just as an atheistic Jew may piously keep kosher in a Reconstructionist synagogue. In the same way, you can visit Messianic Jewish synagogues and see nothing particularly out of place in the order of service—until that is, you start hearing references to Jesus. These folks are believing Christian, acting Jewish, and sincerely doing both.

One of the major Christian misconceptions about Jewish belief is that while Christians believe you are saved by God's forgiving grace, they think Jews believe that they are obligated to keep all the Torah commandments under pain of damnation, like a checklist of things to be done before you have earned your merit badge. Of course, Jews teach that no one can hope to be saved except by the grace of God. No one can earn salvation like earning a vacation cruise by selling enough magazine subscriptions. Salvation comes by the grace of a God who delights to forgive all who truly repent. Jews feel obliged to keep the commandments for a different reason: it is part of their national identity, assigned them as part of their covenant as a people with God. And thus keeping the commandments of God is a privilege, not a chore.

I find it a happy irony that when (usually, I suspect, assimilated half-religious) Jews accept the invitation of Jews for Jesus to become Christians, they often appreciate their Jewish heritage more than before, when they took it for granted. Sure, they believe they have God's grace through Jesus, so if they start attending a Messianic synagogue, it's not because they think they have to in order to be saved. In this matter of motive they think they differ from traditionalist (non-Christian) Jews, whom they falsely imagine to be sweating to accumulate brownie points by keeping Jewish Law. But that's the Christian misconception! How ironic that, having God's grace and salvation as a settled issue, Christian Jews can enter into Jewish custom and liturgy with what turns out to be the same motive Jews really had all along: it's part of the privilege of being Jewish, not an annoying list of curriculum requirements.

SMORGASBORD SEDER

We live in a multi-cultural, pluralistic society unlike any since the cosmopolitan era of ancient Rome. We cannot help anymore being aware of each other's religions, and that fact alone makes it very difficult to insist that you or I have the true religion, that our neighbor of another faith is a benighted heathen. Religious belief tends to become diluted in a society like ours. Beliefs start rubbing off on one another. A friend of mine likes to describe himself as "a Jew who loves Jesus and believes in reincarnation." I know others who are ostensibly Christians in dialogue with Jews and who have given up their belief in Jesus as the messiah. I knew a Pentecostal Christian who devoted himself to keeping all the laws of Judaism. And then there are the "one from column A, one from column B" New Agers who tend to mix a Mulligan Stew of religion. Unitarian churches are filled with mixed-faith couples whose children receive a Comparative Religion course as their catechism. Groups like the Amish and the Hasid communities of Brooklyn are only exceptions that prove the rule. They have erected their walls so high precisely because they see the danger of pluralism and assimilation looming so largely.

In such a context, the question, "Are Christian Jews really Jews at all?" is very much like the tricky question that always comes up in mixed marriages: if a Jew and a Christian marry, what religion do the children belong to? Especially if you raise them to love and respect both parental faiths? What is the child's religious identity? Only the child, ultimately, can decide that one. I am proposing that the Jews for Jesus, Jewish Christians, Messianic Jews are the religiously ambiguous children of a mixed marriage between mainstream Judaism and the American culture. They cannot bring themselves to deny either side of their cultural DNA. Are they really Jews? Like the individual children of mixed marriages, perhaps only they have the right to say. For the rest of us, as always, it is probably safer to try to understand them than to presume to judge or classify them. Sure, it's annoying to be told you're going to be damned unless you believe in Jesus. That's obnoxious. You feel like the pilot in the comedy *Airplane*: you'd like to haul off and slug such nuisances. But that has nothing to do with the nuisance being a Jew or a Christian, neither or both. There are jerks for Jesus, jerks for Judaism, and jerks for neither one.

13

IF YOU DISLIKE CHRISTIANITY, YOU'LL HATE BUDDHISM!

As a teacher of Comparative Religion courses over many years, I have come to notice some surprising and even paradoxical things. It is no surprise to me when certain students keep their minds as closed as a clenched fist because their fundamentalist upbringing demands it. I know to expect it, especially since I felt that way myself when I was their age. But it has surprised me on occasion to discover the same sort of mind set present in other quarters.

Many years ago my wife Carol and I dropped by to visit Maryanne, a classmate of my wife. Carol had told me Maryanne was a convert to Buddhism—which today may mean anything, often denoting more of a New Ager than any traditional sort of Buddhist. After all, if you really believe Cyril Henry Hoskins, AKA Tuesday Lobsang Rampa, is a Buddhist, you may think you are, too, even if you are as far from the Dharma as he was. As we opened a polite conversation, it rapidly developed that Maryanne took a rather non-Buddhistic stance toward Christianity. That is to say, her third eye was somewhat jaundiced when it came to Christianity. She proceeded to fulminate bitterly against its psychological and theological inadequacies. You can imagine the usual line about the destructive self-hatred and guilt over the physical body that Christianity fosters. Then she went on to denigrate the bloody superstition of the substitutionary atonement of Christ on the cross.

As a matter of fact, I agreed with these critiques. My own approach was to try to "purify" Christian existence from these various phobias and superstitions,

128

get to the philosophical/psychological meat of the thing. I made ready to reply, but I sought not to defend Christianity (I couldn't have defended those aspects in good faith anyway). And yet neither did I consider attacking Buddhism, which then as now I revere as a true religion. My chosen strategy was to show how she was reading Buddhism even more selectively than she was reading Christianity.

Surely, I ventured, she could not be unaware of the fact that the very doctrinal features she despised in their Christian avatars were not only present in but absolutely central to historic mainstream Buddhism! I'm not sure what she took Buddhism to mean, but it's a safe bet all the Buddhist faithful in China, Mongolia, Tibet, Sikkim, Bhutan, Nepal, Korea, and Japan (to say nothing of that ancient stronghold of Oriental mysticism, Colorado) would not agree with her. For Mahayana Buddhism is solidly based on the Bodhisattva doctrine. Southern Asian Buddhism, Theravada (or Hinayana, as the Mahayana call it), is a spare and logically simpler scheme of attaining Nirvana through self-effort aimed at extinguishing the apparent self, or ego.

But the Lords of the Mahayana rejected such a goal as selfish in aim and in means. Instead, they believed, all Buddhists ought to emulate Gautama Buddha himself who, after all, did not yield to the temptation of Mara that he should leave this poor world behind and pass forever into his own Nirvana at once. For the sake of poor mortals, Samsara addicts, the Lord Buddha deferred his own rightful Nirvana. And so should we! And given the fact that all beings share the Buddha nature and are thus capable of eventual Buddhahood, it is finally nonsensical to suggest that I can be saved without you and everyone else being saved. It's all or nothing. This means, as the Buddha is made to reveal to his disciples in the *Saddharma Pundarika* (The Lotus of the True Law), that even the 24 previous Buddhas (including Dipankara, the one under whose tutelage Gautama Buddha first heard the Dharma preached many ages before) are still active behind the scenes in the Sambogkhya, the penultimate realm of existence where the Buddhas and Bodhisattvas dwell like celestial gods, answering prayers and otherwise aiding poor mortals who need a hand up.

One ought to take the vow to embark on the path to Buddhahood, and once one does so, one counts as a Bodhisattva (a Buddha-to-be). This is a long and hard row to hoe, but you'd be spending the time in pointless reincarnations anyway, so why not? Through countless lifetimes of toil and self-sacrifice for the good of others, the Bodhisattva earns good karma far in excess of that necessary to win his wings (as Clarence does in *It's a Wonderful Life*). He has to be in the business of doing good works to become worthy of Bodhisattvahood.

Now, who's the Bodhisattva to do these good works *for*? This works out rather well for the vast majority of Buddhist laity who have not the stamina to undertake the Greater Career. They are doing their bit by financially supporting the earthly Bodhisattvas (as they did the Theravadin monks down south) and by praying to the heavenly ones, as their ancestors used to pray to the Vedic gods. Eventually the store of supererogatory merit amassed by the Bodhisattvas was believed so great that they could grant not only worldly boons but actual salvation itself! We think that the Buddha taught that there was no grace upon which to draw to gain Nirvana, since the whole idea was to change your own frame of mind, nullify the ego, which in the nature of the case only you can do. But by hook and by crook, Mahayana Buddhism eventually evolved a salvation scheme by which certain virtuosos, like the Buddha himself, might in fact offer such saving grace to those calling upon them in faith. By such an act of receptive faith the believer is allowed to draw upon the store of good Karma gained by the Bodhisattvas by their good works. It will be transferred to the believers' accounts as if it had been their own achievement. Does this sound familiar? It will sound even more so. For some Bodhisattvas, in order to gain still more abundant good Karma, will voluntarily submit to the tortures of the numerous spectacular Hells of Buddhist eschatology. Avalokiteshvara and his brethren are in this fashion undergoing expiatory suffering in your place and for your benefit.

In Pure Land Buddhism, fantastically popular in Japan where it spread from China and India, we witness the ultimate spinning out of the logic of this redemptive theology. A long succession of Pure Land patriarchs, basing their teachings on the Longer and Shorter *Sukhavati Sutras* (= Pure Land Scriptures), sought to refine the meaning of salvation by grace through faith alone. Their Sutras have Gautama taking the role of John the Baptist, singing the greater glories of Amitabha Buddha, an ancient king who, hearing the preaching of a contemporary Buddha, renounced the throne and took up the discipline of the Bodhisattva. His strategy was to put all of his accumulated Karmic green stamps toward the creation of a "Pure Land," a world in which one need only be reborn to achieve the stage of non-returning, the seventh stage of the Bodhisattva path (something that would otherwise take unthinkable eons of good works, as it did in the case of Amitabha himself). At the end of one lifetime in the Sukhavati, one would infallibly attain Buddhahood.

And how was one to guarantee one's reservations? Aye, there's the rub. The text said one need only call on Amitabha's name three times, and that would do it. But the various patriarchs sought to determine, with all the introspective microscrutiny of a medieval penance manual, precisely what mental condition constituted saving faith. What meditations and attitudes were required? As always happens with introspective pietism (read Watchman Nee, Andrew Murray, etc.) what looked easy turns out to be arduous and confusing—or is made to be so. Each subsequent patriarch narrowed the range of activity required, recognizing that the more a successful faith hinges upon one fulfilling certain conditions, the more salvation after all depends on one's own works ("Self-Power"). And this is incompatible with the doctrine that one needs grace to be saved in the first place. On the one hand, we are so crushed beneath a burden of bad Karma that we would have no hope of ever working it off ourselves. On the other, we live in a degenerate age when the Dharma is but dimly understood. Facing Scylla and Charybdis in this way, we must be saved by grace ("Other-Power"), or we will not be saved at all. Hence the Pure Land theologians tried to circumvent the clever subterfuges of the self-exalting ego by placing complete and utter reliance on the Other-Power of Amitabha Buddha.

In the end, the Japanese patriarch Shinran wound up paralleling Martin Luther and John Calvin: he taught that the first inkling of an inclination one felt to call upon the name of the Buddha was itself proof of Amitabha's prevenient grace. One could never have even sought such salvation without already having been given it! We cannot even seek to repent unless we have already been regenerated by the unilateral grace of God. If we were still sinners, we would think of nothing but continuing to sin. There is no question of subtle Christian missionary influence. It is just that the logic of piety, taught not to believe in its own power, and yet having to *do* something, however minimal and passive, always issues in the same solution, as it did also in Visistadvaita Vedanta Hinduism, which divided into the monkey school (believers must hang on to God's grace like a baby monkey carried by its mother) and the cat school (momma cat simply carries her kittens by the scruff of the neck, like it or not).

Is all this a betrayal of Buddhism with its doctrine of self-reliance? They say no, since a religion based on the negation of self can hardly rely for its success on Self-Power! Interesting point.

So here we have a religion containing the features of crippling original sin, bankrupt and worthless selfhood, salvation by passive faith in the vicarious sufferings of a redeemer (actually a whole stable of them, as in the Catholic calendar of saints), and all of this derived from an infallible scripture, not from one's own cherished intuitions. What is this religion? Buddhism. Christianity. Take your pick. If you prefer something less complex, something more self-reliant, you can always find revamped, streamlined versions of either religion. But, as they stand, neither is all that much different from the other in broad outline. When Maryanne embraced what she called Buddhism as an alternative to Christianity, she had merely exchanged six of one for half a dozen of the other, though she didn't know about at least three of them!

One might contend that Mahayana is a corrupt form of Buddhism, one that has lost sight of the vision of its Founder, whereas Christianity's corresponding doctrines are in continuity with the central vision of its Founder. But this is the worst kind of special pleading. If it happened to the one, it would be surprising if it hadn't happened to the other, too. Max Scheler thought that both religions inevitably suffered the same fate because of the ever-recurrent pattern of religions that exalt a charismatic founder. The founder is first lionized because of his summons for all to follow him in the heroic path. He dies, and the followers form a sectarian community, living out his heroic ethic, necessarily in alienation from the conventional world around them. But time passes and no one finds it any more so easy to live at such a fever pitch of piety and social radicalism. They come to assimilate themselves to the world again, rationalizing this by means of deifying the founder. Now that the life style he taught seems so far beyond the reach of even believers, they conclude his own heroic life must have been the result of his being a superhuman god. Thus no one can be expected to emulate him, and his heroism ceases to be a role-model. Instead, the believers come to regard it as an act done on their behalf so as to absolve them of the sin of not being able to do it! Mediocrity, here we come! And then Luther, Shinran, and the others start in trying to eliminate any vestige of self-effort as impious, even though at first it had been the very basis of the founder's teaching! Such a decline, plainly recognized, at least on some level, in Buddhism, is more characteristic neither of Christianity nor of Buddhism.

Why had my wife's friend been oblivious of all this? My guess is that, like many today, she had really adopted some form of Western pop self-realization therapy and, ironically, called it Buddhism. Harvey Cox foresaw this trivializing trend in his 1977 book *Turning East*. Shirley MacLaine can call it Buddhism, like Jim Bakker calls his religion Christianity, but neither is fooling me.

It might be better to do what Herman Hesse advocated in his novel *Siddhartha*: follow the Buddha's path *not* by slavishly aping him, but by striking out on your own authentic dharma just as he did. How else are you to imitate a great non-conformist except by refusing to conform to him? Have the courage of your own convictions! Don't hide behind supposed authorities by bottling your own product and putting the Buddhist (or Christian) label on it.

14

MYTHS AND MEN:
THREE GREAT RELIGIOUS FOUNDERS

The lives of most religious founders have come down to us, not as straight biography, but as sets of devotional myths and pious object lessons. Their aim is not to inform the reader so much as to edify. As the Buddha might have said, the question of what the founder actually said or did is not among those which tend unto edification. And yet, as the great comparative religion scholar Mircea Eliade said, Western thinkers have been willing to sacrifice everything including religious faith for the sake of pure knowledge. We want to know what happened, if we can, even if that should bar us from the edification of the traditional holy tales. But as anyone who has embarked on the journey of historical discovery knows, the effort is not without a kind of edification of its own. With that in mind let us proceed.

I. BUDDHA

The founder of the Buddhist *sangha* (community) has many names. Siddhartha is his given name. Gautama (or Gotama) is his family name, while he belonged to the Sakya clan, hence the epithet Sakyamuni, "Sage of the Sakyas." His titles include the Tathagatha ("The One Thus Come," which might mean many things), the Jina ("The Victor"), and of course the Buddha ("The Enlightened One"). Western textbook summaries of the Buddha's career must appear startling to any believing Asian Buddhists who chance to read them since these treatments tacitly presuppose a radical "quest of the historical Gautama" as alien to popular Buddhist piety as the modern critical quest for Jesus is offensive to traditional Christian faith. Essentially what any standard textbook will tell you is that Siddhartha was a princeling born to one of many petty Kshatrya-caste noble households. As such his lifestyle would have been slightly above the level of general poverty. What relative affluence he had, he renounced once he found his conscience moved to pity by the plight of all mortals: sickness, eventual infirmity, death—and endless more rounds of the same via reincarnation. Like many young people of his time and his caste, he is pictured as leaving home to seek salvation at the feet of the various gurus who taught techniques of yogic meditation amid shady forest groves, far from the bloody sacrificial altars of the official Brahmanical religion of the priests. The picture is not unlike that of affluent American youths quitting church and business school to run off and join "cults" like the Moonies or the Hare Krishnas in our day.

Having briefly studied with two such gurus and attaching himself to a group of ascetics, he found his questions still unanswered, so he launched out alone and seated himself beneath the spreading branches of the Bodhi Tree ("Tree of Enlightenment"), where he resolved to remain till the light should dawn—and in a matter of hours it did. Returning to his old ascetical colleagues he preached to them the *dharma* (doctrine) of desire as the cause of suffering and the cessation of desire as the key to blissful Nirvana, already in this life. After many years of successful itinerant teaching, the Buddha expired after being accidentally poisoned by a well-wisher who had sought only to provide him a meal.

But all this is only the demythologized version. No Buddhist scripture puts it so simply. Instead, Buddhists are taught, young Siddhartha was miraculously conceived and announced before birth as the savior of the world. As an infant in the crib he already proclaimed his own great destiny. His earthly father, a king with fabulous wealth, sought to influence the boy to a career of conquest like his own and to that end sheltered him on the vast palatial grounds, where he should remain ignorant of the facts of sickness, old age, and death until it came time for him to march forth and unite all India under his booted heel. If the boy did not know the world needed salvation, he would never bother to seek that salvation, or so his father reasoned. But the gods saw to it that the young prince did not escape his destiny. One by one four deities appeared on the palace grounds in the human disguises, first, of a sick man, then an old man, then a corpse, finally a mendicant monk, a seeker of salvation. His father's best-laid schemes in ruins, Siddhartha left the palace, traded garments with his stunned charioteer, and headed off for the woods. There he met one guru after another, then the circle of ascetics, winding up beneath the Bodhi Tree. There he attained his revelation only in the face of some six distracting temptations by Mara, the Buddhist Satan.

How have Western scholars distilled the first version (the "historical Gautama") from the second (the "Buddha of faith")? The best book on the subject is E.J. Thomas's *Life of Buddha as Legend and History* (1927). Thomas easily dispenses with the obvious fairy-tale improbabilities. And like John Dominic Crossan and other historical Jesus researchers, he reconstructs, from what we know of India's political economy of the period, the sort of socio-economic conditions Prince Siddhartha must have lived in, assuming he was an historical individual of the early sixth century BCE. As for specific episodes, Thomas displays the acumen of a David Friedrich Strauss, noting where the existence of a more modest version alongside the better known spectacular version must force us to dismiss the latter, however reluctantly, as legendary. For instance, we might drop the intervention of the gods and yet maintain that the young prince happened to behold a sick man, an old man, and a corpse, and that the shock made all his luxury pale on him. This is the way it is shown in Bernardo Bertolucci's film *Little Buddha*. But then we notice a neglected passage in the scriptures where the Buddha recalls how he was moved to seek salvation by the simple process of cogitation on the unpleasant state of mankind. No gods, not even any "passing sights" (as the sick man, old man, dead man and monk are called in Buddhist lore). We have to admit it is impossible to imagine a Buddhist fabricating the more modest version if the facts were as dramatic as the story of the Passing Sights makes them. But if it were known that the Buddha merely thought out the matter, it is quite easy to picture the pious imagination embroidering these meagre facts to create the tale of the Passing Sights.

Gospel critics defend the historical character of the baptism of Jesus by John the Baptist on the grounds that the story serves not to glorify Jesus but to subordinate him to a prior saintly figure; hence, they reason, it cannot have been a Christian creation. In exactly parallel fashion, Thomas figures that the historical Siddhartha must have studied with two gurus as the story goes, since later Buddhists would hardly have wanted to picture their hero feeling the need for instruction from mere mortals. But here I think Thomas, like his gospel colleagues, is missing a likely option. Both stories actually, I think, finally serve to subordinate the Baptist and the pre-Buddhist gurus to their erstwhile disciples, Jesus and Siddhartha. The stories are symbolic ways of saying that "our" man could not be satisfied even with the best of contemporary teaching—and went on to transcend it. This point comes through with particular clarity in the Buddha's case since one of the two gurus' doctrine is described in terms highly reminiscent of contemporary Samkhya Hinduism which shares the Buddhist "distinctive" doctrine that it is desire, not karma, which causes reincarnation. It was important to try to distance Buddhism from a close rival and predecessor because of what Harold Bloom calls "the anxiety of influence."

There is, then, a surprisingly meagre residue once one scrapes away the historically dubious. Even the notion of the young prince abandoning affluence begins to sound like one more piece of typical stage setting when we realize the same set-up occurs in the hagiography of the Jaina saint Vardhamana (usually called Mahavira, "Great Hero"), who supposedly lived a single generation earlier than the Buddha. Granted, one man might have followed in the other's footsteps, but this is not the only parallel between Buddhist and Jainist hagiography. When Siddhartha sits beneath the Bodhi Tree, he is protected from Mara's assaults by the hood canopy of the mythical Naga King, a hydra-like cobra deity. And so was the Jain hero Parsva, the predecessor of Mahavira! History does repeat itself, but not nearly as much as myth does! The Jainist religion, much like Buddhism in many ways, believed in the periodic advent of a Jina or Tirthankara ("Ford-maker, Bridge-builder, Trail-blazer") in every age, twenty-four in all, Mahavira being the last in this cosmic cycle. It is no wonder that the same adventures should be predicated of any or all of the saviors, who were essentially repetitions of one another anyway. And the same is true for Buddhism itself, since even early Theravada Buddhism, while free of the more extravagant mythology of later Mahayana Buddhism, made Siddhartha Gautama the twenty-fifth in a series of Buddhist avatars that had not yet run its course. Buddhists awaited the coming of a future Buddha, Maitreya. Buddhist doctrine even holds that every single Buddha has repeated all the steps in the canonical life of Gautama Buddha (except for the abortive apprenticeship with the two gurus—here later sensitivities *have* deemed it unbecoming for the Master to have masters, as Thomas suggested).

But it is only the Western critic who would put it this way. Buddhists would say that Gautama Buddha was the repeater. It was he who trod the same path as his predecessors, like Dipankara Buddha. Western scholars argue in a circle at this point, assuming there must have been a historical Buddha, the most recent, and so similarities in the myths of previous Buddhas, all of them mythical, must be derived from the story of the one historical Buddha, the actual founder of Buddhism, Siddhartha Gautama, the Sage of the Sakya clan. But this Gautama-centered perspective would seem strange to many if not most Buddhists. For Pure Land Buddhism, by far the most popular family of Buddhist sects, Gautama is hardly the most important. He yields that palm to Amitabha Buddha, whose salvific labors created the Pure Land where those who call on Amitabha's name in faith can be reborn unto certain salvation. Gautama Buddha is simply the teller of the tale of the far superior Amitabha in the *Sukhavati Sutras* sacred to the sect.

To the average Buddhist none of the twenty-five Buddhas is any more or less historical than the others. And I wonder if they are right. I wonder if Western scholars have simply imported the model of a "revealed religion" with a prophetic founder into a religion ill-suited to that schema. Hinduism lacks it, and no Western critic maintains that there was somewhere back in the past, a "historical Krishna" or a "historical Rama." These two names are among several avatars, or incarnations, of the god Vishnu, and all recognize them as pure myth. An earlier generation of Western scholars of Buddhism, including R. Otto Franke, did relegate Gautama Buddha to the same bin and believed Gautama Buddha just a collective name for earlier generations of unnamed Buddhist teachers who, being vigorous opponents of the ego, would hardly have troubled themselves to be remembered as individuals. That must be true in large measure any way you cut it, since on anyone's reading virtually none of the teaching ascribed to him in Buddhist scripture, all of it written down only some centuries after the traditional date of the Buddha, can possibly be his. What did the Buddha himself actually teach? There is even conflict in the texts as to whether he taught the now-central Buddhist tenet that there is no individual soul (*atman*), or whether, like all yogis, he simply refused to identify such an exalted entity with the ego-personality.

No doubt under the then-pervasive influence of Max Müller, H. Kern thought the Buddha was, like Vishnu and Samson, probably also Hercules, a mythic embodiment of the sun. Müller's theory that all myths originated as solar symbols was too ambitious, but instead of correcting its excesses, typically, scholars pronounced its death-knell and went on to alternative theories, most of them equally over-reaching. This pendulum swing perhaps accounts for the conventional neglect of the possibility that there never was an historical Buddha. I suspect that the scholarly assumption that somewhere beneath the legend there must lurk a real historical founder is a modern case of Euhemerism, the belief of ancient historians that all the mythic gods had first been historical heroes, kings, warriors, physicians, etc. And besides, if one were to admit the gospel-like legends of the Buddha may have gathered like debris around a historically empty Black Hole, why would it not be feasible to raise the same question about those great founder figures of the biblical tradition itself: Moses and Jesus? And that of course is just what we are about to do.

II. MOSES

It is surprising that one does not hear more expressions of doubt as to the historical existence of Moses, the ostensible originator of the Hebrew law. I suspect this is because such suspicions would be heard as attacks upon the Torah itself, and this implicit equation, I shall argue, is a natural one. It is reflected in the ancient custom of the rabbis who used the name Moses as synechdoche for the Torah commandments. "Moses says . . ." Indeed, Moses is essentially a narrative embodiment of the Torah. In the vast majority of biblical tales in which he appears he does not transcend his function of constituting a peg upon which to hang this or that legal precedent. First, let us review this evidence in the broadest possible manner.

One major group of Pentateuchal stories is the class of *ceremonial* and *legal precedents*. The idea here is to secure legitimacy of some later law or rule or detail of religious observance by retroactively fathering it on Moses. Two different versions (Exodus 18:1–27 and Numbers 11:11–12, 14–17, 24–30) have come down to us of Moses receiving divine sanction for establishing a board of jurists or elders to, so to speak, adjudicate legal cases *ex cathedra*, from the seat of Moses (Matthew 23:2–3a). The origin of the priestly order of Levites (actually a *re*-explanation of their origin, replacing their original identity as the priesthood of the serpent deity Nehushtan, as Ignaz Goldziher showed long ago) is ascribed to Moses in Exodus 32:25–29. The temple image of Nehushtan (see 2 Kings 18:4) is re-explained in Numbers 21:4–9 as Moses' version of Apollo's healing caduceus. Similarly, we can detect (in Exodus 32:2–4a, jump to 24, back to 4c-5) the vestiges of a miracle story originally told in the Israelite temples of Dan and Bethel to explain to pilgrims how the priests knew in the first place to represent the invisible God in the form of a young bull (1 Kings 12:28–29). Of course, as we read it, it has become a lampoon of the calf image. Numbers 10:35–36 anchors the war-chant of the Ark of the Covenant (Psalm

68:1ff) in the practice of Moses. Numbers 27:1–11 amends the Torah to allow daughters to inherit.

Cautionary tales form our second category. These are vintage priestcraft as the rationalists used to call it, scare stories appealing to superstitious fear to keep sinners in line even when the authorities cannot see them sinning. Some are aimed at the people as a whole, in the fine sermonic tradition of 1 Corinthians 10:9–10: "We must not put the Lord to the test as some of them did and were destroyed by serpents; nor grumble as some of them did and were destroyed by the Destroyer." We are warned in Numbers 11:10, 13, 18–23, 31–33, as well as Numbers 21:4–9, not to complain to God in times of want. Better not violate the enforced idleness of the Sabbath even in trivial ways (Numbers 15:32–36). Elsewhere we find a warning not to take private booty in war, but to turn all the spoils of holy war over to the priests (Joshua chapter 7). The "uppity" laity are bullied not to give any lip to those who speak as Moses' successors (Numbers 12:1–12).

But it is not only the laity that needed to be kept in line. Most of the cautionary tales are the special concern of the priests for whom the Pentateuch (Genesis, Exodus, Leviticus, Numbers, Deuteronomy) was after all written. Leviticus 10:16–20 warns priests to be sure they finish the sin-offering goat meat, much as Catholic priests today must finish the leftover communion wine and not just pour it out. They must be careful not to mix the incense recipe wrong, or else (Leviticus 10:1–3). God forbid that a priestly functionary dare touch the sacred Ark without proper ritual preparation, no matter how noble the motive (outside the Pentateuch, in 2 Samuel 6:6–8). Numbers 17:1ff tells lower priestly orders not to covet the professional prerogatives of the Aaronide Brahmins. Comparing Numbers 16:1ff with Psalms 84 and 51, especially verses16–17, we gain a fascinating glimpse into Levitical politics. "Korah" in Numbers 16 stands for the later Levitical choral guild the Sons of Korah who penned (and sang) beautiful songs for the temple hymnal. Sacrificial priests were much more highly paid than mere singers, in that the former, sacerdotal butchers, retained a hefty share of the meat they sacrificed. The singers got *nada*. Eventually they protested, and their answer was a tale in which Korah was sent down the shoot to Sheol for his effrontery against Moses (= the Aaronide priests). In reprisals, the singers began to pepper their compositions with dismissals of the whole idea of animal sacrifices (Psalm 51:16–17)!

Geological stories, our third category, sought to satisfy popular curiosity about unusual rock formations, strategic oases in desert places, etc., things formerly ascribed to the potent presence of Baals and other local godlings in these places, which were thus also considered holy places with their own shrines, priests, and fortune-tellers. People continued to visit them, and as Israelite theology changed, new reasons for their holiness had to be found. And Moses figured into most of them. He is responsible for the sweet water at Marah (Exodus 15:22–25), the spring at Massah and Meribah (Exodus 17:1–7 and Numbers 20:1–13), the well at Be-er (Number 21:16–18), the Oasis of Twelve Springs (Exodus 15:27), and even the common desert growth of sweet, flaky manna (Exodus 16:1–36 and Numbers 11:4–9). These brief Pentateuchal notices originated much as the ubiquitous "George Washington slept here" plaques in New England.

Etymological stories provide folk-theories for the origins of certain place names, sometimes also sanitizing former heathenish meanings in the process. These anecdotes include Exodus 15:22–25 ("Marah"), Exodus 17:1–7 and Numbers 20:1–13 ("Massah and Meribah"), Exodus 11:1–3 ("Taberah"), Numbers 11:31–35 ("Kibroth"), and Number 21:1–3 ("Hormah"). The most important is the re-explanation of Moses' own name. Originally it is an Egyptian name, meaning "son of," as in Thut*mose* (son of Thoth) and Ra*mses* (son of Ra), but later Jews wanted it to be Hebrew. The closest Hebrew word available was *mashah*, "to draw forth," so Moses had to have been named for an event in his infancy in which he was drawn out of something, and it had to be eventful enough to commemorate by naming him for it. Hence the story of baby Moses set adrift on the Nile and drawn forth from the bulrushes by Pharaoh's daughter. The "baby set adrift" motif is quite common, e.g.., in the myths of Perseus, Romulus and Remus, Sargon, etc.

The *ethnological myths* of Genesis pretend to account for the current relations between Israel and her various neighbors by telling paradigmatic stories of how their symbolic mythical ancestors related (e.g., Jacob, father of the Israelite tribes, versus Esau, father of the Edomites). In a slightly different idiom, the ethnological stories of Exodus, Leviticus, Numbers and Deuteronomy define the conflicts and alliances of these groups by presenting a gallery of first encounters of Israel with the neighboring nations: were they friendly to God's people or not? If not, they were eternal enemies. Of course, the stories reflected the later politics, not vice versa. These categories mattered a great deal, since they governed the options for Jewish intermarriage, commerce, and admission to the temple. In short, these tales, too, are law.

Moses' role in every one of these stories is to authorize. He is in the stories *for the sake of something else.* Are there any stories told *about Moses*? Yes, but strangely, as Raphael Patai and Robert Graves point out (*Hebrew Myths: The Book of Genesis*, 1983), each of these little Moses stories in Exodus, as well as their linked sequencing, reflect a parallel set of stories told back in Genesis about the patriarch Jacob. Both characters flee eastward after a dangerous altercation (Genesis 27:41–28:5 and Exodus 2:15). Arriving there each hero comes to the aid of native women at a well (Genesis 29:1–12 and Exodus 2:16–17ff). Intending to marry into their family, he enters his father-in-law's employ as a shepherd (Genesis 29:18; 30:29, etc., and Exodus 3:1).God appears to the hero and tells him to return westward (Genesis 31:13 and Exodus 3:1–10ff). He returns with his new and growing family (Genesis 31:17–21 and Exodus 4:20). On the way, astonishingly, God ambushes him (Genesis 32:22–32 and Exodus 4:24–26)! The effect is extraordinary, much like the extensive parallels between Peter and Paul in the Acts of the Apostles. Which cycle, Moses or Jacob, was original? Probably the Jacob version, since each of his stories has a different function (etymological, ceremonial, ethnological) in its own right, whereas the Moses versions seem to have been inserted to move the Moses story along. Thus they seem derivative.

Who was Moses the lawgiver, originally? If all the stories of which Moses' fame now consists are secondary, who was the original Moses whose importance they presuppose? He was, I venture, another sun god. Max Müller being out of fashion doesn't make this any less likely. The basic Moses mytheme is that of the sun (god) which emerges from the tent of concealment, the night, and bestows commandments upon a king. The sun is also the source of both death (by sunstroke) and healing. Psalm 19, as Old Testament scholars uniformly admit, comes from Akhenaten's *Hymn to the Sun*. It speaks of the sun's glorious emergence from his tent, then extols the glory of the commandments, as if there were some connection between the two—which of course there was, since the sun was the origin of the law. We also see this atop the famous stone table of Hammurabi's Code which shows the emperor receiving the law from the hand of Shamash the sun god. Moses was originally the law-giving sun, as we can still glimpse in Exodus 34:29–35, where Moses emerges from the tent of meeting with new commandments, and with his face shining, not coincidentally, like the sun! And like Apollo, he can inflict flaming doom or heal it (Numbers 21:4–9) and even bears the caduceus like Apollo. Like many other Hebrew mythical sun-characters (still reflected in Elijah, Esau, Isaac, Samson, and Enoch), and other gods, too (Gad, Miriam, Jubal, Joshua), Moses must have begun as a god pure and simple, but as Hebrew religion evolved toward monotheism, the stories could only be retained by making the gods into human heroes.

III. MUHAMMAD

For a long time scholars have considered Islamic origins as basically unproblematic. It seemed fairly straightforward: the founder was a figure of relatively recent history, amply documented, and many of his own writings and sayings survived. True, there had been a frenzy of fabrication, but early Muslim scholars themselves had seen this early on and moved to weed out spurious *hadith* (traditions of the founder's sayings and deeds). What was left seemed ample enough, as did the text of the Koran, the revelation of Allah to Muhammad. Even if one could not confess with Muslims a belief in the divine inspiration (actually, dictation) of the Koran, one still agreed the text preserved the preachments of Muhammad. The most recent generation of students of Islam, however, have broken with this consensus. Günter Lüling is joined by many in his opinion that Western scholars of Islam and the Koran had simply accepted the official party line of Muslim jurists and theologians regarding the sources for Muhammad and early Islamic history. The game was certainly simpler that way, just as Church history had been before F.C. Baur. In fact, Western Islamicists had done everything but accept the Koran as the revealed Word of God. In retrospect one wonders why they balked at this last step! Perhaps the most systematic and explosive reconstruction of Islamic origins appeared over twenty years ago, *Hagarism: The Making of the Islamic World* by Patricia Crone and Michael Cook (Cambridge UP, 1977). I will summarize their account here.

Islamic sources offer us a sanitized, party-line account of Islamic origins, one designed to provide a pedigree for a subsequent orthodoxy. Hence the tracks have been covered. If we want to get a critical look at Islamic origins we need to start with the evidence of contemporary non-Muslim reports and then see what light these sources throw on anomalous data surviving in Islamic sources.

It seems that Muhammad first appeared as the prophetic herald of 'Umar (later revered and redefined as the second caliph after Muhammad) *as the messiah*. So we are told in two contemporary Jewish apocalypses. Some Jews were happy to recognize 'Umar as the messiah, even though he was an Arab (an identification not unprecedented). He would shortly drive out the Byzantine/Roman/"Edomite" occupiers of Palestine, which, Crone and Cook maintain, was liberated, contra later traditions, already in Muhammad's time.

The self-designation "Muslim" appears first on the Dome of the Rock in 691 CE and *nowhere else* till the late eighth century. Earlier sources call Muhammad's believers the *Magaritai* (Greek papyrus 642) or *Mahgre* or *Mahgraye* (Syriac papyrus 640s). The Arabic would be *muhajirun*. The early believers were known as Hagarenes because they were engaged in a Hegira/Hijra, an Exodus like that of Moses from Arabia to Palestine, the Promised Land where the messiah must manifest himself. They were organized according to the biblical twelve tribes of the Ishmaelites. The land belonged to Abraham and his seed, which naturally meant Ishmael as well as Isaac, so an alliance of Jews and Arabs in a messianic conquest was natural. Even from the Jewish point of view this seemed natural, since Kenites (understood to be Arabs) had been involved as Moses' allies in the first conquest, and the second should recapitulate it. In the *Secrets of Rabbi Simeon ben Yohai*, "the Kenite" is given messianic status.

They rejected Jesus as a false messiah and scorned the cross. But their own messianism appears to have been more Samaritan than Jewish in orientation, which meant the Promised One would be a prophet like Moses, not a king like David. There was, however, some hope that the Hagarenes, having conquered Palestine, were going to rebuild the temple. They wound up raising the Dome of the Rock instead. Rebuilding the temple would have implied Davidic messianism, but they didn't do it.

Their movement may be understood in many ways as a kind of Samaritanism. There was the non-Davidic Mosaism, the rejection of any books outside the Pentateuch (as attested in Nestorian accounts of debates with the Hagarenes), a non-Jewish biblical covenant (for Samaritans, it was the Mosaic Covenant as opposed to the Davidic; for Hagarenes, it was the Abrahamic promise to Ishmael). The dispensing with the Prophetic books explains why none of the so-called writing Prophets (Isaiah, Jeremiah, Micah, Hosea, Amos, etc.) is ever mentioned in the Koran.

As implied just above, as the winds changed, the Hagarenes found it advantageous to break with Judaism and turn to Christianity. To this end, 'Umar's messianic status was forgotten, his title *al-Faruq*, The Redeemer, explained away as a gratuitous honorific applied by over-enthusiastic Christians (not likely!) or as meaning something else in Arabic by means of a typical etymological story. Accordingly, Jesus was accepted as messiah after all. Though the first Arabic "king" of Jerusalem made a show of praying at Golgotha, Bethlehem, and the Empty Tomb, implying acceptance of the whole soteriology, Islam did not finally go this far. They made Jesus messiah but still rejected the cross. The Koran opts for "docetism," the belief that the crucifixion was a "simulacrum," an illusion or hoax, with Jesus ascending to heaven before he could be executed. But the Koran also refers to the death of Jesus, a vestige of that earlier period of Christianization, and this reference would become the center of desperate theological harmonization among later orthodox Islamic exegetes.

The abandonment of the Exodus (*Hegira*/Hijra) association in favor of that of "sons of *Hagar*/Ishmaelites" reflects the disassociation from Judaism. So does the apparent adoption of "Islam" ("submission" to God) as the new central image for the faith, a *topos* derived from Samaritan characterizations of Abraham as the one who submitted to God. The harking back to Abraham parallels the argument in the Epistle to the Galatians, where Paul leapfrogs the Mosaic Torah and makes Christian believers the direct spiritual descendants of Abraham. In both cases, the retreat to Abraham is a means of undercutting Judaism. And though not preserved in the Koran, contemporary non-Islamic sources say the Muslims originally proclaimed the Commandments of Abraham, circumcision and sacrifice (brought over from prior Arab tradition), rebuking Jews and Christians for abandoning one or the other. Muhammad's role as the one to revive the Abrahamic faith, as well as to bring to the neglected Arabs their own monotheistic faith and scripture, reflects this attempt to distance Islam from Judaism. Muhammad is seen as the successor of various Gentile prophets like Salih and Hud, again, *not* the successor of the biblical Prophets. This prophetology ill comports with the Samaritan-derived motif of Muhammad as the Prophet like unto Moses, which is thus seen to stem from an earlier stage, because the Samaritan-type Mosaic prophetology still locates Muhammad within the biblical tradition, whereas Muhammad as the prophet like Hud takes him outside the Bible but parallel to it.

Muhammad was retroactively removed from his apocalyptic context, as we can readily see when we compare the so-called Meccan Surahs with the Medinan Surahs. In the latter he is no longer the Prophet of the Last Day (much less proclaimer of the messiah 'Umar), but rather the Mosaic theocrat. Similarly, for Islam Jesus' own messiahship is purely vestigial, and Jesus, too, is made over into a prophet like unto Moses, with his own Torah, the Evangel. David, too, is brought aboard once stripped of his messianic associations. He, too, is now a Prophet like unto Moses: Muslims say Moses brought the Law, David brought the Psalms, and Jesus brought the Gospel.

The Koran was assembled from a variety of prior Hagarene texts (hence the contradictions *re* Jesus' death) in order to provide the Moses-like Muhammad with a Torah of his own. (Lüling surmises that as much as a third of the text of the Koran derives from pre-Islamic Christian hymnody!) Some Islamic traditions say that the third caliph, Uthman, destroyed most of "the writings" and kept only one. Does this mean merely variant texts of the Koran itself (as is usually supposed) or something more? Like a creative redaction like that of Ezra after the Babylonian Exile, patching together our Pentateuch from the J, E, D, and P sources? This would account for all the Koranic variants, redundancies, contradictions and harmonizations (earlier revelations "abrogated" by later ones). Perhaps the scraps of anti-Trinitarian Christological polemics are vestiges from disparate sources, too.

The Hagarenes also derived from the Samaritans a precedent for withdrawing from Jerusalem as the central holy shrine, eventually settling upon Mecca, which like the Samaritan center Shechem, was situated near to a patriarchal, but non-Judean, grave, Shechem near the grave of Joseph, Mecca near that of Ishmael. Both were Abrahamic sites as well. There is evidence, though, that Mecca was not the first alternate shrine of the Hagarenes. From some early and anomalous notes and from archaeological evidence (the design of early mosques, etc.) it appears that before Mecca, a place called Bakka (actually mentioned in the Koran and later harmonistically identified with Mecca) may have been the earlier site.

The holy cities Mecca and Medinah are both substitutes for biblical sites originally venerated by the proto-Muslim Hagarenes. Medinah is identified in some Arab sources with *Midian*, which makes sense as the goal of the Exodus (the "hegira" of the "Hagarenes," remember). Midian was the goal of Moses and the Israelites exiting Egypt, and the site of Sinai/Horeb, where Moses received the Torah, just as Muhammad did at Medinah (cf. the legalistic Surahs ascribed to the Medinan period). The fact that Medinah had earlier been called Yathrib suggests that Medinah first actually referred to the Midian of the Bible, then was transferred and symbolically reapplied to Yathrib. And now, of course, since the Hegira has been redefined as Muhammad's personal flight from Mecca, its goal must have been Medinah/Yathrib, not the faraway biblical Midian! But then one wonders whether there might even have been some sort of connection with the biblical Jethro (Hebrew Yithro) and Yathrib!

After the Hegira lost its original coloring as a messianic Jewish-Ishmaelite exodus to Palestine under the messiah 'Umar, this population move was recast as a later *expulsion* of Jews from Arabia *back* to Palestine by the *caliph* 'Umar! The appellation *Ansaru Allah*, Allah's helpers, which had first designated Jewish allies of Muhammad and 'Umar, came to refer to Arabs who heeded the call to holy war.

As for Mecca, this was another later replacement for/relocation of Jerusalem, as is still evident from the acknowledged fact that the *qiblah* (direction of prayer) was early on switched from Jerusalem to Mecca. The idea of the conquest of Canaan starting from a base in *Midian* becomes Muhammad's triumphant return to Mecca after consolidating power in *Medinah* where he had fled from Mecca. But originally, Muhammad himself actually led/partook in the conquest of Palestine. Subsequently, his death was pushed back two years earlier, perhaps in order to reinforce the Moses parallel, since Moses did not get to enter the promised land.

Originally *calipha* denoted not "vicar of the Prophet" as in subsequent Islamic orthodoxy, but rather something equivalent to *rasul* (apostle) or *bab* (gate—cf. John 10:9), the earthly stand-in for Allah himself. The *caliphas* and *imams* were originally a priesthood (Muhammad himself is said to stem from the Quraiysh, a priestly caste) and were even called *kahins* (originally "soothsayer," but in Hebrew it came to mean "priest," *cohen*). This implies that once they de-messianized the movement and demoted 'Umar to *caliph* of Muhammad, the authority structure continued (along one trajectory, leading to Sunni Islam) as an analogue to the Samaritan high-priesthood. Mahdism (the expectation, central to emerging Shi'ism, of an apocalyptic return of a descendant of Muhammad) was equally early but represented a renewal, albeit by deferral, of messianic hopes, based originally on the Samaritan Moses *redivivus* idea (whether of Moses himself, or of the Taheb as a Prophet/Revealer like unto Moses). *Mahdi* is tantamount to *messiah*, as attested by the equation of the two in the Sunni saying "There is no *mahdi* but Jesus son of Mary."

Ali, cousin and son-in-law of Muhammad, was interpreted in two contradictory manners, one by each group. As a priestly successor (fountainhead of the *imams*, a term used for Samaritan high priests/esoteric teachers in Arabic writings by Samaritans), Ali had to be the descendant of Muhammad. And in fact Shi'ite doctrine sees Ali as explicitly playing Aaron to Muhammad's Moses. But as the *sole* successor to Moses, he was analogous instead to Joshua, a layman and not a relative of Moses. The eventual harmonization of the two conceptions made Ali not the son but the cousin of the Prophet.

The rabbinical character of Sunni Islam is not original but came from the influence of Babylonian Judaism. (Thus it is no mere analogy between the Talmud, the Jewish legal code, and the Shariah, the Islamic code.) The category of *Sunni* first referred not to traditions *of the Prophet*, but rather just to "custom" as distinguished from statute law. It still appears this way in early documents. And this means that all we thought we knew of the Prophet Muhammad is really a mass of fictive legal precedents meant to anchor this or that Islamic practice once Muhammad had been recast as an Arab Moses. And the question of the origin of the Koran is no longer "from Allah?" or "from Muhammad?" but rather "from Muhammad?" or "from countless unnamed Hagarene jurists?" The first question was theological ("Do you accept the Muslim gospel?"); the second is historical-critical ("Are you taken in by the Muslim apologetic?"). And it becomes equally evident that the line between the Koran and the *hadith* must be erased, for both alike are now seen to be repositories of sayings fictively attributed to the Prophet and transmitted by word of mouth before being codified in canonical written form.

CONCLUSION

Our survey of the four great religious founders is offered on the cusp of the Millennium. This fact might prompt us to look to the dawning future, but we are drawn rather to the past, gazing down the corridors of lost time, straining to catch what stray traces may still be visible. The sheer magnitude of the centuries separating us from the earliest, the Buddha, as well as the latest, Muhammad, is so great as to raise the question whether historical knowledge of the founders is either necessary or possible. For it has become manifest that the images of these individuals at once began to transform and grow as living symbols of the faith communities whose figureheads they were. This implies that the various believers simply lacked the historical curiosity of us moderns. Their stories were told for other reasons entirely. Insofar as our studies dismantle their edifice of holy myth, we have perhaps debunked only a literalistic distortion of these faiths, itself alien to the traditions it seeks misguidedly to defend. In any event, such scrutiny of the founders and their legends aims only at a greater appreciation of the religions as grand cultural products of the human imagination.

PART THREE: RADICAL THEOLOGY

15

WHAT IS (AND IS NOT) POSTMODERN THEOLOGY?

I recall once going into an automotive store, having been told to buy a can of Wolfshead motor oil. I was immediately confused by the host of similar-looking products on the shelves. For Wolfshead could barely be located in the midst of all its copycat competitors. There, for instance, was Foxhead brand. Whoever invented Foxhead was hoping for customers just like me: people with only a vague knowledge of what they were supposed to be looking for. I think it is the same in the case of what is called Postmodern Theology. There are available today several different theologies that all carry the "Postmodern" or "Postliberal" label, and you have to look closely at the list of ingredients on the side to make sure you are getting what you want.

First, I hasten to write off one option as deceptive advertising pure and simple. This is the position of Thomas C. Oden, first set forth in his 1979 manifesto, *Agenda for Theology* (later revised as *After Modernity, What?*). Oden had previously been, from the later standpoint of this book, the worst kind of bandwagon-hopping, trend-chasing Liberal theologian, writing a raft of books bringing the ill-defined Liberal gospel into line with everything from psychology and existentialism, to ecology and parapsychology. And now he had "come to himself" like the Prodigal Son, munching the loathsome husks of Modernity in a foreign land, and hastened to journey back to the cozy homestead of traditional orthodoxy. His theology is "postmodern" only in the autobiographical sense, it seems to me. He had decided Modernity was a mistake and leap-frogged it backwards to arrive back at an essentially pre-modern pre-critical theology. I call it a theology of the failure of nerve.

Another candidate for which I will not be voting is Whiteheadian Process Theology. A few years ago, I heard John Cobb say he had always understood Process Theology to be post-modern in character, offering an alternative to traditional Liberal theology. David Ray Griffin has edited a book called *Varieties of Postmodern Theology*, in which Process thought figures significantly. He himself had written important books of Process Theology such as his lucid *A Process Christology*.

In what sense is Process thought postmodern? I suppose it has something to do with its claim to break the impasse between the anthropomorphic God-language of biblical narrative and the abstracting "Ground of Being" theologies of Tillich et. al. Process theism proposed a God who changed and was a force of change, a "lure of creative transformation" (as Cobb, *Christ in a Pluralistic Age*, put it in the human potential jargon of the 70s when this theology seems to have reached its peak of popularity).

But the substitution of a Process ontology for one of static substance categories, earth-shaking as it might at first seem, actually did nothing more than to substitute a fluid abstraction for a frozen one. There was no real retreat from the God of the philosophers to that of Abraham, Isaac, and Jacob, only a switch to the God of Whitehead. And besides, especially in terms of Christology, the much-vaunted conceptuality of the Process theologians did not help them move an inch beyond the Christology of Schleiermacher.

John A.T. Robinson said (in *The Human Face of God*) that Process theologians were not trying to jettison the categories of the ancient theology, the combination of divinity and humanity in Christ, for example; they were only trying to say the same thing plugging in the terms of a new philosophical vocabulary. Yet if one looked closely, one readily saw that instead, it was the accents of Schleiermacher and Ritschl, not Athanasius and the Cappadocians, that they were trying to ape. Conservative theologian Kenneth Hamilton was right to dub them "Schleiermacher's modern sons." So this theology, in my reckoning, is simply one more modernism.

Another contender for the Postmodern title weighed in two decades ago, George A. Lindbeck, with his concise book *The Nature of Doctrine, Religion and Theology in a Postliberal Age* (1984). I recall seeing my beloved mentor Robert F. Streetman clutching a copy of Lindbeck's book as he stood on the threshold of his maelstrom of an office. As if to eulogize the work before it left his hand and became lost forever in the abyss of books and papers, Streetman proclaimed that Lindbeck had perhaps marked out the way theology was to follow in the next generation. I am sorry to have to disagree with him.

Theology cannot follow Lindbeck into the future for two reasons. First, his clarion call is too equivocal; as 1 Corinthians 14:8 says, "If the bugle gives forth an uncertain sound, who will prepare for battle?" Second, Lindbeck is a poor guide into the future since it is back into the Liberal theological past that he leads us.

Lindbeck sets forth an alternative to the previously regnant models of understanding doctrines. The first of these is traditional conserve supernaturalism, whether Catholic, Protestant, Orthodox Christian, Islamic, or Orthodox Jewish. It is what Lindbeck calls the "cognitivist" approach. That is, it understands the creedal affirmations of a religion as propositions which are true in the sense that they correspond to an independent, objective reality outside the believer and outside the believer's religious language. For the "cognitivist" Christian to affirm, for instance, that "Jesus is the Messiah" means that Jesus of Nazareth was the one God had in mind when he inspired the biblical writers to speak and write their Messianic prophecies, that Jesus was born to fulfil those prophecies, and that no one else, e.g., David Koresh or Menachem Mendel Schneerson, should they claim to be the Messiah, could be correct. It is difficult to see how ecumenical discussion between Jews and Christians could proceed very far as long as cognitivist Christians and Jews stuck to their guns on this issue. Similarly, it is hard to see how the proposition "God is a Trinity of persons sharing a divine essence in common" would be compatible with the Qur'anic statement that Jesus cannot be made a partner with Allah.

The alternative view, that of Liberalism, which would at first sight seem to show a way beyond the impasse, is that doctrines are merely diverse pictorial or poetic expressions of certain remarkable experiences shared in common by all the religions. This Lindbeck calls the "experiential-expressivist" model. Here, if one can imagine it, in some far-off ecumenical never-never-land, the Dalai Lama and Osama bin-Ladin might be able to agree that they were both experiencing the same "core religious experience" beneath all the divisive theology. "We both receive the numinous Word of God, only you call it the Dharma, and we call it al-Qur'an."

It seems, by the end of the book, that Lindbeck wants to come to a similar amicability with his imagined dialogue partners, so what makes the experiential expressivist model unsatisfactory to him? I will argue in a moment that it is not at all unsatisfactory to him, and that he is in fact simply one more exponent of this position without admitting it. But for now it is enough to note that he thinks he rejects it because of two unfounded liberal assumptions.

The first is that there is some common core experience underlying all the religions. Rudolf Otto argued that there was a primal experience of the Holy, the Numinous, a bipolar experience both of the *Mysterium Tremendum* and the *Mysterium Fascinans*, and that this dual encounter with the wrath/love of the Holy, of fascination and fear for one's soul, was the pre-rational base from which all rituals, myths, and doctrines had grown once the rational and mythopoeic faculties of different cultures had filtered it. Lindbeck contests this claim. All religions may in fact share certain types of feelings, he admits, but their religious experiences are too closely intertwined with their doctrinal, ritual, and ethical frameworks to be understandable or even recognizable as bare "religious experiences." Religious experiences are not identical pearls that different religions have merely placed in different decorative arrangements.

(Perhaps slightly more to the point is Richard Rorty's demonstration that, despite certain similarities in description, it is impossible to get inside the heads of other experiencers and to verify that their experiences are the same as ours even when they use similar terms to describe them (*Philosophy and the Mirror of Nature*).

Why are the experiences of Christian, Nichiren Shoshu Buddhist and Reform Jew so different? Here is Lindbeck's second objection: the experiences are not simple expressions of a universal religious experience, but rather different experiences of different things—or at least produced by different things. The experiences are functions of the various religious life-matrices which spawned them, in which the various religious believers were shaped, and which simultaneously facilitated and dictated the shape and color of the experiences. The experiences are no more interchangeable than the religious systems in which they occur.

Against both previous models, Lindbeck proposes what he calls the "cultural-linguistic" understanding of doctrine. His model is a hybrid spawn of Wittgenstein's language games and Peter Berger's plausibility structures. In his view doctrines are not so much descriptive of extra-linguistic entities as they are prescriptive of practice and experience within particular religious communities.

Contra Liberal understandings, he says, doctrines are prior to religious experiences, since it is the former which produce and shape the latter. But contra conservative cognitivism, for Lindbeck doctrines embody "intrasystemic truth," not necessarily objective, "out-there" truth. A doctrine could only be said to be true to the Christian faith or true to the logic of Christianity. The nature of doctrine would not allow us to go further and say that Christian claims are true as judged by conformity to some external yardstick.

> A comprehensive scheme or story used to structure all dimensions of existence is not primarily a set of propositions to be believed, but it is rather the medium in which one moves, a set of skills one employs in living one's life. Its vocabulary and its syntax may be used for many purposes, only one of which is the formulation of statements about reality. Thus while a religion's truth claims are often of the utmost importance to it (as in the case of Christianity), it is, nevertheless, the conceptual vocabulary and the syntax or inner logic which determine the kinds of truth claims the religion can make. The cognitive aspect, while often important, is not primary. (Lindbeck, *The Nature of Doctrine*, 35)

A good example of the regulative function envisioned by Lindbeck might be the case of Arianism. What was at stake in this pivotal early Christological controversy? Was it simply a point of speculative theology? No, as Robert C. Gregg and Dennis E. Groh (*Early Arianism, A View of Salvation*) make clear, the issue was one of both soteriology and salvation. A close scrutiny of the writings of both sides shows that each side was championing a distinctive way of religious life. For the Arians the way of salvation was an ascetical ascent to spiritual perfection. Accordingly, their Christology modelled a Christ who was a mutable creature who only won through to honorary godhood and to adoptive divine perfection through his own arduous efforts. He was the redeemed redeemer who showed his followers how to work out their own salvation.

By contrast, for Athanasius salvation was more a matter of receiving the grace of *theosis* (divinization) through the sacramental life of the church. For this model Christ had to be a divine dispenser of divine grace, not a changeable creature in need of it himself. He gave the true bread of heaven, and to do the works of God is simply to believe in the one whom he has sent, himself one with the Father's incorruptible essence. Sure enough, in this debate, the issue is how doctrine shall govern the style and shape of the spiritual life, its means and goals.

But all this is nothing new. Insofar as the "theological syntax" model may be judged a new one, the patent must be awarded to the Lundensian theologians, including Anders Nygren, who beat Linbeck to the punch by a good 20 years. Here is Nels Ferre's summary of the Lundensian agenda. He starts by quoting Nygren:

> "religion is a completely independent and unique form of experience that develops according to its own autonomous principles and must be judged from its own center." Theology is thus a special form of religious history with a special working hypothesis, according to which it accomplishes its systematic task, namely the discovery and the systematic exposition of each religion in accordance with its organic distinctiveness. (*Swedish Contributions to Modern Theology*, 58–59) The task of Christian theology is to analyze the historic forms with a view to their inner meaning, and then to test them as to their compatibility with the distinctiveness of Christian faith. (Ibid., 67)

But the novelty of the approach is really neither here nor there. Let us examine the difficulties in Lindbeck's version of it. While Lindbeck often seems to make his "cultural-linguistic" model compatible in theory with either a propositionalist or a non-propositionalist position, it at length becomes abundantly clear that only the latter really fits in:

> There is nothing in the cultural-linguistic approach that requires the rejection (or the acceptance) of the epistemological realism and correspondence theory of truth. . . . Nevertheless, the conditions under which propositions can be uttered are very different in cognitivist and cultural-linguistic approaches; they are located on quite different linguistic strata. For the cognitivist, it is chiefly technical theology and doctrine which are propositional, while on the alternate model, propositional truth and falsity characterize ordinary religious language when it is used to mold lives through prayer, praise, preaching, and exhortation. It is only on this level that human beings exhibit their truth or falsity, their correspondence or lack of correspondence to the Ultimate Mystery. (*The Nature of Doctrine*, 69)

It is right at this point that D.Z. Phillips (*Faith After Foundationalism*) levels an important criticism at Lindbeck. Lindbeck claims to be applying the insight of Wittgenstein that theology is a kind of grammar. And indeed Lindbeck has profited much from Wittgenstein. But, for better or worse, he seems to have imported a kind of reductionism unintended and not implied by Wittgenstein.

Wittgenstein, as Phillips reads him, meant to deny that religious assertions are making merely factual, and therefore dubious and provisional, assertions. Belief in God as held fast by religious believers is primordial and fundamental to religious discourse in such a way that the belief is not the subject of debate, as it is among philosophers of religion and apologists. Doctrines start from such presuppositions and, within the space marked out by them, seek to regulate religious life in the manner of a grammar. What Lindbeck, however, has done is to make the bare bones of Wittgenstein's understanding of the function of doctrine into a doctrine. Lindbeck comes close to saying that doctrines are simply facilitators and regulators of spiritual life/experience, and he seemingly proceeds to strip them of the ideational, propositional content which gave them their facilitating power to begin with. He finally stands exposed as one more Liberal demythologizer whose only theology is that, strictly speaking, there needn't be any.

This tension between two different ways of reading Wittgenstein is reflected, as I read him, in the essays of D.Z. Phillips himself. Sometimes ("Religious Beliefs and Language Games" in *Faith and Philosophical Enquiry*) he seems to be saying that, rightly understood, religious utterances are performative and expressive utterances, and that factual references are imported into them against their natural intent. Most times, though, he seems more in accord with Wittgenstein's concern to safeguard religious claims from reduction to mere factual claims. This also seems to be Bultmann's intent, independent of Wittgenstein, when he seeks to prevent the mythic "objectification" of language about God. There is nothing wrong with either position. The trouble is that Lindbeck seems not to know he must choose between them. Often he sounds uncannily close to Don Cupitt in *Taking Leave of God*, his 1980 manifesto of overt non-realist expressivism. God, Cupitt says, is a meaningful term only within religious language, not outside it, e.g., not in talk about why natural disasters happen, or how the earth was formed. Listen now to Lindbeck:

> Just as grammar by itself affirms nothing either true or false regarding the world in which language is used, but only about language, so theology and doctrine ... assert nothing either true or false about God and his relation to creatures, but only speak about such assertions. These assertions, in turn, cannot be made except when speaking religiously, i.e., when seeking to align oneself and others performatively with what one takes to be most important in the universe by worshipping, promising, obeying, exhorting, preaching. (69)

Lindbeck is explicit in his espousal of an "epistemological non-realism." He even verges on declaring that all the different religions can coexist quite nicely since they are radically incommensurate language games, so different in fundamental terms from one another that the believer in one can not be considered an unbeliever in another. To be an "unbeliever" implies a rejection of the terms of the game from within the game. The only unbelief would be apostasy from within, not aloofness from without. How this posture would serve Lindbeck's apparent goal of a theological convergence between religions is not clear.

He repudiates Rahner's notion of "anonymous Christians" among other religions on the basis that this would imply a silent commensurability between Christians and others—yet he dares to suggest that Christian missionaries might have as their proper business to go into the field to encourage Buddhists to be, not Christians but better Buddhists! Lindbeck simply cannot seem to rid himself of Christian triumphalism in the very moment he appears to be adopting a theology of pure expressivism. But Lindbeck reels back from the expressivist brink and says, like Rahner, that the real problem of ecumenism is whether or not non-Christians may be saved, and his answer is that they may receive a postmortem opportunity to consider the Christian gospel somewhere on the Bardo plane, after which they may be saved or not! (Lindbeck's disciple, William Placher, goes even further toward a traditionalist understanding in his book *Unapologetic Theology*, almost recapitulating the presuppositionalist apologetics of Cornelius Van Til: our faith is the true one, and thank God and Thomas Kuhn, we're not accountable to prove it to anyone!)

Let me return to my earlier statement that Lindbeck is after all an exponent of the very "experiential-expressivist" model he wants to reject. Lindbeck asks us to jeer at a Liberal theology which makes every individual a free lance with no institutional affiliation, each floating like an atom of spiritual autonomy. Traditional doctrines are shucked off as mere husks for ideal and contentless "religious experiences" which arise within the individual and go no further. Liberal theology, he warns, encourages this atomizing, this erosion of any sense of religious communal identity. And insofar as the religious communities have historically been one of the centripetal forces for social cohesion, the break-up of religious community abets the general social disintegration of our time. Lindbeck wants us to begin reversing this deleterious trend by understanding that religious communities still have a place, that religious experience must have such a matrix or it will not flourish, will degenerate into mere humanism.

And to shore up the walls of the churches, we must arrive at an understanding of doctrines that will not drive away free thinkers (hence the absence of any pesky propositional reference from Lindbeckian doctrines), yet will ensure the preservation of the community's distinctives. Lindbeck's is a Liberalism that could politely hold a heresy trial. You may reconceive Christology, but it had damn well better be a new way of saying what Chalcedon said.

I believe we saw exactly such a case of Liberal heresy hunting in the reaction of John Macquarrie and others to the 1977 symposium *The Myth of God Incarnate*. Real conservatives had for decades charged people like Macquarrie with vitiating the doctrine of the Incarnation by watering it down into Christian existentialism. But here came Michael Goulder, Don Cupitt, John Hick and others saying forthrightly that it was time to jettison talk of the Incarnation as a primitive myth which had outlived its usefulness. Macquarrie could not brook this! Neither, it is safe to say, could Lindbeck.

My point is that mainstream Liberal theology has been doing since its inception what Lindbeck now demands as a repudiation of Liberalism. Want proof?

Rudolf Otto never sought to reduce God-talk to religious experience. Indeed, quite the reverse: he argued that the universal experience of the Numinous well-nigh proved the extra-experiential existence of God, else where would the numinous feeling have come from?

Is it news that religious experiences must be mediated by the preaching and the symbols of particular religious communities? Not at all. It was Schleiermacher who warned that "natural religion," religion in general, was a phantom, and that God-consciousness was only to be had through the agency of one of the positive religions. Of these he deemed Christianity the best, but apparently so does Lindbeck. Schleiermacher called the Holy Spirit the Spirit of the Christian Community, so little did he deem Christian experience to be separable from the Christian church. It was through the church's preaching of the Redeemer that a religious experience like unto his own might be made available. This motif was shared in turn by Ritschl and his disciples including Wilhelm Herrmann (*The Communion of the Christian with God*), as well as his great student Paul Tillich, for whom the New Being was communicated through the church via the biblical "picture of Jesus as the Christ." None of these people thought that religious experiences take place in a vacuum.

Lindbeck's talk about the happy incommensurability of religions which prevents us from damning one another sounds much like the "perspectivalism" or "confessionalism" of H. Richard Niebuhr, who in his *The Meaning of Revelation* ventured that we can only affirm our own experience and interpretation of the divine, not deny those of another, since we can never be sure that our vision of truth is so comprehensive as to rule out the other's.

And we have already seen that virtually every recent attempt to redefine Christological doctrine, from Rahner and Schillebeeckx to Cobb, Griffin, Pittenger, and Robinson, to Boff and Sobrino, to Küng and Macquarrie, is careful to try to preserve the classical categories of Nicea and Chalcedon while filling them with new meaning. In other words, they all recognized quite explicitly the regulative but not substantive character of church doctrines.

On his own definition Lindbeck may not be one of those "experiential-expressivists," but then neither were any of the major liberal theologians since Schleiermacher. We had to wait till real radicals like Fritz Buri and Don Cupitt came along. In fact I am not sure Lindbeck has even them in view. His best targets, though never named, would be the religious humanism of Joseph Campbell and the gurus of the syncretistic New Age movement.

I have dwelt at length on Lindbeck because I have gathered that for many he defines Postmodern theology. I will discuss one more type of Postmodernist theology, that based on the Deconstructive anti-philosophy of Derrida and de Man. Theologians in this camp would include Mark C. Taylor (*Erring, Tears, Deconstructing Theology, Alterity*), Thomas J.J. Altizer (*The Gospel of Christian Atheism, The Descent into Hell* and many others), Charles Winquist (*Epiphanies of Darkness*), Carl Raschke (*The Alchemy of the Word*), Robert Scharlemann (*The Reason of Following*), and the later Don Cupitt (*Only Human, The Long-Legged Fly, Creation out of Nothing*, and many others). This is my own theological position. With Derrida, having banished any notion of a "transcendental signified," a logos-center or meaning-center external to language, Deconstructive theology proclaims the Nietzschean gospel of the death of God. But it also proclaims the death of "Man," of a transcendent consciousness as a mirror reflecting a pure vision of truth. All language is cross-referential, referring only to language. All reality is a textual field, a flat surface with much depth beneath it, a depth of unsuspected meanings, but no height, nothing above it to which it points.

To unpack this a bit, the death of God means, for the theology of Deconstruction, that the divine has been poured out into the human, the profane, the secular, which henceforth is seen to glow with a kind of "trace" or witch-fire radiance of the lost sense of holiness. What once was there to be worshipped is now present only in its conspicuous absence. Religious worship for us is like the singing of the Lamentations of Jeremiah amid the ruins of the Temple of Solomon. Over the debris one can make out the word "Ichabod," "the Glory has departed," and in that absence is the lingering trace of the holy, not a Holy Ghost, but a Ghost of Holiness. The rawness of the profane, which is all that is left to us in a world with no transcendent reference, somehow yet retains the hint, the echo, the trace of the Holy that is gone.

With the death of any transcendent source of meaning or value outside language itself, with the revelation that even concept is only metaphor, that even logical argument is only narrative, there can be no religious authority. No book can be more authoritative than any other, because there is no Word of God. No book can even be kept separate from all the others in the light of which we read it. This is what Jabes called "the death of the Book," i.e., as a self contained entity, and what Derrida, following him, called "the birth of the [all-encompassing] Text." All texts are an illimitable field, and the name for that cross-fertilization of each text by our knowledge of what the rest of them say is called intertextuality.

No particular reading of any book can be recovered as the true or binding one. All exists simply as text, a field of signifiers. We as readers break a path through the text as we read, but we can never be sure we are doing more than playing a word-search puzzle, imagining chains of signification where none were intended by the writer. Deconstructive theologians and critics thus have new respect for the subversive reading strategies of the Kabbalah, which did not hesitate to read the text backwards, and as acronyms, and as puzzles and by means of puns. Deconstruction abhors logocentrism, the abstraction of some element of the text and its idolatrous erecting as the key to the meaning of the text. The meaning of the text is the text itself.

It becomes evident that if we for one moment accept the nonconcepts of Deconstruction, as I do, Lindbeck's agenda is ruled out lock, stock and barrel. That one might, for instance, judge one form of Christian theology as more consistent with the central rationale of Christian existence than another presupposes that such a transcendent center of meaning exists. It does not.

Lindbeck's concern to maintain the insular integrity of particular doctrinal, religious communities is a futile attempt, utterly out of touch with the manifest condition of cultural intertextuality. I as a Christian pastor conversant with Buddhism and Islam, can no longer read the texts of my own tradition without reading them in the transforming light of these other texts and traditions. My preaching reflects that.

I judge Michael S. Kogan's proposal for "total dialogue" between the Jewish and Christian houses of faith to be a coming to grips with the intertextualism of the two traditions. Christians have never been able to understand the New Testament without reference to the Tanak, and now Kogan finds it impossible to understand the Tanak without reference to the New Testament, though he might better call it a "Post-Testament." The death of the (self-contained) Book means that the Tanak and the New Testament must remain open at both ends and on every side. Both must come into dialogue with the Qur'an as well. They already are, though they may not know it. And so with the Gita and the Lotus Sutra.

Lindbeck's Yale colleague Hans Frei in *The Eclipse of Biblical Narrative* urged that we stop trying to use the narrative of scripture, in what I would call a logocentric manner, as evidence for something else, not as indirect evidence for primordial (thus prototypical) Christianity or a normative "historical Jesus." Nor as a quarry for true theological statements which might then be worked into a definitive system. He wanted us to take the text as text, as narrative. This is good Deconstruction, too. We salute him.

He also rightly saw that there is no clean boundary line between reader and text. Deconstruction similarly declares that the reader is both a writer of the text as she reads it, configuring it anew, and a character in the story which requires her pivotal role as observer and interpreter. But here we part company with the Yale theologians and prefer to continue with the Yale critics. Lindbeck and Placher agree with Frei that we as readers of the biblical narrative must become part of the ongoing biblical epic, enter its narrative world as our own world of experience. Lindbeck also apparently hopes that we may preserve some of the historic tradition of the West by following Frei's advice, since the Bible, as Jerry Falwell likes to remind us, had so much influence on the life and shape of our republic.

Deconstruction agrees that since the death of transcendent meaning there is only fiction, but with Lyotard, we recognize that the sovereignty of any traditional master narrative has broken down. Harvey Cox was proclaiming this when he celebrated *The Secular City*. There is no longer any totalistic understanding that dominates culture. This is partly because of the creative chaos of the textuality of things. Our society is a text which may mean anything and everything precisely because it means nothing in particular.

But the master narrative of the Bible in particular is unacceptable for another reason, as Don Cupitt shows in *The Crisis of Moral Authority*. It everywhere partakes of phallogocentrism, the violent ideology of a divine despot who is the heavenly rubber stamp of earthly monopolistic priestcraft. The oppressed and rejected are scattered throughout its pages and illumined in ghastly hues: the women, the pagans, the servants of outlawed Israelite Goddesses, the homosexuals, slaves, Jews frying in the Christian hell.

The very universe is defined in self-exalting male terms when we are told that the world was made through the Logos who was, even before the Incarnation, a male, the Son of a male God. He shall rule the nations with a rod of iron, which sceptre is none other than the phallus of the Logos. Besides, the very notion of a master narrative defining a culture is monopolistic and phallogocentric.

Derrida retains from Levi-Strauss the notion of *bricolage*, the opportunistic appropriation of tools and techniques that may once have formed part of a system now rejected as a whole. Navigators, for example, still use Ptolemaic astronomy in their calculations. Indeed, *bricolage* is inevitable once the logos-center is gone. There can be no overarching system that alone could justify a particular method. For Deconstructive theology, this means, "if it seems to work, feel free to use it." Thus particular bits of biblical story or theological language may still have utility as suggestive and empowering fictions (and remember, for us there is nothing available but fiction!).

Rationalistic biblical criticism still seems to make more sense of the text for us than fundamentalist literalism, but we also like the Kabbalah, and no one's trying to stop the fundamentalists! Let a hundred flowers bloom!

Are there spiritual experiences for which our incipient naturalism and reductionism cannot well account? Why not? One thing we don't claim is to have a place for everything. Indeed we would be belying our own claims if we did.

Deconstruction is, in my estimation, the one of our options most appropriately described as Postmodern, though I am quick to admit that the meaning of this, as any, term is in the eye of the beholder.

16

POSTMODERN UNITARIAN UNIVERSALISM

In the gradual evolution of Protestant Theology toward the left, Unitarians and Universalists have played the role of the vanguard of the revolution. Or, in other words, Unitarianism and Universalism have served as the cow-catcher on the front of the theological locomotive: they were the first to clash with and dispense with all the sacred cows, one by one. The mainline denominations would catch up with them on point after point, followed even by the evangelical churches a few generations down the line, but Unitarians and Universalists had already cleared the rails for them. Unitarians and Universalists early took aim at the doctrines of Hell and Trinitarianism. With Nicene and Chalcedonian encumbrances thus sloughed off, they were free next to see new obstacles that stood in the way of "a free man's worship" (Bertrand Russell) and to begin to chip away at these, too. The centrality of Christology, even that of a safely Arian or merely human Christ, was the next bovine roadblock scooped off the track. Theism yielded to mystical Transcendentalism, then to Religious Humanism, then to Secular Humanism.

Unitarian Universalists have decided that the truth is a moving target, or that the motion of the quest for the truth is itself the target: a way, not a destination. In this article I will venture to show how Unitarian Universalism is well on the way into its next evolutionary stage: Postmodernism. This may be more than an abstract exercise in abstract theological taxonomy (or taxidermy!). In his recent article in these pages ("Strained Bedfellows: Pagans, New Agers, and 'Starchy Humanists' in Unitarian Universalism," *Religious Humanism*, Vol.

XXX, #s 1 & 2, Winter/Spring 1996, 7–29), Richard Wayne Lee has documented the increasing influx of New Age thought and practice into once staid and rationalist Unitarian Universalism, as well as the turbulence this development has caused. Lee does a fine job in explaining the change sociologically. Here I seek but to add a philosophical perspective to his compelling account, showing how, despite the fears of some that UUism is threatened with the loss of its historic identity, in fact, the shift Lee describes can be understood as the next logical stage of UU evolution along its natural trajectory of historical evolution. What we are witnessing is the changeover from Modernism to Postmodernism in Unitarian Universalism.

LOGOCENTRISM INCARNATE

What was the Christology Socinians rejected? It was the theological scheme that made the preincarnate Christ the Son of God, the divine Word, eternal in existence and partaking of the identical substance with the Father (and the Spirit). The Father made the world through the agency of the fully divine Son, the latter obedient to his Father's every whim. This divine Word appeared in the flesh to reveal the true doctrine of the Father and to gather his elect to his bosom, promising to take them out of this world to a heavenly mansion. This he will someday accomplish at the final Parousia, or appearing, of the Word of God. On that day we will spurn prophecy and fragmentary knowledge for a face-to-face encounter with the Truth. Then all things shall be revealed, and those unbelievers who gladly accepted a lie in place of the truth will perish ignominiously. The righteous will retire to the Camp of the Saints, where there shall no more be any tears. And those without, all Jews and pagans and apostates, heretics, witches, and sinners, can go to Hell where they belong. All this is what the Unitarians and their twins the Universalists (two sharing one hypostasis?) meant to reject and what they paid a high price for rejecting, braving rack and stake. To be more specific, they meant to deny the division of the divine monad, the exaltation of a mere man (albeit a surpassingly great one) as God, the unreasoning acquiescence in ancient dogma and superstition, and the bigotry of sectarianism.

Unitarianism and Universalism progressively followed the trajectory thus set with remarkable consistency. The God thus rescued from Trinitarian refraction was then more thoroughly purged of irrational elements as the God of Abraham, Isaac, and Jacob was happily traded for the more abstract deity of the philosophers and Deists. Personalism succumbed to abstraction, the merely personal to the Superpersonality of the Absolute, the Oversoul. At length Unitarians and Universalists heeded the prophet-cry of Ludwig Feuerbach and resolved henceforth to seek for the divine attributes where they might truly be found: in human nature, not in some imaginary projection of human perfections onto the heavens. This progressive peeling of the divine onion led to the disclosure that there was no hard center. But this discovery coincided perfectly with the Christ-trajectory. As Christ had been thrust from his Nicene usurpation of the glory of the Father (cf. Philippians 2:6–11!), he began to drop further and further down through the heavens till he became simply one of many saints and prophets in the Unitarian Universalist pantheon, just as we are told Julia Domna had a chapel containing statues of Abraham, Orpheus, Apollonius of Tyana, and Jesus of Nazareth.

But as Christ's stock went down, that of normal human beings went up, and it was no coincidence. The Son of Man, a Hebrew term originally denoting Everyman, had been usurped by the figure of Jesus of Nazareth, but now Everyman had wrested it back. Without theism, Christology had turned into Anthropology. Christocentrism became Anthropocentrism, even a kind of Anthroposophy (with apologies to Rudolf Steiner!). Human nature was exalted, Protagoras' dictum prevailing as the Unitarian Universalist creed: "Man is the measure of all things: of the things that are, that they are, and of the things that are not, that they are not."

And this meant that Humanism was an alias of Rationalism, for it was the faculty of reasoning that made Homo Sapiens the crown of evolutionary perfection: both apex and ex-ape. Enlightenment Rationalism found its religious home in Unitarianism-Universalism as nowhere else, though the Liberal Protestant theology of the nineteenth century and up to the Great War briefly caught up, only to retreat shortly thereafter to the comfortable irrationalism of Neo-Orthodoxy. Unitarian Universalists remained the Righteous Remnant of Rationalism. And one of the cardinal points of Enlightenment Rationalism was the belief that the reasonable person could occupy a God's-eye-view perspective outside the arena of the warring creeds and cultures and perceive the rational-moral essence of them all, perhaps daring even to distill a "natural religion" from all of them. Kant's "religion within the boundaries of reason alone" was such an attempt, though John Locke and others had attempted it, too. Universalism seems to have set out to be such a universal Esperanto of religion, perhaps not a syncretic mix but a synthetic abstraction of the various world faiths. All that a religious Rationalist would consider the best. "World Bibles" were compiled from this perspective, and they tended to major in ethics and Golden Rules with little theology in evidence.

Surely the Twin Tribes had journeyed far from the house of bondage and the fleshpots of supernaturalism and Trinitarianism. But perhaps not so far after all. Is it possible that they had secreted away certain cherished idols, carrying them with them on the way? I believe so, and it is the Postmodernist critique of Enlightenment modernity, as well as Jacques Derrida's deconstruction of Western "presence metaphysics" that make it possible to detect this.

PRESENCE METAPHYSICS

Derrida has traced out the fundamental, sometimes unacknowledged axioms of what he calls presence metaphysics. He begins with Plato and his belief that the mind is by nature a clear mirror apprehending the self-evident truth. On the highest level of contemplation the trained mind, having polished its mirror to perfect clarity, beholds the essences and forms of things. The apprehension of the light of truth is immediate, the mind having fled the allegorical cave where one only inferred and guessed at the truth, seeing only its shadows. No, truth was deemed immediately present to the mind. One simply saw it with the unimpaired eye of the mind.

Derrida (in his seminal essay "Plato's Pharmacy") next focuses on Plato's polemic against writing as a medium of communication inferior to and subversive of vocal speech. Only the latter, Plato insisted, can maintain and convey the immediacy of the speaker's grasp of truth with an immediacy of its own. That is, Plato says, the speaker can almost telepathically convey what he wants to say, what he knows, to the mind of the hearer by well chosen words sped on their way by means of appropriate facial expressions, tones of voice, oratorical flourishes, hand motions, opportunities to double back and explain. The speaker, he says, is "the father of the word" and sends his utterance on its way to do its work. The spoken word says "Father, I go," and indeed goes. But the written word, the tract, the treatise, the epistle, says, "Father, I go," but then does not go. That is, the written word, lacking the presence of the speaker, sent on its way like the community of Israel without the ark accompanying them, may be misconstrued, misinterpreted, misread by the hearer. The writer tries to control the reading of the text, but ultimately he or she must cut it loose. The authorial intent would be the authoritative intent, but it gets lost.

It can only be hypothetically reconstructed by the reader, who may never be able to consult the writer for confirmation. Again, the written word is like the Prodigal, straying into far lands of dissolute pursuits, unintended readings, while the spoken word remains in earshot, faithfully carrying out the intention of the father, the speaker. What the spoken word, the Living Word, ostensibly has that the written word lacks is the living presence of the speaker and thus the immediate presence of the truth the speaker knows. Every written text is plagued by a built-in ambiguity of meaning that vitiates the meaning of any message. Meaning is always a step ahead of us in a wild goose chase. When we read, we decode, we wait to receive a message, even if we read with fluency and rapidity. Meaning temporizes, only to appear later, if at all. We turn from an obscure text wishing we could question the author, because we are sure the Truth would appear with the living word of the father, the author. The true and objective meaning of a text, that programmed into it by the father of the word, the authoritative meaning of the author, is that truth aimed at by the language of the text. It is a truth outside or above the text. Rational, logical explication of the text should cause it to emerge.

All this Derrida calls logocentrism or the Metaphysics of Presence. It is that set of assumptions which has allowed philosophers to exempt their discursive texts from the slings and arrows mere literature is heir to. Philosophers have pretended to have immediate rational access to the Truth and to be able to communicate it to their students in speech, or if need be, in written texts, which strive to mirror speech, as when Plato, Berkeley, Hume and others adopt the dialogue format in their writings. Naive in our confidence that what seems "clear and distinct" in our minds must be the truth (Descartes), we believe we can trust our speculations, following in the footsteps of Descartes, Spinoza, and Leibniz who naively assumed they could reason out reality just as they systematized mathematics, optics, and grammar. We assume the picture we paint inside our head mirrors the reality outside it.

Logocentrism has an architectonic bias as well. It insists that the truth always be a symmetrical system of abstract propositions or axioms, and not, say, a narrative or an experience. And we have limited patience with those who will not or cannot look at things the way we do: the truth seems so clear and distinct, so immediately present to us, we can only imagine our opponents are intellectually lazy or perverse. If they will not step into the neutral commons of rational objectivity as we define it, we write them off as bigots and fundamentalists of this stripe or that. Plato, remember, dreamed of an ideal Republic ruled by Truth-seeing philosopher kings who would not hesitate to execute heretics. Rationalism, then, is an "ism," a dogma, like all its competitors.

Derrida points the finger at Plato as the father of the logocentric tradition in Western philosophy, but he makes Christianity the highest exaltation of logocentrism, logocentrism incarnate, as it were. The Creator God is quite literally the Father of the Word. And the Word is God, which is to say that the order of knowing is imagined as being identical with the order of being, the central assumption of Presence Metaphysics. The Platonic terms have been hypostatized, have become divine persons. What are the divine hypostases but products of the hypostatization fallacy bemoaned by logicians? Every crucial element of the Christian salvation epic can be understood as a hypostatization of logocentric metaphysics. When the Son of Man goes forth as the sower sowing the word of God, we have a dramatization of the Stoic doctrine of the *spermatikoi logoi*, the seeds of rational order permeating all things to give them their intelligible form. This tendency reaches its utmost extreme in Valentinian Gnosticism, where the Demiurge seizes the sparks of divine light from the Pleroma, the Fullness of Divine Presence.

When Jesus, the Incarnate Word, silences the demons of madness because they know who he is, what we have is the attempt of logocentrism to suppress the truth that reason is but the tip of the iceberg that is madness. When Jesus the Logos is exalted as the Pantocrator from whom all authority stems in heaven and on earth, what we are really dealing with is the exaltation of rationalism over all other forms of perception, and with the centered systematizing of reality according to the dictates of an architectonic system. When belief in the gospel truth is made the criterion of salvation, we are saying that ideas and abstractions are the ultimate truth, the Water of Life which to imbibe is to attain unto the ultimate level of reality. To say that human beings are made in the image of God is to project anthropocentric arrogance onto the cosmos, to say "reality is just like us."

And it is no accident that logocentric Christian faith has been androcentric as well, male-centered. Feminist critics speak of phallocentrism, the imposition of a male point of view as the filter of all thought and the embrace of it by women as a kind of false consciousness. Derrida sees that phallocentrism and logocentrism are one, since the exaltation of reason (or potentially anything else) as the single center is a male tendency, a game of "King of the Hill," where only a single victor is left standing as the most powerful. Originally this was an evolutionary mechanism to assure the survival of the hardiest genes: the winner in the duel of suitors became the bull ape in charge of the herd with access to all the females. All talk of a supreme value or meaning-center is "phallogocentrism": a reflection of the victorious ape pounding its chest. Christianity is completely phallogocentric. If the eternal reason according to which all things were created is male, if the Word is the Son, then the universe is ipso facto defined in male terms. And the notion of the Word being the true son, of one nature with the father, is simply the old male paternity anxiety, the care that one's child be truly one's own, one's true-bred genetic stock, *homoousias*. Nicea was male metaphysics from start to finish. And the eschatology of Christianity? When the Parousia of the Logos appears? Here is the hope that meaning will finally issue from texts. And it will be a male meaning: "He shall rule the nations with a rod of iron," and what is that sceptre but the phallus of the Logos?

Just as Christian Christology and theism were found wanting by earlier generations of Socinians, Arians, Unitarians, and Universalists, the presence metaphysics of logocentrism has been repudiated by a number of thinkers, especially Jacques Derrida. Derrida attacks traditional presence metaphysics at many points. Here are a few that I find most illuminating.

AGAINST LOGOCENTRISM

He mounts a frontal assault on the key assumption of Rationalism by denying Descartes's claim that we truly know anything that is clearly and distinctly present to the conscious mind. He is shattering what traditional philosophy sometimes called the mind as "the mirror of nature" (cf. Richard Rorty, *Philosophy and the Mirror of Nature*). There is no pure and unadulterated presence. There is no bare, uninterpreted reality which the mind is able to confront. We always receive the world as inscribed with some prescribed grid of meaning. What confronts us has already been mediated. It stands always already at one remove from us, not really "present" to us at all. What seems obvious to us only seems so because it is force-fed through culturally-prescribed categories and expectations. There is no pure nature, for example, since "nature" is always a projection from culture, the hypothetical extrapolation of anthropologists or philosophers, and thus the "nature" against which culture is so often unfavorably measured is actually a function of the particular theorist's philosophy or theory.

Even the experience of "the present moment" is not real, metaphysical presence. It is instead derived, a product with visible seams, an experience stitched together (as Dilthey already recognized) from the past and the future. The present moment would be a blank slate without echoes of our recollection of the past and anticipations of the future. The "pure" present is actually a composite, the result of a hidden process of relation. Ironically, St. Augustine's attempt to explicate the timeless Eternal Present in which God must live demonstrates the impossibility of presence: Augustine says it must be something like his experience as he recites a familiar Psalm that he knows by heart. He recalls the verses of it he has spoken, as their echoes linger, and he anticipates the parts of it he knows but has not yet reached. So this ever-present now is not present at all, but rather a melding of past and future. This fact of derivation, of having been derived, means that realities are ever deferred, always already at some remove from us. The case is reminiscent of the criticism Plato leveled against writing, that the meaning is precisely not present to the reader, but ever threatens to stay one step ahead of him as a will-o'-the-wisp, ever leading us onward, phrase by phrase, sentence by sentence. And this observation is crucial: the deferring factor, the distancing factor, what Derrida calls *differance*, is characteristic of reality as a whole.

Derrida denies that speech is exempt from the *differance* factor any more than writing is. The speaker cannot be sure he will communicate his intention and very often does not, as any teacher or preacher knows. The very advantage speech possesses over writing, the opportunity to backtrack and clarify, is itself evidence of the inherently ambiguous character of all language whether written or spoken. Else why should clarification be necessary in the first place? The reason all language is ambiguous and indeterminate of meaning, despite the intention of the speaker/writer or the interpretation of the hearer/reader, is the differential nature of meaning. We assume that the meaning of words is referential, words keyed to corresponding things. But as Ferdinand de Saussure has argued, the meaning of words is primarily differential. They are like pieces of a jigsaw puzzle. The shape of each is determined by nothing other than its complementary difference from the adjacent pieces. Words mean this because they do not mean that. The signifier "apple" refers not so much to the familiar piece of fruit as its "signified," but rather (by way of negation) to the meanings of signifiers like "pear," "tomato," "cantaloupe," "apall," "appeal," or "ape." Signifiers receive their meanings by way of differentiation from the other possibilities that they might mean. I can recognize my wife because of her uniqueness, i.e., what differentiates her from all the other women I see.

The fact of *differance* has far-reaching implications, and not only for linguistics. It implies two major things for theology. First there can be no Transcendental Signified, no Reality, no Meaning beyond language, except perhaps meaningless prime matter of some sort, or some Buddhistic Suchness about which nothing can be said. Second, there can be no Ground of Being, no "fundamental" or foundational meaning. This is because every theory of the meaning of things is already infected with the virus of *differance*, the uncontrollable free play of language, the dissemination of meaning. Every use of language unleashes uncontrollable forces of signification that threaten to undermine every intended meaning. Meaning is never present to us, never has a Parousia, because it is always slipping away, draining off, into these cracks between possible meanings. Indeed, this is just where Derrida's controversial hermeneutics of Deconstruction arises. Deconstruction traces out the countersignature of every text whereby it may be shown to argue at cross-purposes with its author's intention.

Tillich came close to seeing how the very Ground of Being he liked to talk about was actually impossible when he defined Being as the affirmation of itself over against Non-Being. In other words, it is grounded on the abyss of *differance* between itself and its opposite. The earth, as Isaiah said, is hung upon the void.

If God is dead for Deconstruction, so is "Man," Descartes's "thinking thing," the Invictus-self of the Enlightenment. Postmodernists learn from Freud that what we call the self is actually the epiphenomenon of subterranean, never-experienced processes in the subconscious. We form our self-concept as we hear our opinions spoken. We are at least as much audience as actor, as George Herbert Meade and Peter Berger have also argued. As writers we are readers of what our creative genius produces. We are language speaking itself. The self is the a posteriori perceiver, not the a priori actor.

Even the axioms of reason are the rules of a game imposed on the ambiguous chaos of the world. The consistency of logic is the consistency of the rules of a game, tautologous, self-referential, the rules of the order of knowing, not necessarily of the order of being. It is the logocentric bias that makes us think otherwise. And the privilege of the supposedly neutral "common ground" from which superior Olympian position Enlightenment Man deigned to judge and mediate all cultures and beliefs turns out to be merely one more among many competing plausibility structures. Having no common ground with rival paradigms, such as the epistemology of militant Islam, of Flat-Earthism or National Socialism, it cannot possibly demonstrate its superiority to them. Indeed it becomes meaningless to claim superiority over them.

POSTMODERN UNITARIAN UNIVERSALISM

Unitarian Universalism seems to be the very incarnation of the Enlightenment paradigm of Rationalism, Humanism, and Logocentrism. And even more ironically, insofar as Chalcedonian Christology was simply a hypostatization of logocentric presence metaphysics, rationalistic Humanism remains essentially just as Chalcedonian as Orthodox Christianity. To finally purify itself of Chalcedonianism, to purge itself at long last from every vestige of Athanasian Christological dogma, Unitarian Universalist theology must needs empty itself too of Rationalism, Humanism, and its bias toward a single "unitarian" synthesis point, or Ultimate Concern. "Universalism" must give way to multiversalism or pluriversalism. And that, I contend, is precisely what is happening with the emergence of New Age, Christian, Pagan, Jewish, and Buddhist factions within Unitarian Universalism. Breaking the hegemony of logocentrism means that there can be no one orthodoxy, and of course Unitarian Universalists have long upheld diversity and pluralism in doctrine. Similarly, the "Unitarian" tag long ago lost the connotation of that monotheism its adherents once sought to free from Trinitarian confusions. Humanism made the monotheistic meaning of "Unitarian" obsolete. Many Unitarians decided the One God was as much a groundless figment of priestcraft as the Three had been. And now the Covenant of Unitarian Universalist Pagans represent an altogether different approach to breaking the monotheistic hammer lock. They seek to restore the polytheism of ancient Israel, banished from the canon by late phallogocentrist editors. There is a lesson for Universalists in Paul M. van Buren's suggestion that, in the wake of the "dissolution of the Absolute," it is only out of habit that we speak of a 'universe' at all. It really depends on how you approach it, we might say, for the 'universe' of one discipline is but the background or a detail for another. All things considered, it appears to be more appropriate to speak of a polyverse (*Theological Explorations*, p. 39). Need we trouble ourselves anymore to define a synthetic harmony of all truth because there is the prefix "uni-" in our trademark? It might be better to follow Van Buren's lead and treat the world as making no one single definitive sense apart from the many different viewpoints from which we and others may view it.

Today a rapidly increasing number of Unitarian Universalists feel the need to transcend (as Schleiermacher, Emerson, and Parker did) the sometimes dry moralism of Kant's "religion within the bounds of reason alone," lacking any mystical, spiritual dimension. Many, as Kenneth Patton did, embrace what some call "ecstatic naturalism," where it is the divine spirit, as Feuerbach said, manifest in human arts and glories that catches away the breath and catches one up to the third heaven. The poems of Rilke and Hölderlin are good examples of ecstatic naturalism, fragments of true inspiration, where the Muse of the subconscious far transcends left-brained rationalism. All this represents, not a repudiation of reason, far from it, but rather a dethronement of logocentrism.

When logocentrism reigns no more, one can feel free to explore spiritual experiences without having to explain them and to account for them first. One need only approach them in the spirit of phenomenology, bracketing the ontological question, temporarily and willingly suspending disbelief as one does in a playhouse or a movie theatre. One may navigate the experience *as* an experience, whatever may or may not lie "behind" it. As Nagarjuna said, one need not despise that which one suspects to be ultimately phantasmal, so long as one does not mistake it for more than a pleasant phantom.

Reason and rational scrutiny must remain our first line of defense against the resurgent superstition of much of the New Age Movement (and here we continue proudly to play our role as sentinels against religious hokum and priestcraft). But we will heed the advice of Paul Feyerabend and embrace the methodological axiom of "counter-inductivity," exploring hypotheses (in this case, religious experiences) not derivable from or even consistent with our base-line theoretical model of rationalism. We may, for example, insist on historical criticism as applied to the miracle-legends of the biblical text, yet be open to visionary experiences ourselves.

The same open-ended, distinctly un-synthesized pluralism seems to mark the emerging UU stance toward the various historic world religions. There is no urgency to figure out a synthesis, an abstraction of what we deem the essence of all the religions (which no single religion would recognize or accept), or to form a syncretism, a new super-religion collecting parts of this and that and hybridizing them into a new system, as the New Age Movement does. Rather, UU ministers and congregations, in their experiments with Sufism or Zen, seem to have adopted the principle of *bricolage*. This term for the unsystematic ad hoc technique of the handyman who patches and contrives a solution from whatever odd bits he may have available, has been adopted by Claude Levi-Strauss and Jacques Derrida to denote the use of leftover techniques, individual ideas or methodologies, from systems that have, as wholes, been deconstructed and dismantled, much as Newton was able to salvage parts of Kepler's earlier paradigm. In our case *bricolage* seems to mean the jury-rigging of whatever spiritual practices or ideas happen to appeal to us, with no attempt to form any kind of comprehensive system. Without logocentric presuppositions, no synthetic system of truth is desirable or possible, so why waste time building one? In the wake of the wreck of all systems of knowledge, one can only pick up what glittering bits of debris as catch one's eye, like a magpie decorating her nest.

The abandonment of Humanism is perhaps the bitterest pill to swallow, as witness the rancor documented by Richard Wayne Lee. Perhaps we need only speak of a chastened Humanism, just as Henry Pitney van Dusen once spoke of a chastened Liberalism in the wake of Neo-Orthodoxy. Indeed I see no retreat from our Protagorean axiom "Humanity is the measure of all things." In fact, in light of the Postmodernist disclosure of the self as a rhetorical construct, this maxim might take on a new meaning. True, we can no longer flatter ourselves simply to be Descartes's "thinking thing," a pure mirror that sees the light of truth undimmed. Perhaps we might rather adopt some sort of Buddhist "no-self" doctrine.

We are less like Aristotle's "thought thinking itself" (Descartes's self concept was pretty much a microcosmic miniature of this God-concept) than "language speaking itself." We are listeners as well as speakers in the same moment, passive in the very moment of activity. We do not measure by use of sovereign reason; rather we are the measuring rod, a tool both of language and of the coded text of the subconsciousness that incarnates language. We must learn to read ourselves. The last frontier is within, that vast ocean of text of which the human self is the epiphenomenon. Humanism, then, is not the sovereign judgment by human selves of everything else. Rather, "the proper study of mankind is man." We must advance to square one as Socrates did, to admit our unwisdom before true wisdom can be ours. We are not blank slates, much less polished mirrors. We are clay tablets already inscribed to the margins, palimpsests with many layers of inscription. We must get down to business decoding that text. And what if that were the best way to understand the continual self-examination beloved of UUs? Instead of denoting a failure of nerve, a loss of mission, what if it denoted an altogether proper turn inward?

In the course of the present essay I have suggested that, thanks to the disclosures of the Postmodernist deconstruction of Presence Metaphysics, we can recognize that in their very embrace of Rationalism, Humanism, a unity of Ultimate Concern and a universal faith, Unitarian Universalism retained the essence of the Nicene-Chalcedonian Christo-theology it sought to reject. The most illuminating way to understand the current shift to neo-Christian, pagan, New Age and other spiritualities in the UU camp is as a natural and inevitable transition to a Postmodernist stance, the next logical step in the ongoing evolution of Unitarian Universalism.

17

LOOSE CANON:
A PROPOSAL FOR A NEW BIBLICAL CANON

OPENING THE QUESTION

If the Father of our Country was supposed to have chopped down a cherry tree, one might say that the Father of the Protestant Reformation sawed off the limb he was sitting on.[1] And few of his spiritual heirs have noticed the perilous position he put them in. Like Wile E. Coyote, running on empty air by momentum alone till, all of a sudden, he notices there is nothing holding him up, Protestants and biblicists grandly thunder about biblical authority, biblical priority, *Sola Scriptura*, all the while seemingly oblivious of the fact that their sacred talisman is just as much the work of human hands as those idols denounced and lampooned by the Second Isaiah. Schleiermacher,[2] Harnack,[3] and Marxsen[4] are among the handful of Protestant theologians who have noticed the fatal inconsistency: how can Scripture sit in judgment over ecclesiastical tradition when all the while the Bible is itself the product of church tradition? And of course none of these men was a biblicist. Many even of those whose exegetical labors have made plain to them the altogether human origin of the biblical writings seem strangely credulous when it comes to the prior question of the limits of the canon. This sacred ark remains untouchable. But why exempt the ecclesiastics who defined the canon from the same critical scrutiny to which we have long subjected the biblical writers themselves?

Strictly speaking, critical ecclesial historiography long ago penetrated the fog of mystification surrounding the canon, but theologians seem to have made up their minds and do not intend to let the uncomfortable facts confuse them. They know well enough how arbitrary, how opinionated, how political, how rationalizing were the choices that made up the holy canon, but they don't care. James Barr holds that "the external limitation of holy scripture" is a "matter . . . full of historical contingency and relativity, full of elements which cannot be given a rational theological justification but which simply are there in their facticity."[5] If this is our piety, we are strange bedfellows with the fundamentalists whose bull-headed invulnerability to biblical criticism we bemoan.[6]

We may quail at the prospect of reopening the question of the canon, as if the task were too Promethean. "Is not the greatness of this deed too great for us? Must we ourselves not become gods simply to appear worthy of it?"[7] Nietzsche was speaking of the death of God. We are speaking, whether we know it or not, though I think we do, of the death of the Word of God. We are able to take unto ourselves the Herculean labor of creating the canon anew because we now know that there was no Word of God. There are and were nothing but human words, and the old biblical canon was but a collection of them. This fact neither erodes nor enhances their inherent value. But knowing it does make it less likely that we will feel entitled to use any biblical canon as a weapon to intimidate belief and to usurp free conscience. We do not have the authority to do what gods once did. But neither did those of old who masked themselves as gods.

James Barr raises, then dismisses, the prospect of reopening the canon. Why? Because "formation of scripture, and canonization of scripture, are processes which were characteristic of a certain time, a certain stage in the life of the people of God. We are in fact no longer in that stage; it is a matter of history to us, and even historically we are not too well informed of the arguments and categories which were employed."[8] Again, agnosticism has mysteriously changed into fideism here, but what of Barr's axiom that canon decisions, the question of their original basis aside, are structurally part of a different stage of religious evolution than we occupy? This reminds me of the maxim "If it ain't broke, don't fix it." But what if it is broke? What if we judge that Christianity is sorely in need of renovation and repair? Even of rebirth and resurrection? Perhaps we find ourselves back at a point Barr thought irretrievably gone. If we concur with Don Cupitt that "classical Christianity is itself now our Old Testament"[9] then, like Ben Franklin at the Constitutional Convention, we may decide we are at the sunrise rather than the sunset of Christianity, and then everything old is new again.

If we wish to consider framing a new canon of scripture, at least we need not begin our task at square one. Theologians in the past couple of decades, though not aiming at such a goal, made a number of observations that might prove helpful in attaining it. The first of these I want to introduce is David Tracy's suggestion that the books of the Bible be viewed as analogous to the "canon" of the classic works of a civilization.[10] His analogy has become all the more helpful for us since this cultural canon has itself become at least as controversial as the biblical canon. The current turbulence over "multiculturalism" mirrors our own unease with the boundaries of the traditional canon of Christianity. We, too, have come to feel that our canon list functions to silence a wider range of voices that once spoke loudly and clearly in the exciting Babel Tower of early Christianity. We want to reopen the canon so as to let those other voices be heard once again. We have taken a great deal of trouble in our studies scrutinizing ancient forbidden texts and literally buried documents on whose account the earth itself cried out as it did on the spot where Abel was killed. We have heard that cry, or that whisper, and we like what we have heard. So we want to widen the scope of the canon so that others, too, may hear.

Our second important consideration is, ironically, an apologetical device employed recently on behalf of the old canon-criterion of "apostolicity" (more on that below), tending to demythologize it in favor of the broader notion that canonical books (should) function as the earliest witnesses to the foundation of the faith.[11] I get the impression that this subtle shift is an attempt to weasel: apologists realize one can no longer take for granted the actual authorship of 2 Peter by Simeon Cephas, of the First and Fourth Gospels by Matthew and John ben Zebedee, the Pastorals by Paul, etc., thus they shift the denotation of "apostolic" to a kind of assumed "apostolic succession" of writers, as if presupposing (without actually saying so) theories such as that the Pastorals were written at Paul's request and contained a couple of scraps of an old note by him, or that Matthew was the compiler of Q, which then bequeathed his apostolic name via metonymy to the whole gospel, etc. The notion is no longer "shake the hand that shook the hand," but rather "shake the hand that shook the hand that shook the hand," a chain of attestations reminiscent of the *hadith* of the Prophet Muhammad. But if even such jerry-rigging fails, a shift is made to "apostolicity" as the best we can do, the earliest surviving witnesses to the foundation of the Church.

The word "apostolic" in any and all of these understandings implies the apologetic of Catholic Christianity. It carries the implication that all of the other Christianities were "Brand X," disqualified, spurious. Only certain early witnesses were to be heard, those who gained state recognition for their hastily minted "apostolic" credentials. But this specificity of reference erodes once we start putting it in terms of the earliest available (anonymous or pseudonymous) witnesses to Christianity. Because then there is no longer any reason for so-called "apostolicity" not to include witnesses from all recoverable quarters of early Christianity, including Gnostic, Judaic, Encratite. As Walter Bauer (*Orthodoxy and Heresy in Earliest Christianity*) made clear, there is no particular justification for according any one early Christian faction chronological or logical priority such as the ancient apologetic awarded Catholic Orthodoxy. Helmut Koester makes the result explicit. In a class I took with him in 1977 ("Heresies Ancient and Modern," team-taught with Harvey Cox), he remarked that "the best canon is the most inclusive."

A third major consideration emerges from current Feminist discussions, albeit inadvertently. Elisabeth Schüssler Fiorenza, repudiating the "biblical authority" of a passage she reads as oppressive of women, announces, "We do not accord to such a patriarchal text divine authority and proclaim it the word of God. Instead we must proclaim it as the word of Luke!"[12] She still doesn't get it: there is no "Word of God." The whole thing is, so to speak, "the word of Luke." What she seems not to see is that any "word" becomes oppressive when idolized as a divine word. That is a mistake we must not make when setting out to form a new biblical canon. That is the mistake made by recent Politically Correct versions of the Bible. They play ventriloquist with the ancient, recalcitrant texts, trying to make them speak the shibboleths of feminism, egalitarianism, etc. It would make sense to play such an implausible trick only on the assumption that, if it's in the Bible, it must be true. So when we find something in the Bible that is manifestly not true, because sexist, racist, whatever, we must rewrite it. It is a caricature of genuine biblicism. A real biblicist (if there are any) would read whatever the Bible says and try to believe and do it, on the assumption that whatever is in the Bible is already true. The Politically Correct biblicist, however, will admit the Bible missed the truth here and there (and there and there and there), but in the goodness of his/her heart he/she is willing to help rehabilitate the Bible. Why isn't it obvious that this strategy is just cynical manipulation? The Bible is still being used as a divine oracle to intimidate the sheep-like flock. The Newspeak Testament.

We cannot pretend to have diversity and orthodoxy ("correctness") at the same time. If we really want an inclusive canon, it's going to have to wind up including ideas and teachings we personally do not relish. For instance, let it not be said of a new canon that, according to it, "the only heresy is orthodoxy." And we needn't feel compelled to have a Bible that is right all the time if we realize up front that it is not the Word of God, since there is no Word of God.

CANONS FOR A CANON: THE CRITERIAL QUESTION

As is well known, the somewhat vague criteria vaguely employed in the series of vague deliberations over the contents of the New Testament canon (and, as Barr notes, we have even less idea how the Old Testament books were chosen) included four principles: orthodoxy, apostolicity, catholicity, and numerology. I want to explore the possible viability of these criteria, once rehabilitated, but first let us review them as an interrelated set.

First, *catholicity*: was a book read all over the οἰκουμένη? If it was not, then it was dubious, since presumably a real apostolic writing would have had sufficient time to circulate more widely. Little 3 John met some difficulty on this score, since few had ever heard of it, but given its "length," it was understandable for it to have gotten lost in the shuffle, and it finally gained admission on the coat-tails of 1 John. In practice this meant that the more widely known a book was, the better its chances for inclusion, since any unorthodox rough edges would have had time to be glazed over by harmonizing exegesis. But if, like the unfortunate Gospel of Peter, it was parochial in use, it would sound strange to outsiders, who could more readily recognize its heretical oddities. The Gospel of Thomas would probably sound less strange to our ears if we had heard it over and over again since Sunday School, like Matthew, Mark, Luke, and John. Conversely, if the faction of the Alogoi had managed to prevent canonization of the Gospel of John, it would still sound as strange to us as it did to them. In any case, to eliminate a little-known book from the list would offend few, since it had few partisans.

Second, *orthodoxy* required of an early Christian document that it pass the litmus test of the Catholic rule of faith in the rudimentary form we find in Irenaeus, Tertullian, and the Apostles Creed. But, again, catholicity could overrule this criterion, since any "heretical" teaching in a book might be, and usually had been, harmonized, if the writing were widely enough beloved. Sometimes, e.g., evidence of Docetism might be enough to sink a book, as it did the Gospel of Peter, but it might take no more than the citation of noncanonical Old Testament books. Barnabas could not survive this strike against it, while 2 Timothy and Jude did, since their value as anti-Gnostic writings outweighed their other eccentricities. Sometimes a book might be suspicious, not because it actually taught heresy, but because it might let the camel's nose under the tent flap. For instance, late apocalypses were suspicious, because if one accepted them, however orthodox they might be in themselves, it would not be as easy to exclude the blasphemous rantings of Maximilla. Finally, in an extension of Tertullian's "prescription against heretics," whereby he sought to disallow his opponents the use of scriptures rightly belonging to orthodoxy, some were willing to reject books they deemed guilty by association from long and notorious heretical use, whether the texts actually taught heresy or not. I believe the Gospel of Thomas was excluded largely because Manicheans and Valentinians used it. John almost met the same fate before Bultmann's Ecclesiastical Redactor salvaged it for orthodoxy by the liberal use of the blue pencil. The same with Marcion's beloved Pauline Epistles.

Third, *apostolicity* was important: was the book written by an apostle or his understudy? If Johnson hadn't actually written a gospel, had Boswell? But this proved to be a wax nose easily twisted. If a book was widely used and deemed orthodox, then an apostolic byline could be created for it (Hebrews) or squeezed out of it by means of *hadith* (Mark, Luke). And if a book proved unpalatable on other grounds, its clear apostolic claim could be contemptuously dismissed as a forgery. There would otherwise seem to be hardly less reason to accept the Gospel of Peter than the Gospel of Matthew if the name tag were all that mattered.

Fourth, there was *numerology*. Irenaeus rationalized the fourfold gospel, no more, no less, by analogy with the four winds, the four directions of the compass, even the four living creatures of the Revelation. Epistles should fall neatly into groups of seven if they knew what was good for them, and the Pauline Epistles would nicely oblige so long as one added Hebrews to their number. It is not unlikely that the eminently forgettable 2 Peter and humble Philemon owe their places in the canon to such *gematria* as well.

The result was to rubber-stamp a variegated collection of books which by no means all conformed to second- and third-century Catholic orthodoxy, but which were being read as if they did. Other, rejected, books such as those buried at Nag Hammadi by the monks of Saint Pachomius in preference to letting Athanasius' inquisitors burn them, either were just too explicitly non-

Catholic or simply had belonged to a different interpretive community.[13] They looked strange to orthodoxy because the bishops had never had the opportunity either to redact or to harmonize them into conformity with the rule of faith.

In our situation, it is the arbitrariness of these criteria fully as much as the narrowness of the result that force us to reconsider the boundaries of the biblical canon. And yet it may prove worth the trouble to ask if there is anything redeemable here. That is, since, by the very act of delimiting a canon, we are walking in the steps of the old ecclesiastics, trying to replace their worn-out edifice with a better one, it may just be that some of their tools and techniques still have some use left in them.

First, what can catholicity mean for us? As already anticipated, it will mean wholeness, something closer to true universality spanning the ancient Christian spectrum. We will strive not primarily for geographical breadth but for theological and gender inclusivity.

And there is another important dimension of catholicity. As Frank Kermode aptly points out, the function of a canon of scripture is to control the resources and results of divination.[14] The Word of God can be drawn only from certain writings, so as to limit God's options as to what to say. When the Saducees challenge the doctrine of resurrection, Jesus must meet them on their own playing field, the Pentateuch. If he wants to win the game, he has to find a prooftext from the Five Books. It was no accident that the Saducees limited their canon as they did. And thus the urgency of Athanasius in circumscribing the New Testament canon to the 27 writings used today. He didn't want people having books like Thunder, Perfect Mind or The Hypostasis of the Archons available to inform and influence their beliefs.

Thus also, and equally important, Constantine's ordering up official copies of an official canon for distribution to the various dioceses. But now the means of production have been democratized, or at least laicized. We need not leave it to the Pope or the King to propagate the true scriptures. In other words, today canonicity is what the market will bear. Already among American evangelicals "the Bible" has come to denote the Living Bible and the New International Version, as it once denoted the King James Version. And all this has less to do with the dictates of any ecclesiastical authority than with mercantile success of these reader-friendly, theologically tailor-made translations. Catholicity, then, in the age of Capitalism, means commercial success. What people buy and read as the Bible *is* the Bible, and that will be no less true of books like *The Five*

Gospels, The Complete Gospels, The Inclusive Language Bible and of any other canon any publisher launches.

YARDSTICK FOR HERETICS

Second, orthodoxy can still have a meaning for us, though one largely transformed. Here I am indebted to a group of neo-evangelical theologians including James D.G. Dunn,[15] John M. Goldingay,[16] and Charles Kraft.[17] All promote the model of the canon as a range of legitimate but different Christian options. Kraft calls it "the tether model"[18] because the canon marks out the outer limits of possible Christian believing and acting. Within that radius there is plenty of room to move. Kraft, Goldingay, and Dunn are reckoning with the wide diversity within the present Javneh/Athanasian canon, but the same principle would obviously apply to a new, even more diverse, canon.

I have already repudiated the notion of a canon of scriptures that any reader must agree with 100% of the time. How is this compatible with the idea of a canon that defines a set of "correct," "allowable" options? Isn't the difference between the tether model and the traditional canon a matter more quantitative than qualitative? A few more correct options, a few less heretical ones? Such an arrangement would be an improvement over traditional Christianity, something more like Hinduism which embraces six orthodoxies though it still damns Buddhism as a false religion. But it isn't good enough. But the tether model may yet serve us.

The trick is to see that to set out a range of "canonical" versus "noncanonical" options (positions represented in the canonical scriptures or not) need not imply exclusivity or excommunication. All we need do is to keep straight the difference between description and prescription. We are accustomed, in our scrutiny of ancient sources, to be alert to cases of a writer seeming to describe when he is really prescribing, stipulating when he seems to be defining, as when the Pastor tells us that women do not (i.e., they must not) teach or usurp authority over men. "It simply isn't done!" We, on the other hand, must make sure all we do is to describe and leave it at that.

To avoid a prescriptive canon we need only count the canonical range of "Christian options" as something like ideal types or even as genre conventions. Ideal types are yardsticks which measure for variation, the goal being, not to disqualify that which varies, but to understand and to appreciate it more fully. If one were to sketch out a range of options that might be considered Christian, what would this imply about those religious movements or beliefs that fell outside the range? Nothing at all! For instance, suppose one noted that the Latter Day Saints Church or the Unification Church were not as Christocentric as the various options attested in the canon? Would this mean there was anything wrong with either Church? Not at all! Rather, the importance of the Prophet Smith or of the Reverend Moon would stand out the more clearly and, with it, so would the distinctives of both movements. And if they were to continue to regard themselves as Christian movements nonetheless, so what?

Here is where the analogy to literary genre conventions comes in handy. As Wayne Booth[19] and Tzvetan Todorov[20] both point out, an earlier generation of literary critics used to damn certain works as inferior insofar as they bent or transgressed the conventions of their genres. Now it seems clearer that such transgressions are simply mutations by which the genres in question evolve. In precisely the same way, to the extent that Mormonism and Unificationism, or the Aladura churches of Africa,[21] vary radically from the parameters of the canon (the old or the new), it simply means that Christianity is evolving into new forms. When and at what point will they shed the designation "Christian" to be called something else? Well, where was the line to be drawn between amphibian and reptile? Such judgments can only be rendered in long historical hindsight, and what's the rush? But the main point is that no value judgment is implied by variations from the ideal type. After all, that is the point of an "ideal" type: *all* actual instances vary from it.

In the same way, to draw a line around a set of "canonical" writings is not to denigrate any writings outside the canon. It is a question of description, not of prescription. Our new canon will not carry any warnings that these and no others must be read, preached from, etc. This is important to keep in mind once we begin the tricky business of deciding which particular writings to exclude (and make no mistake: it will be a matter not of what books to include, but which books to exclude).

POSTCARDS FROM THE APOSTLES

Third, apostolicity can still function for us as it did for the ancient framers of the canon (whether they realized it or not), that is, as a foundation myth. Unlike them, we realize that the claims of any ancient writing to stem from one of the Twelve or other apostles is highly problematical, if for no other reason than that we now approach such claims, even credible ones, as matters of mere probability. And to make canonicity depend on answers to questions that must remain theoretically open would mean having a list of writings that are only probably canonical! But there is no problem at all if we understand and appreciate the nature of the apostolic claim made by the Gospel of John and the Acts of John alike. They both partake of the myth of apostolicity. If the Popes claimed descent from Peter, so did Basilides. All the books that spuriously claim apostolic authorship are really embodying a particular retrospective vision of the foundation and, by extension, of the nature of the Christian religion. When Lukan "nascent Catholicism" is packed by implication into the forty days of Jesus' teaching between Easter and Ascension Day, the point is the same as in the Apocryphon of James, where, however, the Savior vouchsafes quite different post-resurrection teachings to the same apostles. Both writers are making their claims to what Christianity is basically about. The myth of apostolicity is a way of rendering such judgments. The Apostles' Creed says, here's what the Apostles must have said, would have said—not what they actually did say, which no one knows. It may be, as the Shepherd of Hermas has it, that they all followed Jesus down into Hades to preach to the dead (Similitudes 9:16), or maybe as Vincent Taylor once quipped,[22] they did ascend to heaven with Jesus! We'll never know.

The Epistles and Gospels and Acts and Revelations are all "postcards" in Derrida's sense:[23] since we now read them with no assurance of their genuine apostolic authorship, then it must be a structural possibility of the writings for sense to be made of them in light of such uncertainty. The loss of any way to verify apostolic authorship is only a special case of Roland Barthes's "death of the author."[24] The texts must stand on their own, as readable as a misrouted postcard which can now only be read without full background knowledge of author and intended recipient, knowledge which, however, would be absolutely needful if the sense of the text were to be identified with the author's intent. If we accept the critical principle of the death of the author, that authorial intent, even where known, does not control "the" meaning of the text, then the possible authorship of Hebrews by Paul and of Romans by Paul are equally irrelevant.

Apostolicity in the old sense was never a real cause for the inclusion of New Testament books; it only rationalized the rubber-stamping of books already chosen. For us it cannot be a true cause either, since such claims are either demonstrably false or unverifiable. But it can function as a myth that does what all myths do: it can provide the script for a ritual, in this case the ritual of choosing canonical books. Those which treat of foundational truths, in other words, apostolic truths, are the kind we want.

Fourth, numerology seems to be the hardest of the four criteria to redeem for our use. And yet we ought to be able to empathize with the problem the numerological criterion sought to solve: how do you arrive at a specific number of books? How many are there to be? The doctrine of inspiration was another, equally fanciful, tool for setting canonical limits: how many books? Why, all the inspired ones, and only the inspired ones! And how do we know which books are in fact inspired? Simple! The ones included in the canon! No thanks.

Perhaps the deeper issue here is that of an architectonic, even an aesthetic, principle, some design of proportionality such as governs practically any writing. We have a sense, though it is not absolute, of when a book is getting too long, when it lacks a central theme (at which point, if we are biblical theologians, we will pick our favorite theme and declare it the central one), etc. Diversity is already an important principle of design for our new canon. There are other terms and categories which we associate with the very notion of "Bible" which may serve us here, too, including the balance between Law and Gospel; Law, Prophets, Writings; Old and New Testaments; Wisdom versus Kerygma, as well as the simple fact of a stimulating variety of literary genres. We ought to feel at liberty to borrow some of these structures for a Bible of our own making, as long as we are retaining the notion of a Bible at all. And since any boundary is going to have to be arbitrary in the nature of the case, I would suggest appealing to an analogy something like Irenaeus.' How many books should be in our canon? Well, how many are in the traditional Bible? There are 66 in the Protestant Bible.[25] Let's see if we can't go with that. By now, it pretty much goes with the genre. Call it a matter of verisimilitude if you like. Later on, I will invoke the opposite consideration, that of "defamiliarizing" the Bible.

HOW MANY TESTAMENTS?

When we broach the canon question we are in the same breath raising the shade of Marcion, since it seems to have been he who hatched the idea of a distinctively Christian scripture, and he could see that the question of a Christian scripture was automatically and immediately bound up with the question of whether the Jewish Scriptures could serve as part of it. Of course, Marcion said they could not. We must give thought to this matter, or we will be skirting part of the fundamental question we claim we have the courage to consider.

First, let it be remembered that Marcion was neither anti-Semitic nor even anti-Judaistic.[26] His congregations were known as "synagogues of the

Marcionites."[27] He granted that the creator God was righteous by ancient standards, pretty much the same thing Christians and Reformed Jews readily grant today when none of us thinks of himself/herself as a Marcionite. For Marcion, Jews were right not to accept Jesus as the Messiah predicted by their prophets, a Davidic monarch and warrior. Such a Messiah would indeed come to answer Jewish hopes, but Jesus Christ was something else entirely, the Christian Savior. Marcion allowed that Judaism was true on its own terms, and that Christianity was true on its own terms. Or, as we might say, he recognized the difference between the narrative worlds implied by the Jewish and Christian myths and refused to confuse them. He respected the integrity of each and saw no use in Christians trying to co-opt Jewish Scripture.

It seems obvious to me that Marcion's way would have been the way forward to a far better future than the one painted in blood by the Christian supersessionist doctrine implied by retaining, actually insidiously co-opting, the Jewish Scripture. To make the Jewish Scriptures Christian by a wholesale, opportunistic rereading of them[28] was already to pull the rug out from under Judaism, whereas, if the Church had gone Marcion's way, we would have already reached something amazingly close to the "Double Covenant" theology of our own century.

I propose that a new Christian canon learn from Marcion, as Schleiermacher and Harnack were willing to do. Let us live up to the example of post-Soviet Russia and restore our stolen treasures to their rightful owners. Let us abandon the Christian claim to the Jewish Scripture. And this not because we dismiss it as inferior. To the contrary, to insist on retaining it as Christian Scripture is to continue damning it with faint praise: "It's okay as long as it's understood in light of the New Testament." Simply by retaining the Jewish Scriptures as part of the Christian Bible we are, in Karl Rahner's terms, making these books "anonymous Christians," a pseudo-pluralistic strategy that many now dismiss as insufferably patronizing. If we quail at giving Jews our blessing only insofar as we can view them as "anonymous Christians," then what are we doing retaining their Scriptures on the same basis? We are no better than Justin Martyr who smugly informed Rabbi Trypho that the books of the Tanakh were not "your Scriptures," but rather "our Scriptures."

No, a genuine ecumenical respect for these books understood as Jewish writings would admit that they stand alone, self-sufficient, within Judaism. Real respect, as Emmanuel Levinas would remind us[29] means encountering the Other as truly Other, not hastening to make it over in our own image.

We will still love these "other" writings and cherish them. We need not stop reading and preaching from them—just as there should not be any barrier to our reading and preaching from the Koran or the Upanishads (something I have done often enough). Remember, for us, the canon does not mean that non-Christian, non-canonical writings are inferior to ours. It simply means that the books we consider canonical are ours in a special way. These define us in a special way. They show us where we fall on the taxonomical chart, that's all. If, like the Seventh Day Adventists, you want to start letting the Torah define your religious identity, too, well, who's going to stop you? Ditto if you want to be one of those Zen Catholics. Why not? Let a hundred flowers bloom, including new hybrids! Remember, canons (literally, "measuring sticks") are properly only ideal types, heuristic devices, not threats of anathema.

And yet I think that for many of us a New Testament without an Old Testament would seem to float in the air, unanchored. This is probably why proposed jargon like "First Testament and Second Testament" and "Jewish Testament and Christian Testament" falls flat, sounds like barbaric Newspeak. "Second Testament" seems to reverse the perceived sleight rendered to the Tanakh as an "Old Testament" by making the New Testament merely "Secondary," the "Johnny Come Lately Testament." "Jewish Testament and Christian Testament" seems to presuppose a Double Covenant theology and thus patronizes those Jews who believe Christians are just mixed-up semi-pagans. My Solomonic solution is to cut the baby in half! Let's have an Old Testament *and* let's turn the hijacked Tanakh back over to Jews. The Old Testament will not be the text of the Tanakh.

What I'm going to propose has grown from a seed planted one Christmas Eve as I got ready to go to Midnight Mass at Saint Stephen's Episcopal Church in Goldsboro, North Carolina. As I struggled to get my necktie straight, a superfluous effort, since I would soon be vesting as a chalice bearer, I watched a few minutes of a televised service of lessons and carols broadcast from King's College Chapel. To my surprise, the readings included a passage from the Protevangelion of James! I thought, "Well, why not read from the texts that actually tell the story as we imagine it!"

A few years later, pastor of my own Baptist congregation, I experimented with a Christmas Eve service in which many of the "Old Testament" lessons were drawn from Pseudepigraphical writings like the Life of Adam and Eve, the Ascension of Isaiah, I Enoch, and 4 Ezra. My thought was, if you want to trace the course of the Christian myth-epic of the Fall and prophesied salvation, you're not going to get much help from the canonical Old Testament! Genesis 2–3 is more like the Prometheus myth; it has nothing to do with a Fall. Isaiah and Amos weren't talking about Jesus of Nazareth. And I didn't intend to coopt the Jewish Bible by pretending they were! So why not go instead to those off-brand Jewish apocrypha and apocalypses which, unlike the actual Tanakh, did provide the mythemes central to the New Testament epic? And to those Christian midrashes which recast the "Old Testament" sagas and prophecies to make them say what they didn't say: that in Adam's fall, we sinned all, and that Jesus Christ was the seed of the woman who would come in the latter days to die on a cross and redeem the world. When early Christians wrote and redacted these books, they were doing what Josephus did in his *Antiquities of the Jews*, writing a faithful account of what they imagined the Tanakh said. The Old Testament Pseudepigrapha, in effect, really are the Christian Old Testament, in a much more important sense than the co-opted Jewish Tanakh on which they are loosely based. So let's make the *de facto* Old Testament into the *de jure* Old Testament! And these books, unlike the Tanakh, are free for the taking! Nobody else wants them!

The theological result would be much like the Islamic estimate of Jewish and Christian Scriptures. Muslims are glad to recognize a general continuity between the Bible and the Koran; they have genuine regard for the Law, the Psalms, and the Evangel, though they believe these original revelations are but vaguely and partially represented in the extant canons of Jews and Christians. And the Jewish Tanakh and Christian Bible are not, strictly speaking, scripture in Islam, as they are, for instance, in Mormonism. But the Koran does include its own versions of the Tanakh and the Gospels. They are the secret histories of Noah, Abraham, Moses, Mary, and Jesus, revealed by Allah to the Prophet Muhammad.[30] In them we learn how the ancient prophets faced challenges and obstacles precisely parallel to those of Muhammad himself, even down to the same barbs from hecklers! These charismatic *targumim* of the biblical traditions are exactly equivalent to the Pseudepigrapha, especially those like the Testaments of the Twelve Patriarchs, 4 Ezra, and (some think) the Similitudes of Enoch, which have been passed down in Christian versions.

And in terms of biblical exegesis, the situation would change nary a whit. For decades, scientific exegetes have known that the relevant frames of reference for New Testament interpretation are provided not by the writings of ancient Israel or even post-Exilic Judea, already separated by a great impassable gulf from the strange new world of the New Testament, but rather by Josephus,

Philo, the Hermetica, Gnosticism, Qumran, and the Pseudepigrapha. Let's make it official. And when the background of the Jewish Scriptures is necessary, it will be just as easy to refer to them as it always has been. To say, as some have, that the New Testament would make no sense without reference to the Jewish Scriptures, even when true, is no argument for considering the Jewish Bible part of the Christian Bible.

THE UNFAMILIAR

With the New Testament list, no such wholesale replacement is either necessary or advisable. A new Christian canon would want to expand the New Testament, not to shrink it. And we can afford to curtail the Old Testament to make room for a longer New Testament, since we may now admit that the Old Testament we are left with is basically prolegomena to the New. Why not? You'd be grossly underrating the Book of Job to say it was just a running start for the New Testament (in fact, it's probably superior to anything in the New Testament!), but, really, who gives a damn about the Testament of Job except as an interesting precedent for speaking with the tongues of angels in 1 Corinthians 13?

As for which New Testament books to retain, I'm for keeping the four gospels, as well as adding several others. But I'm also for defamiliarizing the four. Each is a case unto itself.

Matthew's Gospel is really a kind of "house name" for a literary tradition, a whole family of versions including our familiar Greek Matthew, the notorious "Hebrew Gospels" of the Ebionites, Nazoreans, and Hebrews,[31] as well as one or more Hebrew versions attested in the Middle Ages,[32] one of which, championed by George Howard, has a real claim to represent an early alternative "original" with links to the Gospel of Thomas.[33] Though the syntagm is the same in all versions, they represent a unique range of simultaneous actualizations of a number of paradigm options. I would like to see us actualize a different one of the options by choosing Howard's Hebrew Matthew as our canonical Matthew. This would give us a fresh Matthew. And there would still be plenty of copies of Greek Matthew floating around to consult.

On the assumption that either John Dominic Crossan[34] or Helmut Koester was right in his reconstruction of the Secret Gospel of Mark,[35] I say we use it in the new canon. Undo the decision which long deprived us of the complete text. Similarly, I find myself convinced by John Knox that Marcion's Gospel was a redaction of a kind of Ur-Lukas, which was in turn embellished and catholicized by the author of Acts.[36] Given the anti-Marcionite tenor of Luke-Acts, my proposal would be to drop the bipartite work in favor of the reconstructed Ur-Lukas and the Acts of Paul (and Thecla). This is not just because Luke-Acts represents the perspective that later became Orthodoxy (orthodoxy must not become a heresy, remember); there is more to it than that. Luke-Acts is a harmonizing whitewash designed precisely to conceal the very variety of voices which we are trying to recover. I say, jettison the Pastoral Epistles for the same reason. And we ought to omit the whole Pastoral Stratum of interpolations identified by Winsome Munro in the Pauline Epistles and 1 Peter.[37]

Finally, it will come as no surprise when I say that I think we ought to canonize the original Gospel of John as it looked before the Ecclesiastical Redactor put his imprimatur on it.

I append my full canon list as a trial balloon.

NEW BIBLICAL CANON

Old Testament

The Patriarchs

1. Life of Adam and Eve/
      Apocalypse of Moses
2. Hypostasis of the Archons
3. On the Origin of the World
4. Apocalypse of Adam
5. The Thought of Norea
6. The Book of Lamech
7. Melchizedek
8. Testament of Abraham
9. Testament of Levi
10. Joseph and Asenath
11. Philo's Life of Moses
12. The Book of Jubilees
13. The Book of Jasher

The Prophets

14. The Book of Enoch
15. The Secrets of Enoch
16. Hebrew Enoch
17. Apocalypse of Elijah
18. Ascension of Isaiah
19. 2 Baruch
20. Fourth Ezra

The Sages

21. Wisdom of Solomon
22. Psalms of Solomon
23. Odes of Solomon
24. Testament of Solomon
25. Testament of Job
26. Akhenaten's Hymn to the Sun

New Testament

The Gospels

27. Mandaean Book of John
28. The Q Document
29. Hebrew Matthew
30. Secret Mark (a la Koester)
31. Ur-Luke (pre-Marcion) (a la Knox)
32. Gospel of John (a la Bultmann)
33. Gospel of Thomas
34. Gospel according to the Hebrews
35. Gospel of Peter
36. Gospel of Philip
37. Gospel of Mary
38. Gospel of Truth
39. Gospel according to the Cathars

The Apostles

40. Acts of Paul
41. Acts of John
42. Acts of Thomas
43. Acts of Peter
44. Acts of Andrew
45. Preaching of Peter
46. Teaching of the Twelve Apostles

The Epistles

47. Romans (a la Munro & Baur)
48. Galatians (a la Munro)
49. 1 Corinthians (a la Munro)
50. 2 Corinthians A/B/C/E/F
    (a la Munro)
51. 3 Corinthians
52. Laodiceans/Ephesians
    (as per Hoffmann)
53. Philippians (a la Munro)
54. Rheginos
55. Ptolemy to Flora
56. 1 John
57. 1 Peter (a la Munro)
58. James
59. Hebrews
60. Barnabas

The Apocalypses

61. Apocalypse of John
62. Thunder, Perfect Mind
63. Apocalypse of Peter
64. Apocalypse of Paul
65. Apocryphon of John
66. Shepherd of Hermas

NOTES

1.   I am aware that Luther did reopen the question of the canon, attempting to relegate certain marginal New Testament writings to an appendix on the basis of their perceived failure to "bear Christ" to the reader. But Luther employed this new canonical criterion in a piecemeal and inconsistent manner, since he left the Old Testament pretty much unmolested. Even on the assumption that whatever Jewish writings bore the Law

to the reader would be counted as canonical, we would have a hard time squaring the Wisdom literature or a great deal of the content of several other books with this principle. (This is, of course, the very same problem faced by Eichrodt, Von Rad, and the rest engaged in the Quixotic task of assembling a unitive "Old Testament theology" that would connect all the dots. There just is no single, unifying theme.)

And Luther freely discarded his principle of the single sense of Scripture when he allowed that the Prophets or Genesis actually predicted the coming of Jesus. The books of the Apocrypha were sacrificed to his desire to escape the Latin Vulgate, since he could not tolerate the presence in the Bible of writings which did not survive in their original language. There could be no inspired translation, or it's back to Popery in one fell swoop. (This is why Francis Turretin shuddered at the prospect of correcting the corrupt Massoretic and Byzantine Texts in light of the early language versions [*The Doctrine of Scripture: Locus 2 of the Institutio Theologiae Elencticae*. Edited and translated by John W. Beardslee III. (Grand Rapids: Baker Book House) 1981, 130-131]). This criterion for canonicity would seem to be a makeshift expedient, and of another sort altogether than Luther's ostensible criterion of bearing Christ (or, implicitly, bearing the Law).

In short, he never carried through consistently the project of reopening the canon, in effect retaining the traditional canon whose boundaries had been set by the very church tradition he had overthrown. His followers nervously retreated from the precipice to which their master had led them. Perhaps they sensed that, as we should say, reopening the canon would mean a de-reifying of the canon, making all too plain the arbitrary, man-made character of the canon, any canon. The Neo-Orthodox did embrace the notion of the Bible becoming the gospel, the Word of God, here and there, now and then, according to the mysterious providence of God's effectual call (a la Calvin), but even they did not dare to discount certain books as not susceptible to such existentialist transubstantiation. So they retained the whole Protestant canon, and, with it, the absurd implication that anyone might feel called to Christian faith by reading Chronicles' dossiers of priestly pedigrees or Numbers' interminable catalogues of bribes offered to Jehovah. What hidden principle guided them? Either an unacknowledged belief in plenary inspiration, or, as seems more likely, simple inertia.

2.   Friedrich Daniel Ernst Schleiermacher, *The Christian Faith*. Vol. 1. Translated by D.M. Baillie, W.R. Matthews, Edith Sandbach Marshall, A.B. Macaulay, Alexander Grieve, J.Y. Campbell, R.W. Stewart, and H.R. Mackintosh.. (NY: Harper & Row, Publishers) 1963, 62,115; *Brief Outline on the Study of Theology*. Translated by Terrence N. Tice. (Richmond: John Knox) 1970, 53: "it must remain permissible . . . to deviate from the ancient Church's practice of uniting the Old Testament with the New Testament into one whole, the Bible."

3.   Adolf von Harnack, *Marcion: The Gospel of the Alien God*. Translated by John E. Steeley and Lyle D. Bierma. (Durham: The Labyrinth Press) 1990, 133–138: "the

rejection of the Old Testament in the second century was a mistake which the great church rightly avoided; to maintain it in the sixteenth century was a fate from which the Reformation was not yet able to escape; but still to preserve it in Protestantism as a canonical document since the nineteenth century is the consequence of a religious and ecclesial crippling" (134).

4.   Willi Marxsen, *The New Testament as the Church's Book*. Translated by James E. Mignard. (Philadelphia: Fortress Press) 1972. "The Protestant . . . faces the dilemma that the canon could not have served as a guideline as the church debated the problem, since the canon did not yet exist! In other words, the church was not able to abide by the principle sola scriptura in deciding what should or should not be canonical" (16). "[W]hoever takes as his only norm the New Testament within its canonical limits travels the road of the Roman Catholics, except that he is less consistent than they" (20). "It is by no means [merely] theoretical, therefore, to suggest that the ancient decision on the canon made on the basis of fourth century experiences is open to revision" (17).

5.   *The Bible in the Modern World*. (NY: Harper & Row, Publishers) 1973, 156.

6.   Again, Marxsen: "From time to time the claim is made that the canon should be treated as an object of faith, although it is beyond me how anyone can propose this. Faith is said to be involved in that we are faced with a decision of faith by the church and are to exercise our faith by consenting to that ancient decision. Acceptance of the canon then becomes a matter of faith. This looks like an easy solution, but it is vulnerable for the simple reason that the canon did not fall from heaven all at once as an entity to be believed in . One cannot emphasize too much that the canon was a part of the fabric of church history" (17–18).

7.   Friedrich Nietzsche, *The Gay Science*. Translated by Walter Kaufman. (NY: Vintage Books, Random House) 1974, 181.

8.   Barr, 155.

9.   *Taking Leave of God* (NY: Crossroad Publishing Company) 1981, 135.

10.   *Blessed Rage for Order: The New Pluralism in Theology* (NY: Seabury Press) 1975, 49–51.

11.   For example, Harry Y. Gamble, *The New Testament Canon: Its Making and Meaning*. Guides to Biblical Scholarship, New Testament Series, ed. Dan O. Via, Jr. (Philadelphia: Fortress Press) 1985. Apostolicity actually need not have entailed a book being the work of an apostle at all, but instead "refers to what was characteristic of the earliest church" (68).

12.   "A Feminist Critical Interpretation for Liberation: Martha and Mary: Luke 10:38–42," *Religion & Intellectual Life* 3, 1986, 32–33.

13. Stanley Fish, *Is There a Text in This Class? The Authority of Interpretive Communities* (Cambridge: Harvard University Press) 1980.

14. "Institutional Control of Interpretation," *The Art of Telling: Essays on Fiction* (Cambridge: Harvard University Press) 1983. 173–176.

15. *Unity and Diversity in the New Testament* (Philadelphia: Westminster Press) 1977.

16. "Inspiration, Infallibility and Criticism," *The Churchman.* January-March 1976, 6–23.

17. *Christianity in Culture* (Maryknoll: Orbis Books) 1979.

18. Kraft, 187, 191.

19. *The Rhetoric of Fiction.* (Chicago: University of Chicago Press). 2nd ed., 1983, 31, 127.

20. "Poetics and Criticism," *The Poetics of Prose.* Translated by Richard Howard. (Ithaca: Cornell University Press) 1977, 29–41; "The Typology of Detective Fiction," Ibid., 42–52.

21. G.C. Oosthuizen and Irving Hexham (eds.), *Empirical Studies of African Independent/Indigenous Churches* (Lewiston: The Edwin Mellen Press) 1992; Marie-Louise Martin. *Kimbangu: An African Prophet and His Church.* Translated by D.M. Moore. (Grand Rapids: William B. Eerdmans Publishing Company) 1975; Gordon MacKay Haliburton, *The Prophet Harris: A study of an African prophet and his mass-movement in the Ivory Coast and the Gold Coast 1913–1915.* (NY: Oxford University Press) 1973; G.C. Oosthuizen. *Post-Christianity in Africa: A Theological and Anthropological Study* (Grand Rapids: William B. Eerdmans Publishing Company) 1968; Bengt G.M. Sundkler. *Bantu Prophets in South Africa* (NY: International African Institute, Oxford University Press) 2nd edition, 1961; Bennetta Jules-Rosette. *African Apostles: Ritual and Conversion in the Church of John Maranke.* Symbol, Myth, and Ritual, series ed. Victor Turner. (Ithaca: Cornell University Press) 1975.

22. *The Formation of the Gospel Tradition: Eight Lectures.* (London: Macmillan Company) 2nd ed. 1935, rpt. 1957, 41.

23. "Envois," *The Postcard: From Socrates to Freud and Beyond.* Translated by Alan Bass. (Chicago: University of Chicago Press) 1987, 3–256.

24. "The Death of the Author," *Image-Music-Text.* Translated by Stephen Heath. (NY: Noonday Press, Farrar, Strauss and Giroux) 1977, 142–148.

25. As Andrew Q. Morton has indicated in a whole series of instructive studies (A.Q. Morton and G.H.C. MacGregor, *The Structure of Luke-Acts* [NY: Harper & Row, Publishers)] 1964; Morton and J. McLeman, *The Genesis of John* [Edinburgh: Saint Andrew Press] 1980; A.Q. Morton, *The Making of Mark.* Mellen Biblical Press Series,

41. [Lewiston: The Edwin Mellen Press] 1996), we ought not continue to overlook the importance of the mundane realities of ancient copying and publishing in the formation of individual biblical books and of the Bible as a whole. A book, whether a scroll or a codex, could be only so long. Even so, any Bible we compile must be of a manageable size, a single volume that people may carry about and which they will not need a magnifying glass to read. It ought to be the size book one might read through in a year, as in popular devotional plans. That seems a pretty good gauge. Otherwise you are talking about a Microfiche scripture.

26. R. Joseph Hoffmann, *Marcion: On the Restitution of Christianity, An Essay on the Development of Radical Paulinist Theology in the Second Century.* AAR Academy Series 46. (Chico: Scholars Press) 1984, 226–234.

27. Ibid. 7.

28. Randel Helms, *Gospel Fictions* (Buffalo: Prometheus Books) 1988: "By a remarkably creative fiat of interpretation, the Jewish scriptures (especially in Greek translation) became a book that had never existed before, the Old Testament, a book no longer about Israel but about Israel's hope, the Messiah, Jesus" (18).

29. Emmanuel Levinas, *Totality and Infinity: An Essay on Exteriority.* Translated by Alphonso Lingis. Duquesne Studies, Philosophical Series, ed., Andre Schuwer, 24. (Pittsburgh: Duquesne University Press) 1969, 212–214; Jacques Derrida, "Violence and Metaphysics: An Essay on the Thought of Emmanuel Levinas," *Writing and Difference.* Translated by Alan Bass. (Chicago: University of Chicago Press) 1978, 79–153.

30. "These are the revelations of the Glorious Book. In all truth We shall recount to you some of the history of Moses and Pharaoh for the instruction of the faithful" (28:1). "That which We have now revealed to you is secret history. You were not present when Joseph's brothers conceived their plans and schemed against him. . . . This is no invented tale, but a confirmation of previous scriptures, an explanation of all things, a guide and a blessing to true believers" (12:102,111). Tell "of Jesus, who said to the Israelites: 'I am sent forth to you by Allah to confirm the Torah already revealed and to give news of an apostle that will come after me whose name is Ahmed.'" (61:6). *The Koran.* Translated by N.J. Dawood. (Baltimore: Penguin Books) 1956.

31. A.F.J. Klijn, *Jewish-Christian Gospel Tradition* (NY: E.J. Brill) 1992.

32. Hugh J. Schonfield, *An Old Hebrew Text of St. Matthew's Gospel* (Edinburgh: T.&T. Clark) 1927.

33. George Howard, *The Gospel of Matthew according to a Primitive Hebrew Text* (Macon: Mercer University Press) 1987; *Hebrew Gospel of Matthew* (Macon: Mercer University Press) 1995; "Hebrew Gospel of Matthew: A Report," *Journal of Higher Criticism* Volume 2, no. 2, Fall 1995, 53–67.

34. *Four Other Gospels: Shadows on the Contours of Canon* (NY: Harper & Row, Publishers) 1985, 119–120. "In the beginning was SGM [Secret Gospel of Mark] . . . Secret Mark was possibly interpolated and certainly interpreted in Carpocratian Mark. . . . In order to eliminate the Carpocratian scandal and redeem Secret Mark for catholicism, this final version, our canonical Mark, carefully dismembered [certain passages in Secret Mark] and distributed the textual debris at various locations in the gospel."

35. *Ancient Christian Gospels: Their History and Development* (Philadelphia: Trinity Press International) 1990, 293–302. The "text of canonical Mark—it is the same text as the one known to Clement of Alexandria as Mark's public Gospel—is not the original Mark used by Matthew and Luke, but an abbreviated version of the Secret Gospel of Mark" (302).

36. *Marcion and the New Testament: An Essay in the Early History of the Canon* (Chicago: University of Chicago Press) 1942, 77–139.

37. *Authority in Paul and Peter: The Identification of a Pastoral Stratum in the Pauline Corpus and 1 Peter.* Society for New Testament Studies Monograph Series, ed., Graham N. Stanton, 45. (NY: Cambridge University Press) 1983.

PART FOUR: FREETHOUGHT

18

ERRORS OF THE ELOHIST:
AN APPRECIATION OF INGERSOLL'S
SOME MISTAKES OF MOSES

We are gathered this weekend to celebrate the life and legacy of the great Robert Ingersoll. At such a time of backward-looking, there are two senses in which we wonder whether his work has stood the test of time. First, is it still well-known? Are readers still conversant with Ingersoll's *Some Mistakes of Moses*? In his day, his lectures of this title were so well beloved (and hated!) that people seemed to regard them immediately as public property, not the possession of the speaker who had created them. So they rushed pirate transcripts into print and circulated them, much like bootleg CDs made from rock concerts and circulated among fans today.

Second, we have to ask if the *value* of the work is abiding. If not, the work is as well forgotten. Sometimes a book with no value stubbornly hangs on because, as the writer of the Pastoral Epistles said, people's ears are itching to hear what it has to say, however worthless. A case of this would be Nicholas Notovitch's bogus *Unknown Life of Christ*, a supposed Tibetan account of the Asian travels of Jesus. Debunked decades ago by the great Orientalist Max Müller, this book continues to be reprinted and avidly devoured by New Agers who find the premise attractive (—which is apparently their sole criterion for truth!). Occasionally Freethought works circulate in the same manner, having outlived their usefulness. For instance, Kersey Graves's *The World's Sixteen Crucified Saviors* is now something of an embarrassment to the cause, since more accurate information on comparative mythology makes many of its claims seem untenable.

Into which of these categories does Ingersoll's *Some Mistakes of Moses* fall? I am glad to report that its value and its power remain undiminished after 120 years, like gunpowder kept dry and ready to fire. It is no mere relic of outmoded polemic. Unfortunately it is generally treated like one, though we owe Prometheus Books a great debt for keeping it available to new generations. One gets the impression that the book is in danger of relegation to the same airless limbo as all the other relics on display in the Ingersoll Home: tokens, mementos, time capsule fodder. This neglect is possibly partly the result of the incautious, tactless manner of Ingersoll, no longer politically correct, though I confess that his scathing style is one of the book's chief attractions for me. Ingersoll understood that, if a proposition is ludicrous enough, we lend it undeserved credibility when we respond too politely. This has certainly been my own policy, for instance, in my contributions to the Internet Infidels collection of replies to fundamentalist Josh McDowell.

But Ingersoll's great book on the Pentateuch certainly does not deserve the obscurity that is gaining upon it. Its scholarship is by no means out of date, as a close, literal reading of the biblical text never is. Ingersoll must have known that the sands of critical opinion shift and drift, and that, even as Christian faith is perilously founded upon historical and exegetical uncertainties, so is the rejection of faith. That is to say, Ingersoll's critique of the Bible and its deity are not predicated upon any particular critical theory, whether in fashion or out. He refers throughout the book to Moses as the author of the Pentateuch, but only in a conventional sense. He shows how the book must have originated long after the time of Moses' supposed dates. But who *was* the author? My title makes reference to one of the critical theories of Pentateuchal authorship, the famous Graf-Wellhausen theory that the five so-called Books of Moses were a textual fusion of four earlier documents. "J," the Yahwist Epic, consistently used Yahweh as the divine name. "E," the Elohist Epic, calls God "Elohim" until the burning bush story and then switches to Yahweh or combines the two. "D," our Book of Deuteronomy, is a law code prefaced by a summary of J and E, already sown together in the Deuteronomist's time. "P," or the Priestly Code, is another vast legal corpus prefaced by stories of the Patriarchs and Moses. This elegant and illuminating hypothesis held the field for over a century. It is only being questioned by critical scholars in our day, though there is of course no thought of going back to Mosaic authorship, let me hasten to say. Had Ingersoll made use of the JEDP hypothesis, he might have been hailed as an astute biblical critic. But if he had, his polemic would have depended on a thousand critical points of debate and would have waned as the theory itself waned.

And besides, it was unnecessary. Colonel Ingersoll was, after all, a military man, and he knew you don't shoot a mouse with an elephant gun. He was not primarily an educator in the right understanding of the Bible. Old Testament critics did and do explain the sources of the Pentateuch, form criticism, and other such matters, because they want Bible readers to plumb the depths of this ancient document unimpeded by the dogmatic blinders of the past. Biblical inerrantism was and remains the worst enemy of the proper appreciation of the Bible. But Colonel Ingersoll was fighting the war for intellectual liberty on a broader front.

> Too great praise challenges attention [Ingersoll wrote], and often brings to light a thousand faults that otherwise the general eye would never see. Were we allowed to read the Bible as we do all other books, we would admire its beauties, treasure its worthy thoughts, and account for all its absurd, grotesque and cruel things, by saying that its authors lived in rude, barbaric times. But we are told that it was written by inspired men; that it contains the will of God; that it is perfect, pure, and true in all its parts; the source and standard of all moral and religious truth; that it is the star and anchor of all human hope; the only guide for man, the only torch in Nature's night. These claims are so at variance with every known recorded fact, so palpably absurd, that every free, unbiased soul is forced to raise the standard of revolt. (pp. viii–ix)

Note, if you please, Ingersoll is no Bible-hater, no village atheist with a tin ear for the beauty of scripture. No, he would doubtless say, we are more likely to stand conscience-stricken at Isaiah's oracles against the exploitation of mortgaged farmers, more likely to warm to the Gandhi-like insights of the Sermon on the Mount, if we do not feel foolishly obliged to pretend that the stupefying pedantry of Leviticus or the bloodthirsty genocide of Joshua are on the same level with them! To listen to some Freethinkers, one might imagine the Skeptic's task to be the mirror image of the fundamentalist's: to make the sublimities of the Bible appear as barbaric as its superstition and priestcraft. This seems to me the bizarre and superfluous approach, for example, of the recent broadside *Queen Jane's Version*. Today's Freethought debaters and polemicists (I am happy to be one of them) could stand to emulate Colonel Ingersoll's balance. He was not like Dracula, recoiling in fear and loathing from scripture, and we shouldn't be either. Not only is it neurotic; it causes us to play right into the stereotypes our opponents have of us. Personally, I approach my debates with the likes of William Lane Craig and Craig Blomberg not as an enemy of the Bible, but as a champion and partisan of the Bible. I love it! I read it as we read all other ancient books, like the Iliad and the Odyssey. I love them, too.

No, Ingersoll's point was that the Bible had become an idol and a tool of oppression wielded with great force and subtle skill by the Grand Inquisitor. It was a bottomless cornucopia of false hopes and empty threats for those cowed, like Dostoyevsky said, by miracle, mystery and authority. His aim might be summed up in a memorable phrase from the Reverend Jim Jones: *I've got to destroy this paper idol!* Ingersoll had to demonstrate what the Bible is *not* by showing inescapably what it *is*. How did he show that the Bible could be a sure guide neither to nature nor to the supernatural?

Ingersoll first shows the untenability of the seven-day creation account as compared not only with the fossil record but with what else we know of ancient history. We need much more history than a single week allows. Knowing that supposedly critical theologians are merely apologists retreating to plan B, Ingersoll then cuts off the escape route of allegory. He will not allow apologists to make the "days" of creation into long periods of millions of years, for then we must ask how plants can have flourished for so long in their allotted "day" with no animals or insects to eat them and help them reproduce? Etc., etc.,. And what of the Sabbath? Were the Deists right, then? Did God take a rest of millions of years after finishing the creation?

So the Genesis One creation story is wrong; it contradicts all known data. If, like Jerry Falwell said on a TV show with Carl Sagan, one proposes simply to close one's eyes to the scientific data and to believe the Bible instead, Ingersoll shows one is no better off—since then which of two contradictory accounts is one to believe? The Garden of Eden story contradicts the seven-day creation story in every particular. It is simply impossible to believe both at the same time. (Fundamentalists, for all their vaunted attention to the letter to the text, either never notice the problems or resort to pathetic spin-doctoring to sidestep them.) Since it is merely the presence in the biblical text that requires the reader believe in either one, the poor biblicist is painted into a corner! You must choose! Yet your choice of either undermines the reason you took either one seriously in the first place!

But Ingersoll, canny tactician that he was, knew his enemy's path of retreat.

He knew the next ploy would be to shorten the line of defense by cutting loose the natural data of the Bible, its erroneous statements about the age and shape and workings of the world, and to defend the inner courtyard instead: to claim that, though the Bible's teaching might be clothed in the terms of an ancient world-picture, its affirmations on morality and religion were still to be regarded as infallible. This is still the approach of sophisticated Evangelical Protestants and Roman Catholics today.

But Ingersoll saw the fortress crumbling and pressed his assault. He had not the slightest difficulty in demonstrating that the Bible, especially of course the Pentateuch, was filled with ancient barbarism: slavery, genocide, human sacrifice, oppression of women. In a particularly devastating tour-de-force, the Colonel laid bare the awful irony of the whole fundamentalist enterprise, what I like to call the *sliding scale of biblical infallibility*. It is this: biblicists start out claiming that the Bible is a divine revelation and should therefore govern both belief and behavior. Robust but naive biblicism lasts only so long before the facts of science (e.g., the sphericity of the earth) become problematical, and then biblicism becomes either *fanatical* (e.g., the Flat Earth Society—it really does exist!) or *sophistical*. In the latter case, it switches tactics and admits science is correct, the earth is round, but says that science has only clarified what the Bible was trying to tell us all along! And then passages will be quoted out of context to make it look like Isaiah or Job envisioned a spherical earth. How pathetic! Biblicists start by trying to lead the way, albeit as blind guides of the sighted, and they wind up playing catch-up, like the Soviets in the 1960s: "We inwented it first!" Ingersoll said:

> A few years ago, Science endeavored to show that it was not inconsistent with the Bible. The tables have been turned, and now, Religion is endeavoring to prove that the Bible is not inconsistent with Science. The standard has been changed. (p. 242)

Ingersoll at least implicitly made the same point in the case of biblicism in morals. Once biblicists led the way, or tried to, demanding that all follow the dictates of the Bible. In the ancient monolithic culture of Israel and Judah, whose mores we may be sure the Bible *reflected* rather than *determined*, there was no great gap between the law and people's lives. But in modern pluralistic America, biblical law has become highly problematic, and it is easy to recognize dogged biblical literalists as fanatical. The counterpart to the Flat Earthers in the realm of biblical law would be the Christian Reconstructionists like Gary North and Rousas Rushdoony, who want to live in an America where adulterers, smart-mouth kids, and loud-mouthed atheists would be executed.

If the Reconstructionists are the *fanatical* biblicists, who are their opposites, the *sophistical* biblicists? They are most Christians of whatever denomination who simply assume that the Bible teaches what is right. And what *is* right? Middle-class moralism. Whatever mulligan stew of Victorianism, Thomism, and pop psychology their pulpits happen to be dispensing at the moment. The Babbit-like Congressmen who want to post the Decalogue in public classrooms could never have suggested such a policy if they had recalled for a moment how the commandments actually read! Monotheism? Aniconic worship? Sabbatarianism? Considering women chattel alongside livestock? No commandments against lying ("bearing false witness" is more specific), fornication, drugs or intoxicants? Ingersoll might have been thinking of our Congress when he wrote:

> It has been contended for many years that the Ten Commandments are the foundation of all ideas of justice and of law. Eminent jurists have bowed to popular prejudice, and deformed their works by statements to the effect that the Mosaic laws are the fountain from which sprang all ideas of right and wrong. Nothing can be more stupidly false than such assertions. (p. 234)

Presupposed in all such public rhetoric, whether from Falwell or from Congress, is an unacknowledged fact: again, the standard has changed! The poor Bible is following, not leading. Of course supposed advocates of biblical morality (except for our Reconstructionist zealots, who thus constitute the exception that proves the rule) do not advocate genocide or slavery any more than they believe the earth is flat, even though the Bible says all these things equally. When pressed about these distasteful teachings, they will start arguing for "progressive revelation." God, we will be told, had to take the ancients as he found them and work with what he had. He couldn't shock their system too severely all at once. Well, this is just absurd; both Old and New Testament writers had more advanced moral standards available to them in their environments, as surviving records show. They were retrograde even at the time.

Once upon a time, some fundamentalists could see that the Bible condoned and even commanded slavery. It was easy for them to recognize that, since they themselves owned slaves. Other biblicists' consciences proved better than their creeds, but they couldn't afford to realize that. They harmonized the contradiction by managing to read the Bible as an anti-slavery text. The Civil War has come and gone, and now all biblicists recognize slavery as a despicable evil; they say that the Bible merely "tolerated" slavery for the sake of the ancients' hard hearts. *Once* all biblicists recognized that the Bible assigns women a secondary role, but when Suffrage came along, some were able to re-read the Bible as an egalitarian document. In both cases, biblicists find themselves, as they did in the case of natural science, playing "catch-up." Their strategy is to follow the distinctive morality of the Bible as long as it does not become as offensive to them as it is to "unbelievers," and when it does, they reverse course, claiming that the Bible, *understood rightly*, is as enlightened as secular morality any day. What damning faint praise! And what pathetic self-deception. By such a process of gradual assimilation liberal theology was born from fundamentalist: by and by, all that made Christianity a distinctive option, even if an obnoxious one, has bled out, and Christianity has humanized itself by moving ever closer to Humanism. Why not just go all the way?

The same is true even in the area of philosophical theology. Ingersoll is everywhere concerned to rub the reader's nose in the biblical depiction of God as a mythical being on pretty much the same level with Zeus. He will have none of the apologetical hogwash that has always tried to say "God's image," in which human beings were made, referred to rationality or some such abstraction. No, Ingersoll insists that we read the text literally and not take Jehovah to be some Anselmian abstraction when "Moses" clearly presented him as a temperamental tyrant whose "grace" is just the arbitrary "thumbs up" of a Nero at the Coliseum. Alfred North Whitehead recognized the biblical Jehovah for what he was:

> As for the Christian theology, can you imagine anything more appallingly idiotic than the Christian idea of heaven? What kind of deity is it that would be capable of creating angels and men to sing his praises day and night to all eternity? It is, of course, the figure of an Oriental despot, with his inane and barbaric vanity. Such a conception is an insult to God. (in Lucien Price, *Dialogues of Alfred North Whitehead*, p. 277)

Colonel Ingersoll—the title always reminds me of the Dayton Tennessee Scopes Trial, immortalized in the film *Inherit the Wind*, because of the titular elevation of both protagonists, Brady and Drummond (Bryant and Darrow) to the rank of honorary colonel in the State Militia. It was silly, and yet it was right on target as Colonels Brady and Drummond blasted away at each other with salvos of unequaled oratory. Colonel Ingersoll, too, fought on that battlefield. And what a delightful coincidence that the chief theoretician of 19th century American fundamentalism was Benjamin B. *Warfield*!

I think it is Warfield's kind of thinking that Ingersoll has in view when he repeatedly asks if we must be damned to hell for not believing this or that biblical absurdity. Did fundamentalists ever claim belief in biblical inerrancy was a condition of salvation? It sounds like Ingersoll is bayoneting a straw man. But I don't think he is. You see, Warfield was trying to close the door on liberal theology, which might otherwise tempt his Princeton Seminary students. Liberal theology said you could very well accept Jesus as savior without believing in the infallibility of scripture: two different issues, no? But Warfield said you were not much of a disciple of Jesus, not much of a follower of Christ, if you picked and chose which of his teachings you felt like accepting. And as it happens, Warfield reminded his students, Christ and the apostles can be shown to have shared the contemporary Jewish scholastic doctrine of scriptural infallibility. Had Christ not addressed the point, we would be left to our own best speculations, but as it is, like it or not, a good Christian must share his Lord's doctrine of scripture. Doesn't this imply that anyone who fails to share this belief is no disciple of Jesus? And thus damned! In case you hadn't noticed, fundamentalists simply do not believe what they *say* they believe and *think* they believe: that one is saved by the simple grace of God. There are too many shibboleths for that.

I started by observing that a once-great book might become outmoded in two senses. *Some Mistakes of Moses* has been left behind in the popular consciousness, and that is a tragedy, since it is far from outdated in the cogency of its arguments. A third sense of outmodedness, however, is this: *is the book still timely? Is it relevant?* And plainly Ingersoll's *Some Mistakes of Moses* is at least as important to the perennial struggle for intellectual and social liberty as it ever was, perhaps even moreso. And I am convinced that at least some of us must join that battle using the same techniques as Colonel Ingersoll used: debate, polemic—in the opponent's home stadium! As Ingersoll did, if we hope to show biblical fundamentalists the error of their inerrantist ways, we have to debate with them as they do with each other in their more-or-less friendly sectarian disputes. To be taken seriously we must, as Ingersoll sought to do, demonstrate a superior understanding of the text of the Bible read literally and in detail. We must not retreat into the vagaries of allegory and demythologizing as liberal Christians do. We must join fundamentalists in their disdain for such sleight-of-hand. We must ask what reading of the text makes the most sense, answers the most questions, solves the most puzzles. That is the only argument a biblicist can respect, and rightly so! After all, it was precisely such honest, unblinking scrutiny of the biblical text that led many of us out of fundamentalism and into Humanism in the first place. To this end, I invite your support for three strategic measures:

First, of course, the renewed propagation of Ingersoll's own *Some Mistakes of Moses*. It is as winsome and as powerful as the day it was written. Second, the funding of translations of several foreign language classics of biblical criticism which have, thanks to Christian control over religious publishing, never been rendered into English before, notably the works of Bruno Bauer and W.C. van Manen. And third, the publication of what I call a *Skeptic's Annotated Bible*, a study edition of the Old and New Testaments with notes and articles detailing the prescientific and fictive character of most of the narrative, as well as the shocking moral and religious ideas tactfully smoothed over by Christian study editions. Introductory essays would explore the questions of who chose the books to go into the Bible, why and when, the political issues involved, etc. Where this and that Bible passage point in a "heretical" direction, the *Skeptic's Bible* would hasten to point it out. Cross-references would highlight contradictions, not paper them over. A critical, scientific, and skeptical perspective on the Bible would become clearer than ever, and the Freethinker would have at his fingertips all the ammunition he requires for the battle into which our brave Colonel led us these many years ago.

19

IS THE BIBLE MEIN KAMPF?

Let me assume the role of Rod Serling for a moment. Imagine yourself in a world in which there is a powerful militant sect devoted to the worship of the gods of ancient Greece. These strange zealots not only believe in the literal, personal existence of Zeus, Athena, Hera, and the others. They also hold Homer's *Iliad* and *Odyssey* to be inspired and inerrant scripture (even though the more educated among them sometimes suggest that the epics are to be taken allegorically, when things get too messy, e.g., all those seductions of mortal females by Zeus). These well-meaning but obnoxious believers are insistent in the media and from every public soapbox that Western society was founded upon the culture of the ancient Greeks, and that, in an age of moral decadence, only a return to the faith and scripture of the ancients can save us from wholesale ruin. Among others, or so they urge, the hero Achilles must have been a historical figure, else how can one explain the well-attested fall of Troy, which Heinrich Schliemann vindicated? What room is left for doubt? And wouldn't you like to accept Asclepius as your personal savior?

What would your reaction be? You would, number one, be astonished that twenty-first century men and women with any degree of education could take these myths, and their attendant worldview, literally. Second, you would recoil from their invitation to join them. And third, you might think it worthwhile, especially if this sect were gaining ground among the young and naive, to mount a counter-attack, showing the untenability of the whole thing. And as part of this Freethought crusade, you would probably delve into the historical and other inaccuracies in the Homeric epics. You would apply the canons of historical and literary criticism to show we are dealing with ancient fiction, and that it is neither inerrant history nor divine revelation. And you would easily be able to enlist in this effort the aid of classicists who are most familiar with the ancient Greek writings.

What would you expect them to say? Well, I am pretty sure you would hear none of them condemning the *Iliad* and the *Odyssey* as the bane of mankind, something better never written in the first place, containing nothing edifying, but only the most perverse nonsense, worthy of the attention of none but fools and knaves. Not one of them would say any such thing, and for the simple reason that they approach the olden texts as ancient human artifacts, warts and all, the products of a civilization still barbaric but glowing with frequent flashes of dramatic and poetic genius. Classicists would oppose this thankfully-imaginary Olympian fundamentalism not because they hate the sources of the movement but rather because they *love* them and bristle to see fools and knaves appropriating them for a perverse purpose.

Outrageous as the whole scenario seems, you knew paragraphs ago that I am drawing an analogy with biblical fundamentalism, which is regrettably all too real. My point is not so much to invite you to marvel at the gross silliness of fundamentalism (though I won't much mind if you do), but rather to suggest a second look at the type of response we offer to it. Here is a cameo of what I mean. Once I heard of a Pro-Choice rally where the sponsors held a public Bible-burning. Why would they do this? Simply because their Pro-Life opponents claimed the Bible was on their side, that it forbade abortion. And the Pro-Choice people took them up on it. Damn that Bible! But in fact, the issue of abortion never once comes up in the Bible! We do know early Christians vehemently condemned abortion in non-canonical writings like the Didache, the Epistle of Barnabas, and the Apocalypse of Peter, but none of these is in the Bible. Pro-Lifers simply infer a ban on abortion from "Thou shalt do no murder." And that is an understandable, though not an inevitable, inference. But the Bible does not just *say*, "Thou shalt not abort." The Pro-Choicers made the error of accepting the fundamentalist caricature of the Bible, and then vilifying it. And too many in the Freethought movement do the same. Thus they are in an ironic position: accepting the fundamentalist reading of the Bible, albeit not liking it. Not believing the Bible is the Word of God, they seem to believe it is the Word of Satan, even though they do not believe in Satan. Well, maybe *some* do: I have met atheists who do seem to have a shadow-belief in God as the Satan of Atheism! They pursue him with stake and garlic like Van Helsing after Dracula! This is no surprise, since many in the Freethought movement, obviously and properly, are here because of a bitter disillusionment with fundamentalism. Me too. But this sort of pendulum- swinging runs out of steam after a while (though new recruits keep it swinging high), and it will be interesting to see if our movement ever collectively outgrows it. What will we achieve? What will we *try* to achieve?

But back to the Bible. I began to study the Bible avidly as a teen-age fundamentalist because I believed that it was God's inspired Word. It was largely the study of the Bible that led me to reject this view of the Bible. I could see that the actual texts simply did not match the dogmatic definition of the Bible. As Evangelical theologian Clark H. Pinnock (who wouldn't mind being quoted in pages like these) once quipped: "The fundamentalists don't like the Bible they've got!" But by that time I was hooked! I found the Bible fascinating, and still do! In fact, more and more all the time! As I have learned new methods of biblical "criticism" (analysis), the Bible has come to make sense in new ways. The very contradictions and errors that so threatened the dogmatic view of the Bible are in fact clues to a proper understanding of the book, a book which, like the *Iliad* and the *Odyssey*, has much to say. It is as a lover of the Bible, not a hater of the Bible, that I take exception to fundamentalists and their apologetics. Why one would hate the Bible, as many do, I cannot understand, except that I understand their error in blaming the Bible for what fools have made of it. We should not become fools, repeating their error in reverse.

No, the Bible is not *Mein Kampf*. It is not a compendium of evil spewed up from Hell's bowels. Sorry. If you want to condemn such a book, you might try something by the Marquis de Sade, I don't know. Or, of course, Hitler. But it would be as absurd to put the Bible on the shelf alongside such books as it would be to place Homer there. Do you recoil with loathing to read that Jephthah sacrificed his daughter to gain victory over the Ammonites? I understand. But do you feel the same way when you read of Agamemnon sacrificing his daughter Iphigenia for victory over Troy? Both are ironic tragedies of the same type. We do not get on our high horse to protest the "gross immorality" of the ancient epics because no one is surprised to read of barbarity in a book from a barbarous age. Why should the Bible be any more blameworthy in this respect than other ancient books?

Nor is there any use in pretending there is not plenty of ethically and socially profound teaching in the Bible: verses, psalms, oracles, maxims which shine like torches in the darkness of the ancient world. Dr. King didn't seem to have any trouble finding material there! The fundamentalists, like a stopped clock, are occasionally right, if only by accident: they dimly recognize what I am saying whenever they point to this or that biblical verse and claim it is so advanced for its time that it must be a piece of divine revelation. No, but such texts *are* flashes of human genius (the only kind there is), and it is against the barbaric background of the rest of the text and its implied world that these insights shine. When we pretend the noble ethics of Jesus or Isaiah are not sterling, we are just as disingenuous (or ignorant) as the fundamentalists are when they claim there is nothing reprehensible in the Bible! We are, again, fundies in reverse!

And in terms of our practical approach or response to fundamentalists: we can never expect to be taken seriously by zealots for the Bible as long as we pretend the Bible is what they know it is not: a book of evil. We need, if possible, if it is true, to tell them that *precisely as people who care about the same book*, we do not wish to stand by and see it misinterpreted, misrepresented. It is we who are the true friends and champions of the Bible, not those who invite ridicule for the scriptures by inflating them into a garish idol. (Maybe you're not a lover of the Bible. I'm not saying you should be. I'm just saying that I'm the sort of person you want to call on for a debate or to recommend books by!)

The fundamentalist, as I tell my students, has no right to pontificate about the Bible until he or she has studied the Bible in great detail and from many perspectives. And even then one will not be able to pontificate! One will have come to realize pontificating is a sport forever denied the intellectually honest individual. And the same is true for Freethinkers: we dare not make the Bible into another *Mein Kampf* before we study it seriously. If there are religious fundamentalists who blithely accept dogmatic claims of behalf of the Bible to save them the trouble of thinking for themselves, there are plenty of sophomoric atheists, too. One suspects they are eager to accept sweeping polemics against the Bible in order to give their immature consciences license to do what, under the fundamentalist yoke, they dared not. What we need is a group of Atheists, Humanists, Freethinkers, whatever, who will have *rejected the right thing* from fundamentalism: the mythicizing of the Bible as an excuse to make things easier for ourselves, when in truth we need to rethink all the issues for ourselves.

20

HUMANISMS:
A THEOLOGICAL CLASSIFICATION

Today we are witnessing a many-sided debate over something (or some things) called "humanism." Fundamentalists claim that secular humanism is a religion and that the theory of evolution is the "creation myth" of that religion and should not be taught in public schools. Similarly, any kind of textbook that advocates an open-ended approach to problem-solving or decision-making is thought to promote secular humanism's "doctrine" of relativism. Some religious humanists have joined fundamentalists as very strange bedfellows, claiming that secular humanism is indeed a religion, though religious humanists embrace it instead of attacking it. By contrast, secular humanists reject this religious status and are surprised to find themselves joined by equally strange bedfellows when their fundamentalist critics lump them together with the New Age movement, seeing both as part of a conspiracy to stamp out Bible-believing Christianity. And then there is the widespread tendency, both within and without the Freethought movement, to equate Humanism with Atheism. I believe that most of this confusion can be sorted out by means of some insights from theologians Paul Tillich and Harvey Cox.

THE DEATH OF GOD AND THE DEATH OF MAN

Many Atheists describe themselves as also Humanists and affirm that (double? Single?) identity by joining groups with both titles, say, American Atheists and

American Humanist Association. The same holds true for many Humanists. Probably most self-described Humanists would include Atheism as one of their axioms, implying that, once one abandons faith in God, one replaces it with faith in humanity and human resources. But it is important to note that the two terms are not equivalent. There are certainly Atheists who are not Humanistic. In a moment, we will discuss the Christian Atheism of Thomas J.J. Altizer, but for the moment, let us note the existence of long-established religious Atheists including Samkhya Hindu mystics, who believe in souls and salvation, but in no God. Carvaka and Mimamsa Hindus and Theravada Buddhists might be considered religious Atheists, too.

But there is also the phenomenon of misanthropic Atheism. One need not embrace a sentimental or optimistic view of human potential or goodness in order to qualify as an Atheist. One might even find that belief in the goodness or potentiality of humanity is an illusion kindred to Theism, just a kind of "Theism Lite." Similarly, one might have broken with one's naïve loyalty to the human race in favor of, say, radical environmentalism or Animal Rights. One might have come to despise one's humanity as some White liberals hate their own ethnic and economic identities because of what their ancestors did to African slaves or American Indians. (In the interests of historical accuracy, I refrain from the Politically Correct label "Native Americans," since all these fine folks hail originally from Asia. The only surviving "Native Americans" are probably the buffalo!) Once my wife asserted in an on-line debate that she was both a Humanist and anti-abortion. Her interlocutor declared that impossible and charged my wife with being a Christian who wouldn't admit it! Some kind of mole or spy! But my wife replied that she saw the most Humanistic option as giving human fetuses the benefit of the doubt, not relegating growing proto-humans to the status of an unwanted appendix to be excised without mercy. In view of this, her dialogue partner admitted that she thought abortion worth the risk of slaughtering what might turn out to be a real human person. She figured humans no longer deserved the benefit of the doubt, given their crimes against the environment and the animals. "Humanist" was probably not the right term for her, though she was undoubtedly some type of Atheist.

Similarly, there is the Postmodern Atheism typified by Michel Foucault, which proceeds from the insight that the "self" is merely a rhetorical fold, a piece of grammar falsely hypostatized as a metaphysical entity. The self, the unique humanity of men and women, some Postmodern thinkers contend, is a figment of the imagination, a fiction of logocentrism and "Presence Metaphysics," as when Descartes thought he had demonstrated his own existence at least as a thinking entity by means of an inference, the validity of which was "clearly and distinctly" known to the mind. Foucault thought Descartes had been kidding "himself." And if you believe something along these lines, I think you might prefer another label to "Humanism."

So the relation between "Humanism" and "Atheism" is neither automatic nor obvious. Even so, many Atheists still decide to sport the term "Humanist" along with the "Atheist" nametag because they happen not to be misanthropic or Postmodernist, etc. But not so fast. One must still lay out the nuances of Humanism. Humanism is a more complicated matter than one might at first suppose.

RELIGIOUS VS. SECULAR HUMANISM

An old exchange between the late, great Paul Beattie, Unitarian minister and President of the Fellowship of Religious Humanists, the equally late and equally great Joseph Fletcher, author of *Situation Ethics* and Episcopalian turned secular humanist, and others,[1] threw into stark relief the basic question of what makes a religion religious. Beattie argued that secular humanism is in fact religious. Beattie claimed that the religion which religious humanists embrace is "the religion of secular humanism." He admitted that his values and beliefs stemmed more from secular Western culture in the wake of the Renaissance and the Enlightenment than from the Christian tradition and that he did not believe in God.

What, then, was religious about humanism as he practiced it? His humanism was a profoundly felt commitment to a set of values, a humanist credo, and it was expressed and reinforced in a community setting, a like-minded congregation encouraging one another to faithfulness and collectively celebrating rites of passage. Beattie argued that secular humanism is already essentially a religion because of its deeply held convictions but that it should become more overtly religious by adopting a congregational form of organization (like a Unitarian-Universalist Fellowship, for instance). He seemed to imply that a firm commitment to any credo is a sufficient criterion for one's being called religious. He argued that there is only a difference in organizational patterns between avowed secular humanism (e.g., American Humanist Association, Council for Secular Humanism) and religious humanism (e.g., Friends of Religious Humanism, Ethical Culture).[2] Both are religious.

To all this Fletcher replied that the whole point of "secular" humanism is to dispense with what is usually intended by the word "religion," especially any dependence on the guidance or blessing of higher powers. When humanists proclaim themselves "secular," they are saying they want no more to do with religion. Secular humanism is the philosophy, the worldview, the creed they hold instead of a religion. It is an alternative *to* religion, not an alternative *kind* of religion. A credo and a religion are not the same, unless one wants to inflate the term "religion" to the point of meaning everything, and therefore meaning nothing in particular.[3]

What Fletcher does not quite say is just the converse of what Beattie says: if Beattie's religion is secular humanism as he avows, then Beattie is actually no more religious than Fletcher! Implicitly Fletcher (and others who share his position., e.g., Paul Kurtz) are denying there is anything really religious about either secular or self-proclaimed "religious humanism"! I believe there is indeed a subtle but important difference between secular and religious humanism beyond mere organization. Religious humanism is indeed genuinely religious and secular humanism is truly non-religious. Paul Tillich's distinction between theonomy, autonomy, and heteronomy may help us to see this.[4]

THEONOMOUS VS. AUTONOMOUS HUMANISM

Tillich believed that some cultures, or aspects of culture, are more open to (or transparent to, or in tune with) their ontological Ground than others. There is a depth dimension, a grounding of transcendent meaning, that Tillich judged to be alone worthy of the appellation "religious." Religion, thus construed, Tillich said, is the substance of culture, while culture is the form of religion. It is this assumption that made possible Tillich's "theology of culture," the interpreting in art, architecture, etc., of a given culture's quest for meaning.

Tillich felt that the High Middle Ages were a period in which culture was completely transparent to its divine Ground, which was reflected in Medieval art, music, architecture, etc. Such a culture is "theonomous," or spontaneously in harmony with the divine law (nomos) of its being, its own inner essence. No conflict was yet perceived between reason and faith.

But when scientific and historical advances threatened the prevalent religious mythology that symbolized the culture's divine Ground, the Church reacted in a hostile and mistaken fashion. Failing to see the non-literal character of the truth of symbolism, the Church tried to suppress new knowledge in the name of God. At that moment the theonomy of the culture was lost. As soon as the hierarchy sought to suppress genuine knowledge by imposing alien dogma (e.g., the case of Galileo), "heteronomy" replaced theonomy. Heteronomy is the domination of culture by an alien (*heteros*) law: that of religious dogma now alienated (and alienating itself) from the culture with which it had hitherto been in deep harmony.

Thus threatened and persecuted by heteronomous religious authority, the forces of rational, critical inquiry rebelled against religious heteronomy, rejecting any religious allegiance. Thus they became "autonomous" (a law or *nomos* unto oneself); scientists and philosophers rejecting obscurantist Medieval religion became humanists, secular humanists.

When theonomy prevails, no tension is perceived between the religious dimension and rational inquiry (or art, etc.), but when heteronomy replaces theonomy, the connection with the divine Ground is forfeited, since the religious authorities themselves have confused the religious Ultimate with a concrete symbol for it (e.g., a mythical creation story) which should not be taken literally. The rejection of rationally discovered truth in favor of cherished myth in this way, Tillich called idolatry.

Heteronomous religious authorities no longer actually represent the Holy, the Ground of Being, but they still claim to. Persecuted thinkers may mistakenly accept this claim, and so they want nothing to do with religion. They, too, confuse the Ultimate with an idol. It is an act of faithfulness to Truth that they reject the idol, but in so doing they throw the baby out with the bath water and no longer believe in the Ultimate. In another sense they do, so long as they believe in Truth, but they no longer realize the connection, the identity, between Truth and the religious Ultimate. This condition, again, is autonomy. Autonomy may indeed be in closer touch with the Ultimate than is idolatrous heteronomy, which values concrete (perhaps outdated) symbols of the Ultimate more than the Ultimate itself. The difference between autonomy and the lost theonomy is that, while both are in touch with the religious Ultimate, theonomy knew it, while autonomy does not. To borrow Schleiermacher's terms, such "cultured despisers of religion" are "absolutely dependent" on "the Infinite" no less than the religious person, but the religious person is aware of it, or has "the feeling of absolute dependence." The non-religious person does not.

Theonomy can eventually be regained after a period of readjustment as religious people come to see the difference between outmoded symbols and the Ultimate, and how one need not deny the truths of reason and science in order to know the Ultimate. New symbols may be born (e.g., "Theistic evolution") or old ones deliteralized (or "demythologized," though Tillich did not like Bultmann's term).[5] Heteronomous religion will look askance at a newly theonomous religious position, complaining that it has "accommodated itself to the spirit of the age," while autonomous skeptics will distrust theonomous religion as inconsistent and still dangerous to free thought.

I believe we see here pictured precisely the relation between heteronomous fundamentalism, theonomous religious liberalism (e.g., religious humanism), and autonomous secular humanism. Religious humanism is very definitely religious. This is easy to miss, even in Beattie's presentation, since the central symbol of religious humanism is, of course, humanity. What makes it religious is that humanity is a symbol (in Tillich's sense), a symbol for the divine Ground. Religious humanism claims that there is a transcendent reality in the universe, and it is seen most clearly in humanity, in our intellectual, cultural, and artistic achievements. Human beings participate in this transcendent greatness; we concretize it in works of art, literature, philosophy. This understanding of religious humanism is nowhere better set forth than in Ludwig Feuerbach's *The Essence of Christianity* (1841). There Feuerbach demonstrates that all the traditional "moral predicates" or "communicable attributes" of God are simply the moral qualities of humanity self-deprecatingly projected onto an illusory abstraction, "God." In fact, "in religion man contemplates his own latent nature."[6] Feuerbach sought not to reject religion in favor of humanism, but rather to show that humanism was the true essence of religion. The humanist is not irreligious: "he alone is the true atheist to whom the predicates of the Divine Being, -for example, love, wisdom, justice,-are nothing,- not he to whom merely the subject of these predicates is nothing."[7] These qualities inherent in human nature are themselves divine. To believe thus is religious humanism.

Religious humanism really believes in "revealed" (= evident, discoverable) truth; it simply sees the human mind as the organ of this revelation, not as an obstruction to it or as being bypassed by it, as in much traditional supernaturalism. Religious humanism even finds this truth in the religious myths of the ancient scriptures and legends, Christian and other. It employs Bultmann's demythologizing hermeneutic, the key insight of which is that all myths embody understandings of human existence. Though Bultmann himself was a theist, Joseph Campbell would seem to be an example of a pure religious humanist for whom the myths speak "only" of humanity and the human life-cycle. Religious humanism does not reject miracle in rejecting supernaturalism;

rather, like Schleiermacher, it simply says, "To me, all is miracle."[8] By contrast, secular humanism rejects any such transcendent inference. "To be a secular humanist, to thus qualify the noun, means to be a certain kind of humanist. . . . No residual wonderings about the 'transcendental' or searching for the 'ultimate.'"[9]

RELIGIOUS HUMANISM AND SECULAR THEOLOGY

I believe we can see today's religious humanist movement as the natural heir of the secular theology of the 1960s. "Religious humanism" and "secular theology" make an interesting pair, both thought by critics to be exercises in self-contradiction, but I believe neither is. Several aspects of the radical theology of Harvey Cox and others foreshadowed today's religious humanism. For instance, the complex and poetic metaphysics of Thomas J. J. Altizer's "Christian atheism" included the assertion that God's transcendence had, in Jesus, been poured forever into the mundane world. The Word was made flesh once and for all, the Sacred emptying itself into the Profane in a paradox recalling the Mahayana Buddhist belief that Nirvana is to be found within Samsara. "God," the deity transcending humanity, was therefore dead, immanent forever in the material world, especially in humanity. Christian atheism, for Altizer, was the logical outworking of the doctrine of the Incarnation. Henceforth Christians must rejoice in the death of the once-separate God in a world newly suffused (or newly seen to be suffused) with divine presence.[10]

Harvey Cox similarly spoke of the modern process of secularization as a continuation of the biblical salvation history in which nature was desacralized, i.e., not to be worshipped as a god (Baal), and the state with its divine king was deabsolutized, relativized and debunked as a merely human creation. Even the eclipse of God is part of the biblical process of *Heilsgeschichte*, since God's goal for humanity is full maturity, no longer to be like children helplessly dependent on their heavenly Father.

Here Cox drew on the thought of Dietrich Bonhoeffer and Paul Lehmann. From Bonhoeffer came the notion that God wants mature men and women to stand on their own feet, "living without God before God." Cox wrote "As Bonhoeffer says, in Jesus God is teaching man to get along without Him, to become mature, freed from infantile dependencies, fully human. . . . He will not perpetuate human adolescence, but insists on turning the world over to man as his responsibility."[11]

From Lehmann's *Ethics in a Christian Context* Cox derived his understanding of the Christian mission in "a world come of age" (Bonhoeffer). "Lehmann suggests that what God is doing in the world is politics, which means making and keeping [human] life human. . . . Theology today must be that reflection-in-action by which the church finds out what this politician-God is up to and moves in to work along with him. In the epoch of the secular city, politics replaces metaphysics as the language of theology."[12] Humanity takes center stage, because God wants it that way. And Cox ventures that perhaps to "speak in a secular fashion of God" (Bonhoeffer), requires our dispensing with the word God in order not to confuse the One who reveals Himself in Jesus with the gods of mythology or the deity of philosophy . . ."[13]

The "secular theology" and "Christian atheism" sowed by Cox, Altizer, and others have born fruit in today's religious humanism with its focus on humanity as the living incarnation of the Ultimate. The important thing is that Cox and others provided a genuine theological undergirding for humanism, a nontheistic humanism logically and theologically derived from the Bible and the Christian gospel.

Secular humanism is built on no such foundation. In the case of secular humanism, "Reality has lost its inner transcendence or, in another metaphor, its transparency for the eternal. The system of finite inter-relations which we call the universe has become self-sufficient" (Tillich).[14] Secular humanism is pretty much what Paul calls "the flesh": finite humanity confident of its own worth without God and capable of self-salvation.

Both religious and secular humanism put humanity at the center. As Protagoras said, "man is the measure of all things." But whereas religious humanism sees human nature as the symbol of the Ultimate, secular humanism sees no Ultimate. For secular humanism, humanity is the highest known reality, but there is no Ultimate Reality.

SECULARISM VS. SECULARIZATION

Fundamentalists, then, are mistaken to consider secular humanism a religion. They object to the teaching of evolution in public schools on the supposed grounds that evolution is part and parcel of an anti-Christian religion. Tillich aptly summed up the situation as fundamentalists see it: "if a scientific theory with a high degree of probability is rejected in the name of a religiously consecrated tradition, one must find out precisely what is rejected. If it is the theory itself, a heteronomous attack on the idea of truth takes place and has to be resisted in the power of the Spirit. If, however, it is an underlying metaphysical-and ultimately religious-assumption which is attacked in the name of religion, the situation has ceased to be a conflict between heteronomy and autonomy and has become a confrontation of two ultimates which may lead to a conflict between religious attitudes but not to a conflict between autonomy and heteronomy."[15]

Just so, fundamentalists believe evolution is propaganda for the "religion of secular humanism," and not truly science at all. However, they are simply mistaken. Evolution neither presupposes nor promotes any religious or non-religious worldview. In fact if one closely examines fundamentalist "scientific creationist" literature, one finds that evolution is abhorrent mainly because it is inconsistent with the fundamentalist exegesis of Genesis. "[It] is this author's belief that a sound Biblical exegesis requires the acceptance of the catastrophist-recent creation interpretation of earth history. If this interpretation is accepted, the evolution model of course, becomes inconceivable."[16] So it is, at bottom, a case of heteronomy trying to stifle autonomy.

There is an insidious confusion in the fundamentalists' attack on the teaching of evolution and their advocacy of "equal time for creation science." Sidney Hook hits the nail on the head: "The fundamentalists assume that the absence of instruction in their own particular faith is tantamount to a commitment to the teaching of a non-religious or irreligious faith. This assumption is mistaken both in logic and in fact."[17] Whence this mistake?

Fundamentalists are confusing secularism with secularization. As Harvey Cox describes it, secularization is an opening up of a society into pluralistic freedom, a society in which there is no official worldview or ideology, where a hundred flowers are allowed to bloom. "Secularism, on the other hand, is the name for an 'ideology, a new closed world-view which functions very much like a new religion. . . . Like any other ism, it menaces the openness and freedom secularization has produced; it must therefore be watched carefully to prevent its becoming the ideology of a new establishment. It must especially be checked where it pretends not to be a world-view but nonetheless seeks to impose its ideology through the organs of the state."[18]

Now this is a letter-perfect description of the situation fundamentalists claim prevails: secularism (= secular humanism) is secretly and insidiously trying to control our society, and fundamentalists are valiantly trying to prevent it. But secular humanists are doing no such thing. What fundamentalist zealots really cannot stand is not secularism but secularization, true pluralization. As Hook intimates, fundamentalists will not rest until their heteronomous view is imposed as the new "sacred canopy"[19] of American society. They do not want to prevent secularism from locking up the American worldview; they want, rather, to lock it up themselves.

NOVI SAECULI HUMANISTS?

Fundamentalists often lump together secular humanists with the New Age movement, a linking that seems at first to be very strange, given the fanciful pseudoscientific beliefs of the latter and the skepticism of the former. In fact the claims of the New Agers come in for constant ruthless scrutiny in every issue of the humanist *Skeptical Inquirer*. What has Athens to do with Esalen? I believe that there is indeed a link, or better, a fundamental similarity between the two that fundamentalists have instinctively discerned. The New Age movement is in fact another kind of humanism. Brooks Alexander of the Spiritual Counterfeits Project has correctly pegged the movement "cosmic humanism." One of the central tenets of New Age thinking, according to Alexander, is that "Man is a Divine being (the Divine within). . . . All forms of occult philosophy are united around the central belief that the inner or 'real' Self of man is God."[20]

This is a very important insight, but I think Alexander Immediately strays into serious confusion when he identifies this cosmic humanism with Vedanta Hinduism and Mahayana Buddhism. He is thinking of the nondualist atman=Brahman doctrine. The self = the Godhead. But far from being self-centered or deifying the individual self, the intent of nondualism is to dispel the illusion of individual ego. The atman is not the ordinarily perceived everyday self but rather the Infinite that lies concealed behind the false ego. Vedanta and Buddhism are anything but humanistic.

The New Age movement, however, is indeed humanistic. Despite its frequent use of Hindu and Buddhist concepts and terms, New Age thought is fundamentally a Western pop-psychological human potential movement. (Cf. the advertising claims that TM will improve your relaxation, or that Ramtha's soul speaks from ancient Atlantis to help you lose weight.) In theological terms New Agers make the fatal error of confusing the individual, illusory ego (*jiva*) with the universal Self (*atman*, Brahman, Sunyata). They ascribe the divine attributes of infinite Brahman to an individual self which is pitifully finite. In

Eastern mystical theory, it is precisely such *avidya*, ignorance, from which liberation is sought!

Again, Harvey Cox accurately perceived where all this was headed years ago in his book *Turning East*: "The Western proclivity for narcissism has been given a new baptism. . . . Buddhist practitioners would be shocked to learn that meditation might be used in the pursuit of something as phantasmagoreal as the 'self.' I expect this Westernized pseudo-Oriental pastiche to spread, and even at points to label itself religious or Christian." Cox bemoaned the "use of meditation . . . to enhance the exploration and realization of the insatiable Western self."[21]

One outstanding example of the New Age movement's psychologizing Eastern metaphysics is its use of the doctrine of reincarnation. While Hindus, Buddhists, and Jainists seek to escape the wearying and futile treadmill of transmigration, New Agers view reincarnation as a long educative experience, many eons' worth of Rogerian "becoming a person." The goal of the New Age movement is not Shankara's Hindu Self-realization but rather Maslow's humanistic "self-actualization."

FUNDAMENTALIST HUMANISM

One last type of humanism must claim our attention, and that is, perhaps surprisingly, fundamentalism. Up to this point I have cast fundamentalism in the role of the villain heteronomy and the nemesis of autonomous humanism, but fundamentalists quite often ape the quality of humanism that they hate the most: they elevate merely human, "man-made" ideas to Ultimacy.[22] They place human utterances in the lofty niche reserved for God's Word. How do fundamentalists do this? To borrow Karl Barth's critique of Schleiermacher, fundamentalists are like a man who shouts into a ravine, hears the echo of his own voice magnified, and mistakes it for the voice of God addressing him. Fundamentalists never tire of saying "God said it! I believe it! That settles it!," when they actually mean "I said it! God believes it! That settles it!"[23] How can fundamentalists loudly assure us that God condemns abortion when the subject is never once mentioned in scripture? How can they insist we must believe that if the Bible is inspired, it must also be inerrant in matters of science and history, when no biblical text says so? Of course fundamentalists infer both the immorality of abortion and the inerrancy of scripture from other matters that *are* mentioned in scripture. But they can see no difference between their inferences, their human reasonings, and the Word of God. Is this not the most dangerous kind of self-magnifying humanism of all?

NOTES

1. The symposium, "Is Secular Humanism a Religion?," featured an essay by Paul Beattie ("The Religion of Secular Humanism"), with responses by Joseph Fletcher, Sidney Hook, and Paul Kurtz, all included in the Winter 1985/86 issue of *Free Inquiry* (Vol. 6, No. 1), pp. 12–21.

2. Paul H. Beattie, "The Religion of Secular Humanism," *Free Inquiry*, pp. 12–17.

3. *Joseph Fletcher, "Residual Religion," Free Inquiry*, pp. 18–19.

4. See especially the section "Humanism and the Idea of Theonomy" in Paul Tillich, *Systematic Theology*, Vol. III (Chicago: University of Chicago Press, 1976), pp. 249–252. Interestingly, Tillich himself has been charged with being an atheistic humanist. See Leonard F. Wheat, *Paul Tillich's Dialectical Humanism* (Baltimore: Johns Hopkins University Press, 1970).

5. Paul Tillich, *Dynamics of Faith* (NY: Harper & Row, 1958), pp. 50 ff.

6. Ludwig Feuerbach, *The Essence of Christianity*. Trans. by George Eliot (NY: Harper & Brothers, 1957), p. 33.

7. Ibid., p. 21.

8. Friedrich Schleiermacher, *On Religion: Speeches to its Cultured Despisers*. Trans. John Oman (NY: Harper & Row, 1958), p. 88.

9. Fletcher, p. 19.

10. Thomas J. J. Altizer, *The Gospel of Christian Atheism* (Philadelphia: Westminster Press, 1966); *The Descent into Hell* (Philadelphia: J. B. Lippincott Company, 1970).

11. Harvey Cox, *The Secular City* (NY: Macmillan, 1966), pp. 258–259.

12. Ibid., P. 255.

13. Ibid., P. 267.

14. Paul Tillich, "Aspects of a Religious Analysis of Culture" in *Theology of Culture* (NY: Oxford University Press, 1977), p. 43.

15. Tillich, *Systematic Theology*, p. 252.

16. Duane T. Gish, *Evolution: The Fossils Say No!* (San Diego: Creation-Life Publishers, 1979), p. 64. See also Gish, *Evidence Against Evolution* (Wheaton, IL: Tyndale House, 1972), pp. 19–20; John C. Whitcomb and Henry M. Morris, *The Genesis Flood* (Phillipsburg, NJ: Presbyterian and Reformed Publishing Company, 1980), p. xx.

17. Sidney Hook, "Pluralistic Humanism," *Free Inquiry*, p. 19.

18. Cox, *Secular City*, pp. 69, 21.

19. Peter L. Berger, *The Sacred Canopy: Elements of a Sociological Theory of Religion* (Garden City: Doubleday Anchor, 1969), passim.

20. Brooks Alexander, *Occult Philosophy & Mystical Experience* (Berkeley: CWLF, n.d.), p. 2.

21. Harvey Cox, *Turning East* (NY: Simon and Schuster, 1977), pp. 77, 82, 90.

22. This understanding of fundamentalism as hubris and humanism comes from Edward T. Babinski.

23. I owe this succinct way of putting the matter to Methodist minister and wag, the Reverend Anthony Jarek-Glidden.

21

THE RETURN OF THE NAVEL:
THE "OMPHALOS" ARGUMENT
IN CONTEMPORARY CREATIONISM

Surely one of the most bizarre efforts to defend biblical Creationism was that of Philip Gosse in his nineteenth century work *Omphalos*. The word is Greek for "navel," and the book addressed itself to the old biblical stumper, "Did Adam have a bellybutton?" Why should he, if he were created, *ex nihilo*, as an adult? More about this line of reasoning in a moment, but for now suffice it to say that Gosse contended that Adam did indeed have a navel and that he was not alone. For though God created the world in 4000 B.C.E., a la Genesis, he created it with simulated signs of age and development. Thus all evidence of evolution, biological or otherwise, might be safely ignored by Creationists. This argument may be new even to readers who have followed the creation-evolution debate, for now it is seldom if ever adduced. Instead, fundamentalist debaters tend to concentrate on debunking evolutionary theory with appeals to its allegedly fatal flaws. How seriously could they expect to be taken if they appealed to a logical circle like the "omphalos" argument? Yet, I will contend, this old rationalization underlies much of their allegedly "evidential" polemic. Having established this, I shall go on to consider "Scientific Creationism" in the light of Thomas Kuhn's theory of "scientific revolutions."[1] Finally, I hope to show how, seen in the light of Kuhn's work, the Creationist "navel" argument actually tends to argue *for* evolution instead of against it.

As I said above, Gosse's "omphalos" argument allowed him simultaneously to admit *and* to dismiss all the biological and geological data for the great age of the earth and the evolution of life.

He reasoned that if God were to create a functioning planet, he must have created it already "rolling." Understood this way, the creation might be compared to a movie, the first frame of which depicts an action scene. No sooner does the film start than a hold up or an air battle is already in progress! Now if the earth were born full-grown (like the legendary sage Lao-tzu, fully age 75 from the womb!), there must have been telltale signs of age, but the tale they told was false, at least fictitious. A flowing river (let us say, the Euphrates at the border of Eden—Genesis 2:14) from the first moment of its creation must have already possessed an alluvial deposit along its banks. But strictly speaking, it was never deposited! So with Adam, who had the mark of an umbilical cord which never existed save in the mind of God. And so with the earth's crust, pregnant with fossils of strange life-forms which never walked the earth. All were created *as if.* So all those unbelieving biologists and geologists had gotten the story *correct*—the problem was that they didn't realize it was only a story.

Why did this argument fail to attract any supporters, even among Creationists? Simply because all (but Gosse) could see what extreme special pleading it was. Certainly it was all beyond disproof, but so was the Hindu claim that the world was *maya* (indeed a very similar claim!). For that matter, who could prove that the world had not been created only ten minutes ago, with Gosse recalling his formulation of a theory he had never actually formulated? Alas, solipsism has never been very attractive. Not even to modern Scientific Creationists who know too well that such an argument would get them laughed out of the courts and off the debating platforms.

Yet, if one carefully examines Creationist polemical literature, one is surprised to find that the "recessive" argument has newly surfaced, though anonymously. A few brief examples will indicate the unacknowledged debt of "scientific" Creationists to this strange old argument. The most obvious instance known to me occurs in the 1973 work *Science and Creation* by William W. Boardman, Jr., Robert F. Koontz, and Henry M. Morris. In a discussion of astronomy and its implications for the age of the universe, the authors zero in on a trouble spot.

> The Biblical record places the creation of the universe at ten thousand years or less in the past; whereas, the presently accepted distance scale held by

astronomers measures the universe in billions of light years. If the light rays now reaching the earth were created in transit at the time of the creation of the stellar objects, they must have been created carrying information descriptive of historical physical events (such as super novae) which never actually occurred, because we would now be observing light rays which were created *in transit* and never were radiated from the stars which they seem to image.[2]

OMPHALOS!

Less easy to recognize at first glance is the same book's approach to the question of geographical distribution. For instance, doesn't the dominance of marsupials in lonely Australia, together with their recapitulation of non-marsupial parallels on other continents (e. g., marsupial versions of the rat, woodchuck, bear, and dog) count in favor of evolution? In isolation from competition with more efficient non-marsupials, the Australian forms seem to have evolved in parallel fashion to their far off counterparts. Now what does Creationism have to say of this phenomenon? Our authors hastily disclaim:

> The general concept of world-wide dispersal of living things, including . . . limitation in migration by barriers and by diversification of isolated populations into related varieties or sometimes species is not disputed by Creationists. [Nevertheless,] the Creationist believes that the basic forms of marsupials were created like the basic stocks of mammals and that they survived in Australia because of lack of competition due to isolation.[3]

To begin with, it is not at all clear that the authors are actually denying what they think they are denying! They almost seem to be espousing in the name of "Creationism" what really amounts to a "theistic evolutionary" view, that God "created" the various species by evolving them in the manner Darwin suggested. But since this would be merely to "refute" an opposing view by renaming it, we should look for an alternative meaning. In fact, the meaning seems to be that the processes which lead scientists to posit evolutive speciation really do work as the scientists imagine them to, but *God specially created* the various marsupials despite appearances! Why did God impose such patterns in nature which lead naive scientists to so faulty a conclusion? Well, God just wanted it that way! Omphalos!

We can find the return of the navel implicit in some forms of the Creationist attack on comparative anatomy and physiology:

On the assumption of creation, it is reasonable that there would be resemblances between creatures and that these resemblances would be stronger between those creatures living in similar environments and with similar physiological functions to fulfill. One could hardly imagine any more probable an arrangement than now prevails, if the origin of all things actually were special creation.[4]

What makes this or any other "arrangement" by a divine creator, "probable"? Couldn't God theoretically have made birds that swim instead of fly, whatever that might mean? Keep in mind that, as a fundamentalist, Morris believes in precisely such zoological marvels, for he envisions the day when "the wolf and the lamb shall feed together, and the lion shall eat straw like the ox" (Isaiah 65:25). He must believe that before the time of Noah, carnivores created in Eden did not eat meat (Genesis 1:30). So anything goes, or should, in Morris's frame of reference. Nothing should be more "probable" than anything else since "with God nothing shall be impossible" (Luke 1:37). Now all this is not mere carping. The point is that by talking in terms of what is "probable" given the earth's environmental conditions, Morris is quietly admitting the evolutionist's criterion of environmental "fitness." In other words, he recognizes the validity of the processes of evolution but merely short circuits the whole business at the last minute by appealing to the prescientific notion of teleology. Granted, it looks like creatures must be fitted to survive in certain environments, and indeed they are so fitted. And why is this? Because God arbitrarily wanted it that way! So he created in such a way as to have framed a riddle which would seem to call for the solution of evolutionary biology (i.e., an explanation of how life-forms are fit for their environments). But instead, the answer is unrelated to the question. The answer is arbitrary fiat. God could have created grass-eating lions; he did in Eden, and will again in the Millennium! But he put us on a false trail by creating the interlocking web of life that suggested the theory of evolution. Omphalos!

Finally, let us look at the Creationist repudiation of the line of human evolution, the "descent of man." Despite appearances, there wasn't any! The Creationist, when he doesn't adopt the expedient of simply denying the existence of fossil "cave men," finds himself (and hopes no one else will find him) in an odd position. He cannot deny the rather obvious chain of creatures (let's not prejudice the case by calling them "pre-human ancestors") which start out looking like lemurs and monkeys, and end up looking more and more like man. But these must not be admitted to be "transitional forms." So they must be simply extinct but independent life forms that just happen to look like they fall somewhere in between monkey and man. I am aware that there are other approaches taken by Creationists, e.g., the "cave-men" were descendants of Noah corrupted by sin, or that all were merely deformed or arthritic individuals who coincidentally were the only survivors of their otherwise normal tribes, etc. But this particular line of reasoning is repeated in the case of Eohippus and its kin. . . oops, one should say those others which *seem* to be, but must not be, its kin! The same with Archaeopteryx. Transitional forms they may appear, but the Creationist knows better! Why do these fossils have the appearance of chains of development which never actually occurred? Omphalos!

Notice, please, that in none of these cases has the Creationist explained the rationale of the omphalos argument as Gosse did. He may not be aware of it himself! But the implicit logic is the same—the evidence points in the direction of evolution, but that is because (for whatever reason) God simply wanted it that way. This is a throwback not only to Gosse's esoteric argument, but also to the prescientific shrugging off of such questions by the catch-all appeal to teleology. Why do birds fly south? Because they were made to do this. As Jacques Monod[5] has observed, the notion of teleology is inimical to scientific inquiry, and has always served to nip it in the bud. How "scientific," then, can "scientific creationism" be? Let us pursue this question along a slightly different avenue for a moment. Then we will be in a position to recognize the final irony of the Creationists who often assume the pose of righteous prophets crying in the wilderness, ignored by pharisaical "establishment" scientists. If only their voice of truth were heeded! We would have a scientific revolution! Thomas Kuhn, in his celebrated work *The Structure of Scientific Revolutions*, has drawn a compelling picture of the history of science involving a series of turnabouts just such as the fundamentalists anticipate. Now it is far from clear that the Creationists are in reality the "scientific revolutionaries" in the scenario. But we will see that their polemical efforts are helpfully illuminated by Kuhn's schema, which I will briefly review here.

Kuhn writes to correct the naive notion that the progress of science is simply the accumulation of new discoveries. No, while new empirical discoveries do occur, real movement in science comes when scientists accept a new "paradigm," a conceptual model in the light of which the same old data may be better understood. A scientist will notice certain troublesome data which the current paradigm cannot accommodate. An example would be the retrograde motion of the planets in the Ptolemaic paradigm for astronomy. Everything else in the heavens moved like clockwork, and was tidily accounted for by Ptolemy, but a fantastic and elaborate series of "epicycles" (celestial wheels-within-wheels) was needed to make retrograde motion predictable. Copernicus was eventually to find this unsatisfactory. Could not some new paradigm be formulated that would deal more naturally, more economically, more inductively, with *all* the data, instead of dealing fairly with part of it and imposing contrivances on the rest? So Copernicus set to work and, going Archimedes one better, he moved the sun. He transferred it from the earth's periphery to the center of our orbit. Now *everything* seemed naturally explainable—no more epicycles. The lesson we are to learn from this brief history lesson is that a scientific revolution occurs when somebody offers a new, more natural, way to construe the data. The new model must make economical sense of as much as possible of the data in its own right; it must make the most possible sense of it without reference to extraneous factors (e.g., invisible epicycles, dictated not by the evidence, but by the Ptolemaic model itself). Though the model is imposed on the data by the theorist, he has derived the model from the suggestion of the evidence itself. It is like one of those puzzles where one must connect all the dots with the fewest possible lines.

On this basis, might the Creationists be justified in expecting to usher in a new revolution in biology? How closely do their efforts match the pattern traced out by Kuhn? First, note that much (perhaps most) Creationist literature concentrates on only half the job—pointing out epicycles. Creationists never tire of indicating troublesome data regarding the theory of evolution, data supposedly far more troublesome than evolutionists believe. Whether their claims are correct or not, Creationists could expect no "scientific revolution," according to Kuhn's scenario, until they supply an alternative model capable of doing a better job. But insofar as they restrict their efforts to demolition, they are committing one of the most blatant of logical fallacies. They assume that there are but two options, and that one must be true. And, as if we were all playing "Let's Make a Deal," the elimination of evolution automatically vindicates Creationism! Not so fast: Lamarck, Lysenko, and a host of other contestants are waiting backstage.

My second observation is that when Creationists occasionally do try positively to defend the elusive "creation model," they violate the necessary criterion of inductiveness. That is, a paradigm must be derived as much as possible from the data themselves, and as little as possible from outside considerations. But Duane T. Gish is forthright in his admission of where his model comes from; "a sound Biblical exegesis requires the acceptance of the catastrophist-recent creation interpretation of earth history. If this interpretation is accepted, the evolution model, of course, becomes inconceivable."[6] Henry M. Morris is equally clear that "the general method of [Bishop] Ussher—that of relying on the Biblical data alone—is the only proper approach to determining the date of creation."[7] So the hidden agenda is revealed. After all, "There is nothing hid except to be made manifest" (Mark 4:22). The "Scientific Creationists," it would seem, are closer to the Inquisition than to Galileo in whose footsteps they claim to follow. They begin with a biblical dogma imposed heavily *on* the data, rather than an experimental hypothesis derived tentatively *from* the data. It will put the efforts of Creationists in proper perspective if we compare them to another famous school of pseudoscience, the offbeat astronomy of Immanuel Velikofsky. In fact the parallel is virtually exact. Velikofsky read in Exodus that the Nile turned red ("to blood"), and in American Indian myths that the sky once turned red. First he concluded that once Mars must have very nearly collided with the earth; then he shuffled astronomy accordingly. Even so, Gish and Morris discover in Genesis that the earth is merely thousands of years old with a six-day period of creation; then they practice ventriloquism with the data of geology and biology. In both instances, the dusty pages of ancient legend dictate in advance the results of scientific "research."

And thirdly, we must note the methodological outworking of this a priori dogmatism. With their "paradigm" thus derived from an entirely different quarter, it would seem the wildest stroke of luck if the data happened to conform spontaneously to the predetermined pattern. So it must be squeezed into place. With a skill well-developed in dealing with the contradictions found in the Bible, fundamentalists go to work harmonizing the data of science.

Let us return momentarily to the deliberations of Morris and company on the question of starlight. Listing other options besides the unvarnished "omphalos" approach, they point out that

> There are several possible approaches to the solution of this problem, each worthy of careful study by Creationists. Some propose that the distance scale represented by the Hubble constant which relates distance to observed red shift is greatly in error and that the distance scale should be drastically reduced. Another proposal made by Creationist scientists is based upon the

hypothesis made by Moon and Spencer in 1953, namely, that light travels not in Euclidean but in Riemannian curved space with a radius of curvature of five light years, so that no transit time could exceed 15.71 years. And a third proposal. . . is that further study of "the meaning of the scriptural terms" ["the heavens were] stretched out," etc., may give an understanding of how vast distances correlate with Biblical chronology. It is hoped that Creationists may be able to gain a fuller understanding of this problem and attain a satisfactory solution in the near future.[8]

What of the insistent claims that the "creation model" fits the data better than the evolution paradigm? For suddenly the data has become a "problem" requiring a "solution." Notice how various hypotheses are being preferred on the basis, not of their inherent cogency, but rather of how much aid and comfort they provide for the creation model. And this case is symptomatic of the dilemma of creationism in general. The model is prior to the data, and the latter will be coerced and manipulated in any fashion in order to fit the Procrustean bed of the former. Alas, the creation paradigm is almost all epicycle! Obviously, this is the very opposite of what we would expect if the Creationist model were the harbinger of a new "scientific revolution."

Finally, what is the bearing of the unannounced rehabilitation of Gosse's omphalos argument on all this? Remember that the tendency of the navel argument is always to admit implicitly that the evidence actually does favor evolution, but that it is misleading. Fortuitously, God merely "did it that way." In the original version, Gosse's, there were two possible explanations for this. Either God made it all look like evolution in order to test our faith (this was actually suggested by some fundamentalists in order to explain away dinosaur bones). Or, as Gosse himself preferred, God created the world as if the very real processes now observed in nature (e. g., alluvial deposit) had always been in operation, just so that the curtains could open on a fully set stage. In either case, every time the omphalos argument is invoked, even anonymously, Creationists are admitting that they hold to their "new" paradigm despite the fact that the old paradigm (evolution) fits the data better.

Creationist arguments evolve as everything else does, reluctant though some are to admit it. And just as in biological evolution we occasionally run across cases of atavism, such a throwback reveals the origins of fundamentalist pseudoscience. No matter how much "Scientific" Creationists would like to forget that "black sheep of the family," the omphalos argument of Philip Gosse, now and then its characteristics reappear in the population. And where they do, we see what sort of animal we have been dealing with all along—not scientific theory but religious propaganda.

NOTES

1.   Thomas S. Kuhn, *The Structure of Scientific Revolutions* (Chicago: The University of Chicago Press, 1962).

2.   William W. Boardman, Jr., Robert F. Koontz, and Henry M. Morris. *Science and Creation* (San Diego: Creation-Science Research Center, 1973), p. 26.

3.   Ibid., p. 91.

4.   Henry M. Morris, *Evolution and the Modern Christian* (Grand Rapids: Baker Book House, 1978), p. 23.

5.   Jacques Monod, *Chance & Necessity* (New York: Vintage Books, 1972).

6.   Duane T. Gish, *Evolution: The Fossils Say No!* (San Diego: Creation- Life Publishers, 1979), p. 64.

7.   Morris, *Evolution and the Modern Christian*, p. 63.

8.   *Science and Creation*, pp. 26–27

PART FIVE: BIBLICAL EXPLORATIONS

22

HOW THE GOSPELS SUBVERT APOLOGETICS

Let me first affirm that personally I do not approach them with the notorious "naturalistic presupposition" that miracles cannot happen. How could a mortal pipsqueak like me ever know such things? But I do ask you to keep in mind that, even if miracles may occur, that in no way means that every report of a miracle must be accurate. And does the possibility of *miracles* have anything to do with whether particular *sayings* ascribed to Jesus are really his?

George Eldon Ladd, the dean of evangelical NT scholars, thought so. In his book *The New Testament and Criticism,* he said he believed that the Holy Spirit providentially kept the transmission of Jesus' sayings and deeds accurate and free from unhistorical accretions. In other words, it boiled down to a belief that the gospels are divinely inspired and thus accurate. That, I believe, is the controlling assumption, the *supernaturalistic presupposition,* of evangelical apologists. But it is not much of an apologetic. If it took divine supervision to keep distortions out, that implies such distortion was ordinarily to be expected, doesn't it? That it would be probable, not improbable, *without a miracle stopping it.* Ladd's is a faith statement, not a *defense* of the faith. Apologists seem unable to tell the difference.

Apologists argue that the gospels stem from eye-witnesses and are too close to the events for any false reports or spurious sayings to have crept in. The disciples would have been vigilant, we are told, to reject and suppress any such false accounts or sayings. We even hear that the high Christologies of Paul, John, and the Writer to the Hebrews must reflect the self-understanding of Jesus since they were circulating while disciples of Jesus were still alive, and they would have nixed any exaggerations.

All these assumptions are gratuitous. Someone's idea of what the apostles would have or might have or should have done is mere speculation. If fact, it is all circular: "Now let's see, first we need the gospels to be trustworthy. What would have to have happened for that to be the result?" Apologists reason backwards from their preferred conclusions. But, ironically, as I hope to show, it is the gospels themselves that cast doubt on their arguments.

Again, we are told Jesus' disciples would have spent their time quashing false or exaggerated reports of miracles, so that any stories that survived must be legit. The disciples are pictured here as a sort of first-century version of Snopes, that internet site where they track down and debunk urban legends. Well, if the apostles didn't have time to spend waiting on tables, I doubt they'd have time for this either. Besides, had the twelve been on hand to document every single thing Jesus might have done or said? "What's that, Andrew? Someone told you the Master did (or said) *what?* Well, *I* don't remember it, but I guess it could have been while we were away on that missionary journey. Who knows?" To tell such a person to stop telling his "unauthorized" story would be like John telling the lone exorcist to stop casting out demons in Jesus' name because he was working their side of the street!

But what do you know? Mark tells us (7:36) that Jesus himself *did* try to hush up certain miracle stories—*and he couldn't do it!* He would tell those he healed not to tell anyone, presumably because he didn't want to get mobbed all the time. But the more he told them, Mark says, the more they blabbed it! I know what you're thinking. Mark tells us these stories were true reports, not false rumors of miracles. But that is not the salient point. The point is: here we see Jesus himself trying to scotch miracle stories he didn't want circulating for whatever reason, and *it was impossible to suppress them.* Would the disciples have had any better luck?

Form critics suggest that certain Jesus sayings originated as prophecies of the Risen Lord from heaven, as when he said to Paul, "My grace is sufficient for you, for my power is made perfect in weakness." Isn't this anticipated when Jesus says, "Whoever hears you hears me" and "Do not worry about what to say, for in that hour I will give you wisdom they cannot answer"? People remembered the sayings but may not always have bothered to segregate historical Jesus sayings from Risen Jesus prophecies. Apologists hate this idea, but why? If they believe in the resurrection, and in prophecy, aren't these sayings just as good, just as authoritative, as quotes from the Galilean teacher? Surely the ancient Christians thought so! Indeed, it seems to me, to keep the two categories separate implies a value judgment their faith would not have allowed them to make, namely that a prophecy from Jesus wasn't *really* from Jesus; you just made it up. That would have been blaspheming the Holy Spirit.

Apologists point to 1 Corinthians 7 as proof that all early Christians were always careful to segregate their own statements from historical Jesus quotes. "Now concerning the unmarried, I have no command of the Lord, but I give my opinion as one who by the Lord's mercy is trustworthy." "To the married I give charge, not I, but the Lord, that the wife should not separate from her husband, etc." "To the rest I say, not the Lord, that if any brother has a wife who is not a believer, but she is willing to live with him, etc." Keep in mind that Paul regards his own inspired rulings as "commands of the Lord." "If anyone thinks that he is a prophet or a pneumatic, he ought to acknowledge that *what I am writing to you is a command of the Lord*" (1 Corinthians 14:37). In 1 Corinthians 7:10 Paul fears that what he is about to say may not be taken seriously enough, so he makes sure his readers understand that he has God's will on the matter and no tentative opinion that they may take or leave as they see fit. In verse 12 Paul is back to more slippery issues that do not allow absolute answers. When things are inherently "iffy," one cannot simply lay down the law. But in clearer matters, one *can*, and with divine authority. What Jesus of Nazareth may or may not have said is just not in view.

Might false reports about Jesus have survived attempts of Christians to stymie them? Presumably the historical Jesus was neither a drunkard nor a glutton, not a demoniac or a Samaritan, yet we still hear these reports in the gospels, neither suppressed nor, come to think of it, even denied. Likewise, Matthew tells us that the report of Jesus' disciples absconding with his body and faking the resurrection had spread unchecked for decades and was still current as he wrote! I am assuming these reports are false, but it demonstrates that the disciples, if they even tried, could not purify the Jesus tradition of false reports.

Did "heretical" views about the nature of Christ get suppressed as long as his disciples were around to keep an eye out for such things? Well, Mark 8:27–28 tells us that already during Jesus' ministry people held all sorts of views of him that we would consider heresy, yet Jesus made no attempt to clamp the lid on them. So *what* if some imagined him to be the returned Elijah or Jeremiah? He told the disciples not to try to set anyone straight, but to keep the truth to themselves. And he certainly cannot have been publicly teaching his messiahship or his divinity as C.S. Lewis said, since that option is the only one no one in the crowd proposes!

Skeptics have suggested that on Easter morning, the disciples did not see Jesus himself, but only chance passersby, whom, in their desperation, they later inferred must have been Jesus alive again—even though it did not look like him! In other words, a false belief in resurrection stemmed from cases of mistaken identity abetted by wishful thinking. Is this scenario some contrived, modern fabrication, alien to the gospels? Maybe not. According to Mark 6:16 and 8:28, there are joyful reports among the disciples of the martyred John the Baptist that *their* master has been raised from the dead and seen by many witnesses! But Mark says it was all a case of mistaken identity: it was really *Jesus* these people were seeing. They only *thought* it was their much-missed master. Keep this in mind when you read the Easter stories where Mary or Peter or the Emmaus disciples first think they are seeing someone else and later "realize" that it *must* have been Jesus.

Paul's teaching was drastically misrepresented already during his career. Some viewed him as a libertine. "Why not do evil that good may come? – as some people slanderously charge us with saying. Their condemnation is just" (Romans 3:8). Others circulated the distortion that Paul told Jews not to circumcise their children (Acts 21:21). Others claimed Paul still preached the need for circumcision (Galatians 5:11), or that he had gone to Jerusalem for the approval of the Twelve as soon as he was converted (Galatians 1:15–20), a version of events that he denied vociferously, but which Acts repeats! Paul had, it seems, little control over the distortion of his own teaching during his own career. How can you be so sure the Twelve had any better luck safeguarding the teaching of their Master—if they even tried? They may have been the ones adding to it!

The idea that no one could have fabricated teachings in Jesus' name and gotten away with it is absurd once you think of the Gnostic Gospels, like the Pistis Sophia, the Dialogue of the Savior, the Secret Book of James, the Gospel of Mary, and so on and so on. "But," you may say, "they *didn't* get away with it! We true Christians reject them as forgeries!" Plenty of other ancient Christians treasured them. Don't you see what is going on here? It is theological, not historical, reasoning: "Oh, we can ignore that evidence because it's not in the canon."

Did the gospel writers know what Jesus had and had not said? John, like the Gospel of Thomas, has Jesus warn that, if this temple be demolished, he will raise another in three days. John admits Jesus said it, but he immediately allegorizes it: Jesus must have meant his *body*, not the Herodian temple. But for Mark and Matthew, Jesus said no such thing, and only false witnesses say he did! Luke says *Stephen* said it, or was *reported* to have said it, though he leaves it out of the trial of *Jesus* altogether.

People are quick to misinterpret what they hear, filtering it through their expectations and biases. What preacher has not been chagrinned to learn what his parishioners *think* he said in a sermon? I have had students complain to their parents at what they thought I was teaching, only to have the parents calm down once I explained what I had actually said, that junior, half-listening, had distorted. Maybe it was just too new to them. Similarly, I have found myself frequently misquoted in the newspaper and edited misleadingly on TV, for instance, on the *Faith under Fire* program.

In an interview on an Australian podcast, I quipped that, even if the gospels had been written ten minutes after whatever events transpired, the historian still could not simply accept what they said because of the typical ease and speed of distortion. But Dr. White took me to mean, as I heard him say on his own podcast, that I have a total skepticism about the past and our ability to reconstruct it. Dr. White means well and is after the truth, yet even he misconstrued what I said. How much more easy must it have been to misunderstand and misrepresent Jesus' sayings for disciples as stupid as Mark makes the Twelve? And in Mark chapter 4, Jesus flatly tells the disciples that the crowds, though they idolize him, understand his teaching not at all. So much for oral tradition!

Many apologists appeal to the theories of Riesenfeld and Gerhardsson who suppose that Jesus must have made his disciples memorize his sayings verbatim and pass them on, just as the Rabbis supposedly did. It was said of Rabbi Johannon ben Zakkai that he was "like a plastered cistern that loseth not a drop," i.e., of the teaching, the sayings, entrusted to him. But the very fact of spotlighting him in this way implies he was *unique* in his fidelity, not *typical*. And Jacob Neusner has made it plain that no one in rabbinic Judaism could keep straight who said what when. The same saying will be ascribed to three or more Rabbis, generations apart, as if each were the first to say it. Neusner shows how individual teachings cannot be dated with any certainty earlier than the documents in which they first appear, that back-dating them to earlier sages was often just a way to win an argument, giving one's opinion a bit of additional clout by associating it with a big name.

This is precisely what form-critics think happened in the case of Jesus. Someone believed Christians should never fast because the Kingdom had arrived, and it would be futile to pour the new wine of the Kingdom into the threadbare skins of Jewish practice. So he attributed the opinion to Jesus. But someone else thought it was time to take up fasting again in remembrance of Jesus, the Bridegroom, now taken away. So now Jesus was made to say that, too. Someone else just couldn't imagine Christians not fasting, any more than not praying, so he has Jesus say that Christians fast all right, just not in order to be seen by others, unlike the hypocrites. Well, which is it? Did Jesus say any of these things? If he somehow said them all, he was a first-century Robert Gibbs or Janet Napolitano.

Oh, you can always try to reread (really re*write*) the various sayings in such a way as to split the difference, but don't you see what you're doing? You might as well admit the statements are incompatible and that you only want to jam them together because your real concern is the inerrancy of the Bible which you hold as a matter of dogma before you ever look at the evidence. No one who lacked that controlling presupposition would treat the texts the way apologists do.

Did Jesus want to restrict the preaching of his gospel to Jews alone, skipping Samaritans and Gentiles, as in Matthew 10? Or did he throw open the gates to the whole world, as in Matthew 28? Peter and the Jerusalem elders debate this issue in Acts 11 and 15 with no one mentioning that Jesus ever said anything on the subject. And if he had, these debates never would have happened. It seems natural then to suggest that Matthew 10:5–6 was produced by someone who was against the Gentile Mission, while the Great Commission of Matthew 28 was the product of a supporter of the Gentile Mission. Each sought to add dominical clout to his position, pulling rank by imaginatively citing opinions of Jesus no one had ever heard before.

It's the most natural thing in the world. In the more recent case of Islam, we know that many holy men fabricated so-called traditions of the Prophet Muhammad to claim his sanction for favorite teachings or practices. Many even later admitted that they made them up, and no one blamed them, since it was all for the sake of piety. That sounds exactly like what form-critics picture happening in the Jesus tradition..

Now, just because it *might* have happened doesn't mean it *did*, any more than the mere *possibility* that the disciples suppressed any invented sayings or stories means they did. You have to weigh each case, which the Jesus Seminar spent eleven years doing.

That is hard work, and we cannot wish it away because we prefer the simplicities of Sunday School.

WHY DON'T THE GOSPELS DEAL WITH ISSUES OF CONTROVERSY IN THE EARLY CHURCH?

The issue of whether Gentile converts must eat only kosher food, as in Galatians 2:12–14, must be the point of Mark 7:14–19, where we find an echo of Romans 14:14: a rationalistic repudiation of the idea that nonkosher food renders one unclean.

Must Gentile Christians accept circumcision? That must be the point of Thomas 53: "His disciples say to him, 'Is circumcision worthwhile or not?' He says to them, 'If it were, men would be born that way automatically. But the true circumcision in spirit has become altogether worthwhile.'"

Do the gospels make Jesus address the issue of a gospel mission to Gentiles, debated in Acts 10 and 11? As Peter's vision shows, the sticking point was the necessity of Jewish missionaries eating Gentile food. But Jesus addresses it plainly in Luke 10:7, where the seventy, in contrast to the twelve (in other words, future missionaries to the Gentiles), are told to "eat and drink what they set before you."

The Gentile Mission as a whole? What do you think the Great Commissions (Matthew 28:19–20; Mark 16:15; Luke 24:47–48; John 20:21), not to mention the distance-healings of the children of Gentiles (Mark 7:24–30; Matthew 8:5–13), are all about?

Table fellowship with Gentiles, as in Antioch? That's why Jesus is depicted as dining with "sinners."

Eating meat offered previously to idols? Someone must have realized that Jesus could not plausibly be pictured addressing this in Jewish Palestine, so they left this one in the form of a post-Easter prophecy (Revelation 2:20), a concern for verisimilitude not often observed.

Paul tells Gentile Christians not to cause Jewish converts (neophytes, babes) to stumble by railroading them into disregarding Jewish dietary scruples (Romans 14:13). The same language, and I think, implicitly the same issue, occurs in Mark 9:42 about "causing these little ones who believe in me to stumble."

The role of women in the community is the point of Luke 10:38–42, where, depending on how one understands it, the issue is either women serving the Eucharist (like Martha) or women embracing the contemplative, celibate life of the so-caled "widows" and "virgins" (like Mary).

Speaking in tongues? Matthew 6:7 ("When you pray, do not say '*batta*" as the heathen do.") is against it; the late Mark 16:17 ("they will speak with new tongues.") is for it.

23

ACTS 14 AND THE EQUINOX OF THE GODS[1]

GREATER FESTIVAL OF MASKS[2]

Purim is the Jewish Halloween, a festival of costumes, parties, and carnivals. In it people often don masks which conceal one's true identity beneath the visage of a favorite biblical character. The Book of Esther is a large-scale etiology for this feast, dignifying an old, pre-Jewish game of "Lots" (Assyrian *purim*) as a commemoration of a (probably fictive) feat of deliverance of the Jewish Exilic community from the envious hostility of their Persian neighbors.[3] The feature of masks associated with the modern observance of the holiday is appropriate when we realize that the Jewish hagiographer has adapted for his purposes some old myth which treated of the transition between archaic Elamite deities and those of their Babylonian conquerors. The Elamite god Hu-man and goddess Mashti reappear as the Persian aristocrat Haman and the fallen Queen Vashti. For very different reasons, in the Bible, these two fall from power to be replaced by Jews, Mordecai (a mask for Marduk, the chief god of Babylon) and Esther (the goddess Ishtar). The story of Esther is one of a surprising number in the Bible which witness the ossification of raw myth into history-like legend, gods into heroes and mighty men of renown. "This transposition of myth to heroic saga is a notable mechanism in ancient Indo-European traditions, whenever a certain cultic system has been supplanted in living religion and the superannuated former apparatus falls prey to literary manipulation." In the case of the Old Testament, it was the gradual move from polytheism to monolatry to monotheism that perforce led to the diminution of former gods to heroic status as the only way for them to retain a foothold in the sacred literature once Samson and the like had worn out their welcome as gods.[4] In such fashion, as an earlier, less-church-blinkered, generation of Old Testament scholars knew, the goddess Hebe became Mother Eve; the god of luck, Gad, became an Israelite patriarch; the musical god Jubal became the inventor of pyre and pipe; Joshua son of Oannes became Moses' lieutenant; and several solar deities were demoted to humanity (Samson, Jacob, Esau, Enoch, Elijah, even Moses).[5]

The story has had some marginal relevance for New Testament scholars who appreciated only its membership in the class of "Suffering Righteous" stories written for young folks' edification in the Diaspora, tales in which fine young Jews like Joseph, Moses, Daniel, and Esther prove the superiority of a Jewish way of life by following its path to surpass their pagan contemporaries, despite the advantages of the latter. The story of Jesus is seen to be a distant cousin of these stories.[6] That is as may be. But in the present exercise I propose that Esther has another relevance: it helps us see what is going on in the fascinating fourteenth chapter of the Acts of the Apostles. This chapter of Acts, it seems to me, is written on the same general plan as Esther, and it is, like its canonical Jewish predecessor, a veritable festival of masks and games. Let us seek to figure out the rules, so we may join in the fun!

FIFTEEN MINUTES OF APOSTLESHIP

Acts 14 begins with a case of "the *pseudo-iterative*—that is, scenes presented, particularly by their wording in the imperfect, as iterative, whereas their richness and precision of detail ensure that no reader can seriously believe they occur and recur in that manner, several times, without any variation."[7] Verses 1–8 provide a fictive summary which (like so many in Mark, Luke, and Eusebius)[8] seems to summarize a series of typical cases but is actually a specious generalization drawn from a single example. The missionary preaching of Paul and Barnabas, its reception by Gentiles, its envious rejection by spiteful Jewish fanatics (Oberammergau puppets, as Jack T. Sanders shows),[9] the persecution and expulsion of the missionaries, etc., is a recurrent Lukan template, and if he derived it from any single earlier story (whether traditional or his own prior creation) it was likely the ensuing episode set among the barbarians of Lycaonia (verses 8–20). The passage features various points of interest and curiosity. The brief speech in verses 15–17 is a dry-run for the longer Areopagus speech in 17:22–31, and is no doubt based on it, though both are Lukan compositions. And both partake of the Apologists' theology of the second century.[10] More interesting is that Paul and Barnabas, so carefully denied the dignity of apostleship by Luke elsewhere in the book (an anti-Marcionite gesture), are here, as if by a slip of the pen, twice called "apostles" after all (verses 4 and 14, though Codex Bezae lacks the term in verse 14),[11] but never again. Why should this be? When we are done, we may have an answer, though perhaps not a very compelling one.

LUKE-AONIA

Some may question the propriety or the viability of such an inquiry as we are pursuing here on the grounds that the apostolic adventure in Lystra is a piece of history, not a vestige of mythopoeia. History or fiction: how may we decide? Remember where one finds the proof of the pudding: insofar as the interpretation presented here is illuminating or convincing, this judgment will itself militate in favor of the literary, fictive, character of the narrative, since presumably factual historical accounts do not lend themselves so neatly to such exposition: "the more complex the purely literary structure is shown to be, the harder it is for most people to accept the narratives as naively transparent upon historical reality" (Frank Kermode).[12]

But let us not rely on a circular argument. Are there features of the narrative itself that would signal the reader as to whether the story is history or fiction? Indeed there are. First, there is the strictly dramaturgical arrangement of Paul's speech in the context. Dibelius observed concerning the Acts speeches generally that "the speeches are not, in fact, bound to the historical events in the setting in which we find them." "All this explains itself if we ignore completely the question of historicity and see here the author's hand fashioning the material."[13] Just so, in the present case, we must picture Paul and Barnabas plunging into the surging chaos of an unruly, enthused mob (v. 14) precisely while speechifying, as if any such sermonette could be heard amid the tumult (cf. Paul's shipboard sermon given over the crashing of the storm in chapter 27[14]). Surely John writes with more verisimilitude when he has Jesus take one look at such a crowd of admirers—and make a hasty exit (John 6:15)! Second, we cannot help but feel that the priest of Zeus manages to wrangle those oxen and produce them on-site a bit too quickly and easily (14:13), as if from right off stage.[15] Admittedly, Luke may have prepared for this problem by having the incident take place at the city gate, with the temple of Zeus hard by, but even this detail is introduced as an afterthought, only when it comes in handy, as if that is why it is there at all.

Third, the very coincidence between the Acts 14 story and the setting in Lycaonia of the Baucis and Philemon story, which is sometimes claimed in behalf of the historical basis of the episode, rather seems to imply the fictitious character of both. Apologists seem to assume that the residents, proud of their mythic stardom ("Zeus ate here"), were just the kind of folks to mistake an eloquent speaker for God! As it happens, I live one town over from Smithfield, North Carolina, a tiny burg whose main claim to fame is that Ava Gardner was born there. Tourists are directed proudly to the Ava Gardner Museum. The road into the Wal-Mart is Ava Gardner Avenue. But suppose an attractive woman arrives in town; are the locals likely to jump to the conclusion that Ava has returned from the dead? I think not. No, the Acts episode is Luke's equally fictive response to Ovid.[16]

Fourth, the denouement of the story features the spectacle of Paul being stoned to death by an angry mob (v. 19), then getting up and brushing himself off with no harm done, like Elmer Fudd, incinerated by a bomb blast in one frame, hale and hardy, albeit slightly smudged, in the next. And we are simply told that a crowd, a moment before desirous of worshipping Paul, have been turned in a moment into a howling lynchmob, all by some seductive whisperings of Luke's ubiquitous Elders of Zion. And then, to top it all off, Paul and Barnabas nonchalantly return to the city shortly thereafter (v. 21) to check on the welfare of their converts as if the apostolic portaits were not tacked onto the post office wall. Once the original episode's action has concluded, Luke has no use for the memory of it.

It seems there is precious little to convince us that the author of Acts 14 ought to be called "Luke the historian" (not that he would have fancied the name). Haenchen is right: "It is indeed merely right to acknowledge that in applying to Luke the yardstick of the modern historian we do him an injustice."[17]

STEREOSCOPIC GODS

The basic structure of Esther as a tissue of mythic associations, and of substitutions of one tier of deities for another, is as follows. We begin with the pair *Hu-man/Mashti*. To these are opposed, in the original supplantation myth, another pair of deities, *Marduk/Ishtar*. We do not know what narrative trick the first author chose to bring about the supplantation of one pair (synechdoche for pantheon) of gods for another. For our purposes, it is enough to see that the action was one of supplantation. There is a second level of supplantation, as the gods of myth are reduced to mortal heroes and villains: Hu-man becomes Haman. Mashti becomes Vashti. Marduk becomes Mordecai. Ishtar becomes Esther. But the direction and dynamic of supplantation remains, only now it is mortal sovereignty that witnesses a changing of the guard. Evil (Haman) and disobedient, though dignified (Vashti)[18] Persian rulers lose their positions to the worthier Jewish Mordecai and Esther. This latter change prefigures both the triumph of Jews over Persian enemies in the story and the eventual Persian sponsorship of the Exilarchs and their resumption of authority in Jerusalem under Ezra and Nehemiah. The conversion of divine sovereignty to human rule is natural, since on the game board of history, the victories of the gods were thought to be reflected in those of mortals. If Babylon defeated Judea, Marduk must have defeated Yahve.

We can, I propose, still discern pretty much the same structure of double supplantation in Acts 14. We find our two opposed pairs of mythic immortals standing behind two pairs of Luke's characters. First there is the pair Zeus and Hermes. We are to understand them playing their roles familiar from the famous myth of Baucis and Philemon (Ovid, *Metamorphoses*, Book VIII). This myth parallels both the Flood and Sodom myths of Genesis. Ill rumors have inclined Father Zeus to flood the world, particularly the cannibalism of the Lystragonians. But young Hermes prevails on Zeus to undertake a fact-finding tour and canvas a representative sample of human homes, just as Yahve's lieutenants/avatars go down the valley into the Cities of the Plain to check out the rumors that rise from it like the stench of garbage. In both cases, the immortals operate incognito. Any fool, knowing himself to be in the very presence of the gods, would approximate his best behavior (Matthew 25:44–45), hence the need to appear as mere humans so as to gauge everyday morality and fellow-feeling. In Genesis, of course, Lot and his daughters Patty and Selma are saved from the ensuing melee, but the rest of the Sodom xenophobes, Procrustes and his ilk,[19] are destroyed with as little mercy as they used to show hapless travelers. Likewise, various ugly incidents serve to confirm Zeus in his original opinion, whereupon he unleashes the Flood after all. But the judge of all the earth is just: having run across a single righteous couple, the elderly Baucis and Philemon, he sees to their rescue. How had they demonstrated their worth? Spotting a pair of weary wayfarers, neither knowing them nor needing to, the old man and woman welcomed them into their cramped hovel and shared their pitiful stock of stale crusts and wine dregs. But how strange that, through the convivial evening, the wine never seemed to run out! The question would remain unspoken no longer: were they after all the gods? Indeed so. And as a reward, Zeus and Hermes granted the old couple a boon. They should together tend a shrine to Zeus to be built on the site of their home, and when their natural span of days was spent, they should be immortalized as a pair of trees whose intertwining canopy of branches should evermore shade the chapel. The incident, myth said, occurred in the very province of Lycaonia, whose surviving coins yet commemorate the event. So we have two pairs of immortals: *Zeus/Hermes*, born immortal, though each in his day had narrowly escaped death. And *Baucis/Philemon*, born mortals, but raised to immortality (symbolically, at least, as long-lived magical trees in the garden of the gods—as if a prelapsarian Adam and Eve had eaten of the fruit of immortality and been transformed into the twin trees of Eden!).

APOSTLES AND EPIPHANIES

For the moment, we shall skip the first layer of supplantation we should expect to find if the cases of Esther and Acts 14 are true parallels. We shall leap from the question of the first substitution, i.e., of one pair of ancient gods by another pair of pagan deities. Let us jump all the way to the biblical whitewash. It is obvious that in Acts, the virtues of the old gods have been Christianized, because Zeus has become Barnabas, servant of the living God.[20] Hermes, lord of divine eloquence and salesmanship, has become Paul, chief evangelist and fast-talker for Christ. This is explicit in the story (verse 12). But what about Baucis and Philemon? Their costumes are more concealing, but we can still recognize them. They (re)appear here as the man lame from birth (verses 8–10) and the local prelate of Zeus (verse 13). They need not much resemble the actual characters; the actantial roles are all that is necessary.

And they do match up. Paul's healing miracle corresponds to the subtle multiplication of the wine in the jar. It is this act that causes the crowd to suppose, as Baucis and Philemon did, that the gods had appeared in mortal guise among them (though not a disguise very difficult to penetrate!). More, it corresponds to the wish granted to the old couple, that they may *stand* forever, no longer infirm, before their god. And then it becomes obvious who the priest of Zeus is: he is just what Baucis and Philemon became as part of their reward: *priests of Zeus*, specially custodians of a particular temple of his, exactly like the priest of Acts 14.

The order of events has changed, on purpose, in accord with the Christian belief that the apostles were not gods but merely messengers of Christ, mortals like their audience. The acclamation of the apostles as gods is hotly rejected by Paul and Barnabas[21] just as eagerly as it was fatally gobbled up by Herod Agrippa I (Acts 12:22–23) and Simon Magus (8:10). In the Greek myth, this acclamation was a confession of faith rewarded by the gods Zeus and Hermes. In Acts, it is blasphemy uttered by ignorant idolaters. It must be overturned, by the preaching of the gospel, before a proper confession of faith can even become possible. Priesthood to Zeus was identical with the blessing of salvation in the original version, but it represents the paganism from which salvation must needs be sought in the Acts version. And of course, this envisioned shift from pagan Greek religion to the Christian religion, a matter of human allegiances and sovereignties, parallels that at stake in the Esther story: from Persian to Jewish sovereignty/blessing. Even the outcomes of the stories of Esther and Acts 14 are similar. In Esther, Jews escape persecution and take vengeance on their pagan enemies. In Acts, however, Christians have taken the place of Jews, and Jews have become the persecutors of the righteous in a particularly cruel twist.

It is time for our guess as to why here and only here Paul and Barnabas are called apostles. As Walter Schmithals has shown,[22] the root concept of "apostle" comes from a network of Syrian Gnosticism and related Oriental[23] mysticism, where it first denoted a heavenly avatar of the world-soul or of a deity. It meant pretty much the same thing as the epiphany of a god in human form. It occurs to me that the title may retain some of its original meaning here in Acts 14, where the missionaries are taken for the gods themselves. While they can never be such for Luke, he may have allowed them the title "apostles" to catch this nuance. Who knows? But in the absence of competitors, even a pretty slow runner takes the prize.

THE MISSING PAIR

Now what of the missing pair of substitutions? If Acts 14 parallels the supplantation sequence of Esther and its underlying myth, where is the layer corresponding to the Babylonian deities Marduk (who will become Mordecai) and Ishtar (who will become Esther)? Thus far we have followed the explicit identification of Paul as Hermes and Barnabas as Zeus, as well as the evident identification of the Lycaonian Zeus hierophant and the congenital cripple as Baucis and Philemon. But who are the other gods whom Paul and Barnabas directly or indirectly displaced? You will have no difficulty in recognizing the next set of identifications as speculative, and this is usually considered dangerous, at least distasteful. But consider this: if the evidence for a thing has survived in mere fragments, no reconstruction can ever be compelling, only more or less plausible. And we may have to be satisfied with that." Many literary critics seem to think that an hypothesis about obscure and remote questions of history can be refuted by a simple demand for the production of more evidence than in fact exists. But the true test of an hypothesis, if it cannot be shown to conflict with known truths, is the number of facts that it correlates, and explains."[24] We cannot pretend the best guess in such a case, the best of a bad lot, is a firm conclusion, but it is worth considering until something better comes along.

The set of correspondences I have tried to trace so far is striking as far as it goes. We cannot simply assume it must continue any farther at all. That would be exactly what Samuel Sandmel called "parallelomania."[25] But when a set of footsteps seems to be headed in some definite direction, and they suddenly stop, washed out by the rain, it is reasonable to assume that they continued, and then to try to discern that last known trajectory. Here goes.

IS THERE A DOCTOR IN THE HOUSE?

First, Paul. I suspect that in Paul we are to recognize (as Margaret Morris has argued)[26] a Christianized version of Apollonius of Tyana. Some make "Paulus" a Romanized form of the name "Apollonius." The correspondences between the careers and even the itineraries of the two are striking. Paul is a born citizen of Tarsus (Acts 22:3), while Apollonius is declared the second founder of Tarsus (*Life of Apollonius of Tyana* 6:34). Both spend a preparatory period in Arabia (Galatians 1:17; *Life* 1:20). Both cover much ground, much further afield than Jesus, accompanied by disciples and working miracles. Both visit cities including Antioch (Acts 11:25–26; Galatians 2:11 ff.; *Life* 1:16), Paphos (Acts 13:6; *Life* 3:58), Ephesus (Acts 19 *passim*; *Life* 4:1), Caesarea (Acts 21:8; Epistle 11), and Corinth (Acts 18:1–17; *Life* 4:25; 7:10). Upon his arrival in Philippi, Paul's preaching receives the surprising endorsement of the local oracle (Acts 16:16–18), just as Apollonius does when he reaches Ephesus, where the oracles of Colophon, Didyma, and Pergamum direct seekers to him for healing (*Life* 4:1). Just as Paul's first missionary journey takes him from Antioch to Seleucia to Cyprus, and then to the mainland of Asia Minor, so does Apollonius begin in Antioch and continue to Seleucia, Cyprus, and Ionia (Acts chapter 13; *Life* 3:58). Both head finally to Rome where they are to appear on trial before Caesar (Acts 27–28; *Life* 7:15–16). In the course of this journey, each is deserted by a companion who heads back east, one named *Demas* (2 Timothy 4:10), the other *Damis* (*Life* 7:41). Apollonius also has associates named Lykon (Luke) and Timasio (cf. Timothy). Both are on record in epistles as eulogizing the Roman conquest of Jerusalem (1 Thessalonians 2:16; Romans 11:3, 9; *Life* 6:29) Both bequeathed travelogues and sets of epistles.

These comparisons need mean no more than that Luke has borrowed Apollonius traditions to tell his story, no surprise after all, since Luke elsewhere borrows fast and thick from Homer, Vergil, the Septuagint, Plato, Euripides, Arrian, Epimenides, and Cleanthes. Luke's Paul is equally Pentheus and Heliodorus, even Dionysus in Acts 16.[27] He might as well be Apollonius here. And if he is Apollonius, that means he is the incarnation/son of Proteus, as that god informs Apollonius' mother in his annunciation (Philostratus, *Life of Apollonius of Tyana* I. iv).

An early adventure of Apollonius concerns his youthful apprenticeship at the healing shrine of Asclepius at Aegae (*Life* 1:7–8). Just as Mark's Jesus makes conventional medicine look like charlatanism by comparison (Mark 5:26–28), and John's Jesus puts to shame the tall claims of the Beth-Zatha spa (John 5:1–9), so Apollonius proves able to heal a suppliant when even the god cannot (1.9).[28] In the same way, I see in Acts 14 a story in which Paul heals a cripple, proving his superiority as a Christian apostle over Hermes, bearer of the Caduceus, the healing staff with the intertwined serpents. And he does so playing the role of Proteus, the god incarnated in Apollonius. And remember that Proteus was the shape-shifting god whose chameleon-like nature provided the prototype for the divine polymorphousness of both Christ and his apostolic avatars in every single one of the Apocryphal Leucian Acts![29] (That is, the divine transcendence of physical limits is manifested by the ability of the god to assume different forms at will, even simultaneously.) Paul is Apollonius, i.e., Proteus.

AVATARS AND APOSTLES

Barnabas, on the other hand, plainly bears a pagan theophoric name, "son of

Nebo/Nabu," the Babylonian ruler of fate and fortune.[30] As the god of writing (like Cadmus, Thoth, and Enoch), it was he who inscribed the heavenly tablets of destiny which the king of Babylon glimpsed each year at his heavenly ascension on New Year's Day. Typical of biblical writers from the Yahvist on down,[31] Luke has tried to conceal the pagan character of the name Barnabas by making it a pun on "Son of Encouragement" (Acts 4:36)—an astonishing piece of heresy in its own right, as it implies Barnabas was thought to be the incarnate Paraclete, an honor accorded also to the Fourth Evangelist, Paul (by Marcionites whom Origen mentions), Montanus, Maximilla (mentioned in the Acts of Thomas?), Priscilla (mentioned in the canonical Acts?), Mani, and Muhammad. As Bultmann observes: "the figure [of the Paraclete] itself must have originated in a body of opinion, according to which the revelation was not exclusively concentrated on *one* historical bearer, but shared amongst various messengers following upon each other, or repeated in them."[32]

As far as I know, there was no imported Mystery cult of Nabu in Hellenized Rome, but Nabu was equated with the Roman Jupiter (Dyus-Pitar, "Father Zeus"), just as Luke makes Bar-Nabu (Barnabas) into Zeus, and there certainly was a veritable epidemic of interest in astrology as the art of mastering fate and destiny.[33] Like Nabu, the owner of fate, astrology was indeed a Babylonian import. In the "age of anxiety" autopsied by Arthur Nock and E.R. Dodds,[34] both Apollonius' Pythagoreanism and "Nabu's" astrology were largely replacing traditional Olympian gods, whose worship was superannuated.

Nabu, Nebo, was known to the Mandaeans for hundreds of years CE, and they considered him a false messiah. They also considered Jesus a false messiah, as is well known, exalting the Old Testament Enosh (cf. *bar-nasha*, Son of Man) to this role instead, making of him a divinized patriarch like Enoch. Though archaeological evidence for any early Nebo-worship in Israel is lacking, it cannot, it seems to me, be mere coincidence that a significant Old Testament peak is named Mount Nebo! Surely, contra A.R. Millard,[35] this demands that a high place devoted to that god once existed there. Nabu had long since begun to surpass his father Marduk in importance, and in turn, as astrology moved west, he himself had to yield his planet to Hermes (our planet Mercury). This development is interesting, as it might imply a further wrinkle in Luke's schema, whereby Paul ("Hermes") is set to eclipse Barnabas ("Nebo").

So I see, on one end of the sequence, an initial pantheon of Olympian gods, represented in Acts 14 by Hermes and Zeus. On the near end I discern the Christianization of the ancient world, with Paul replacing Hermes and Barnabas replacing Zeus. In the background, I believe I can make out the traces of Proteus as Apollonius (scion of Pythagorean ascetic wisdom and soul-healing) and Nabu (a symbol of astrology as a way of salvation) standing behind Zeus. Just as Esther attests a historical/religious progression from Elamite to Babylonian to Jewish religion, so does Acts 14 preserve traces of a later extension of the same evolution: from Olympian worship; to popular philosophy and astrology; finally to apostolic Christianity.

EPILOGUE JAM

In the neglected second part of *Faust*, Act Five, Goethe retells the story of Baucis and Philemon with the same sovereign freedom as Acts, only he combines it with the tale of Naboth's vineyard, Faust feeling Ahab's pathetic covetousness for the old couple's garden and seizing it. As Thomas L. Brodie has demonstrated,[36] Luke has composed the stories of Ananias and Sapphira and of Stephen from equal parts of Achan's crime (Joshua 7) and Naboth's vineyard (1 Kings 21:1–19). And who, by selling a field and donating all the profits, serves to introduce the Ananias and Sapphira tale but Barnabas, who forms the antitype to the couple as Lot does to the men of Sodom. Now Barnabas functions in this story, a variant form of Naboth's vineyard, as a "second Naboth," a *bar-Naboth*! So here he is again in *Faust*, silently standing in the background of the myth of Baucis and Philemon as if he had a right to be there! Surely Claude Levi-Strauss was right:[37] "Our method thus eliminates a problem which has, so far, been one of the main obstacles to the progress of mythological studies, namely, the quest for the *true* version, or the *earlier* one. On the contrary, we define the myth as consisting of all its versions." Thus we can discern a deep structure in common in all the various versions and tellings of the same myth, all the more, as there can be no "original version" in any case.[38]

NOTES

1.   See Aleister Crowley, *The Equinox of the Gods* (privately printed 1936; facsimile ed., Scottsdale: New Falcon Publications, 1991).

2.   See Thomas Ligotti, "The Greater Festival of Masks" in his collection, *The Nightmare Factory* (NY: Carroll & Graf, 1996), pp. 159–165.

3.   Otto Eissfeldt, *The Old Testament: An Introduction*. Trans. Peter R. Ackroyd. (NY: Harper & Row, 1975), pp. 508–510.

4. Jaan Puhvel, *Comparative Mythology* (Baltimore: Johns Hopkins U. Press, 1989), p. 39. See also Hermann Gunkel, *Genesis*. Trans. Mark E. Biddle. Mercer Library of Biblical Studies (Macon: Mercer U. Press, 1997), p. xii–xiii.

5. Ignaz Goldziher, *Mythology Among the Hebrews, and its Historical Development*. Trans. Russell Martineau (NY: Cooper Square Publishers, 1967 [orig. 1877]); Chapter V. "The Most Prominent Figures in Hebrew Mythology," pp. 90-197.

6. George W.E. Nickelsburg, "The Genre and Function of the Markan Passion Narrative." *Harvard Theological Review* 73 (1980), pp. 153–184. According to this analysis, much admired by Crossan, Jesus' eventual appearance before Pilate's tribunal is supposedly equivalent to the advancement of Joseph, Moses, Daniel and Esther to high positions in the "courts" of pagan rulers. One need not be Bar-Timaeus to fail to see the similarity.

7. Gerard Genette, *Narrative Discourse: An Essay in Method*. Trans. Jane E. Lewin (Ithaca: Cornell U. Press, 1980), p. 121.

8. Robert M. Grant, *Eusebius as Church Historian* (NY: Oxford U. Press, 1980), e.g., p. 27: "When we get to Book VIII, then, where he is arguing from single examples to the universality and the intensity of the persecution, his method is completely inadequate. Indeed, while it is likely that there were very many martyrdoms in Egypt, Eusebius' own *Martyrs of Palestine* shows that his generalizations exaggerate the number of martyrs. The effect is apologetic. He is trying to prove a case."

9. Jack T. Sanders, *The Jews in Luke-Acts* (Philadelphia: Fortress Press, 1987), p. 263: "They have therefore behaved like good puppets in response to Luke's string-play and have rejected the gospel."

10. J.C. O'Neill, *The Theology of Acts in its Historical Setting* (London: SPCK, 1961); Philipp Vielhauer, "On the 'Paulinism' of Acts," in Leander E. Keck and J. Louis Martyn (eds.), *Studies in Luke-Acts* (NY: Abingdon Press, 1966), pp. 33–50; Charles H. Talbert, *Luke and the Gnostics* (NY: Abingdon Press, 1966).

11. On the other hand, it may be that Luke does not grant Paul and Barnabas the dignity of apostleship even here. Notice how verse 4 mentions "the apostles" as the opposite factional allegiance, over against "the Jews," without actually naming Paul and Barnabas. If we follow the lead of D, "the apostles" did not originally belong in verse 14 and has been added to the names where it is cumbersome and superfluous. I wonder if "the apostles" in verse 4 is really synecdoche for "Christianity," the apostolic message, as in Acts 2:42, and does not intend application to Paul and Barnabas personally. It may be that some copyist added "the apostles" to the names in verse 14 in order to apply the honorific specifically to Paul and Barnabas so as to secure for them the status Luke had carefully denied them.

12. Frank Kermode, *The Genesis of Secrecy: On the Interpretation of Narrative*

(Cambridge: Harvard University Press, 1979), p. 62.

13. Martin Dibelius, "The Speeches in Acts and Ancient Historiography," in Dibelius, *Studies in the Acts of the Apostles* (London: SCM Press, 1956), pp. 177, 164–165.

14. Ernest Haenchen, *The Acts of the Apostles: A Commentary*. Trans. Bernard Noble and Gerald Shinn, rev. R. McL. Wilson (Philadelphia: Westminster Press, 1971), p. 709

15. Ibid., p. 432

16. Ibid.

17. Ibid., p. 434.

18. What did Queen Vashti do wrong? We admire her for refusing to be made a spectacle for the king's masturbating beer buddies, nor is there any hint that Esther would have so degraded herself either, though, lucky for her, the issue seems not to have arisen again, the king having apparently learned his lesson, not wanting to risk losing face a second time. But we might understand the narrator's attitude by comparing Vashti with Lilith. Created alongside Adam in Genesis 1, ancient harmonists posited, she refused to submit to him, demanding to be on top during sex, so she left him to become Samael's concubine. Thus the need for Eve as a subsequent replacement in chapter 2. In both cases, Vashti and Lilith, female pride stands almost as a source of numinous astonishment, not precisely reprehensible, but nonetheless impossible to brook. See Raphael Patai, *The Hebrew Goddess* (Avon Books, 1978), p. 183. Joshua Trachtenberg, *Jewish Magic and Superstition: A Study in Folk Religion* (NY: Atheneum, 1975), p. 37.

19. Robert Graves and Raphael Patai, *Hebrew Myths: The Book of Genesis* (NY: Greenwich House, 1983), pp.167–168. The *Sepher Hayashar* transplants the story of the Procrustean "one size fits all" bed to Sodom's salty soil. Only there it is the common citizenry of Sodom, not a single wicked innkeeper, who perpetrate such outrages upon strangers, and in broad daylight.

20. Paul's description of the bountiful deity in verses 15–17 could as easily refer to Zeus as to his Jewish cousin Jehovah! No wonder the poor Lycaonians were confused!

21. Gerd Theissen, *The Miracle Stories of the Early Christian Tradition*. Trans. Francis McDonagh (Philadelphia: Fortress Press, 1983), p. 168.

22. Walter Schmithals, *The Office of Apostle in the Early Church*. Trans. John E. Steely. (NY: Abingdon Press, 1969), Part Three, section IV, "The Apostle in Gnosticism," pp. 114–192. See also Geo Widengren, *The Great Vohu Mana and the Apostle of God: Studies in Iranian and Manichaean Religion*. Uppsala Universitets Årsskrift 1945:5 (Uppsala: A.-B. Lundequistska Bokhandeln, 1945); Ibid., *The Ascension of the Apostle*

and the Heavenly Book (King and Saviour III). Uppsala Universitets Årsskrift 1950: 7 (Uppsala: A.B. Lundequistska Bokhandeln, 1950).

23. And to hell with Edward W. Said, *Orientalism* (NY: Random House, 1979). Despite his finger-wagging, I like the category and will continue to use it. Sue me.

24. Francis MacDonald Cornford, *The Origins of Attic Comedy.* Ed. with a Foreword and Additional Notes by Theodor Gaster (Garden City: Doubleday Anchor, 1961), p. 191.

25. Samuel Sandmel, "Parallelomania," *Journal of Biblical Literature* 81 (1962), pp. 1–13. Sandmel did not mean to discourage inference from striking parallels between ancient religions and myths (as apologists misrepresent him—their condemnation is just). His gripe was that, when one has a set of *fragmentary* texts or myths, one cannot gratuitously assume they would continue in parallel where we lack the text just because they are parallel where we *can* verify it.

26. Margaret Morris, *Jesus-Augustus: From Emperor Cult to Christianity* (unpublished, 1999), Chapter 26, "Paul's Real Identity," pp. 413–461. D. Surmani Murdock ("Acharya S"), *The Christ Conspiracy: The Greatest Story Ever Sold* (Kempton: Adventures Unlimited Press, 1999), pp. 173–175. See also R.W. Bernard, *Apollonius the Nazarene: Mystery Man of the Bible* (Pomeroy: Health Research, 1956), pp. 7–8, 22, 33.

27. Lilian Portefaix, *Sisters Rejoice: Paul's Letter to the Philippians and Luke-Acts as Received by First-Century Philippian Women.* Coniectanea Biblica New Testament Series 20 (Stockholm: Almqvist & Wiksell International, 1988), pp. 169–170.

28. A modern example of the same hagiographic motif may be found in an episode of *Xena: Warrior Princess*, where Xena, having brought a number of wounded into a nearby shrine of Asclepius, is astonished and disgusted to see that the priests merely pray over their charges, administering no medicine, reasoning that the god will heal them if he wishes. They oppose her when she then applies what rough battlefield medicine she knows. But she gets results, not them. We get the message.

29. David R. Cartlidge, "Transfigurations of Metamorphosis Traditions in the Acts of John, Thomas, and Peter." In Dennis Ronald MacDonald (ed.), *Semeia* 38 (1986), pp. 53–66. See also Robert M. Price, "Docetic Epiphanies: A Structuralist Analysis of the Apocryphal Acts," *Journal of Higher Criticism* 5/2 (Fall1998), pp. 163–187.

30. The great fantasist Gardner F. Fox perfectly represented Nebo/Nabu as the comic book superhero Doctor Fate, wearing the mystic amulet and helmet of Nabu. Doctor Fate first appeared in *More Fun Comics* # 55, 1940.

31. Gunkel, *Genesis*, pp. xix-xx.

32. Rudolf Bultmann, *The Gospel of John: A Commentary.* Trans. G.R. Beasley-Murray, R.W.N. Hoare, J.K. Ritches (Philadelphia: Westminster Press, 1971), p. 567.

Tor Andrae, *Mohammed: The Man and his Faith.* Trans. Theophil Menzel. (NY: Harper Torchbook, 1960), p. 35; Chapter IV, "Mohammed's Doctrine of Revelation," pp. 94–113.

33. Franz Cumont, *Astrology and Religion among the Greeks and Romans.* Trans. J.B. Baker (NY: Dover Books, 1960).

34. Arthur Darby Nock, *Conversion: The Old and the New in Religion from Alexander the Great to Augustine of Hippo* (NY: Oxford U. Press, 1933); E.R. Dodds, *Pagan and Christian in an Age of Anxiety: Some Aspects of Religious Experience from Marcus Aurelius to Constantine.* (NY: W.W. Norton & Company, 1970); Walter Burkert, *The Orientalizing Revolution: Near Eastern Influence on Greek Culture in the Early Archaic Age.* Trans. Margaret E. Pinder and Walter Burkert. (Cambridge: Harvard U. Press, 1992).

35. A.R. Millard, "Nabu," in Karel van der Toorn, Bob Becking, Pieter W. van der Horst (eds.), *Dictionary of Deities and Demons in the Bible (DDD)* (Leiden: E.J. Brill, 1995), col. 1146: "there is no compelling reason, apart from the identical spelling, to associate the places in Judah (Ezra 2:29; Neh 7:34) and Moab (Num 32:3 etc. Moabite Stone 14, written *nbh*), or the mountain in Moab where Moses died (Num 33:47; Deut 32:49; 34:1), with the Akkadian god" Nabu. Huh? Seems to me that's a good mouthful of evidence right there!

36. Thomas L. Brodie, "Luke the Literary Interpreter: Luke-Acts as a Systematic Rewriting and Updating of the Elijah-Elisha Narrative in 1 and 2 Kings." Ph.D. Dissertation, Pontifical University of St. Thomas Aquinas, 1981, pp. 271–287.

37. Claude Levi-Strauss, "The Structural Study of Myth," in Levi-Strauss, *Structural Anthropology.* Trans. Claire Jacobson. (Garden City: Doubleday Anchor, 1967), pp. 213–215.

38. Albert B. Lord, *The Singer of Tales* (Cambridge: Harvard U. Press, 1960), Chapter Five, "Songs and the Song," pp. 99–123.

24

HEAVENLY BRIDEGROOMS:
THE SEX ACTS OF THE APOSTLES

The Apocryphal Acts of the Apostles seek to depict the exploits of the apostles as they heeded the command of the Risen Christ to take the gospel to all corners of the earth. But they do not take just any gospel. It is the gospel of celibacy: "Blessed are the continent, for to them will God speak" (Acts of Paul). While it was generally considered reprehensible for Hellenistic women to defy the authority of their husbands by converting to strange new faiths from the east (see, for instance the sober warnings of Plutarch in his Advice to the Bride and Groom or the scathing mockery of Juvenal in his sixth satire), conversion to encratite Christianity, "the word of the virgin life" (Acts of Paul), would obviously cause more domestic controversy than any other cult. Newly Christian women spurned their husbands' advances as if the latter were drooling rapists. Indeed they considered them as little more, since now all sexuality was held to be sinful, "horrid intercourse" (Acts of Thomas).

The Apocryphal Acts end with the martyrdoms of their blessed protagonists. And it is not hard to guess what leads to these martyrdoms! In most cases the apostle is done in by the ire of an estranged husband who has connections with higher-ups. Once the husband complains about the "sorcerer" who has "deceived" his poor wife, the governor generally agrees with him and decides the home-wrecking apostle is too much of a public nuisance to go on living.

But let us be more precise. The pagan husbands, left with an empty bed, are not only angry at losing a good wife. True, hell hath no wrath like an encratite's husband scorned, but suppose the husband not only blamed the apostle for teaching celibacy, but suspected the apostle of cuckolding him?

When Charisius entreats his estranged wife Mygdonia to return to their life together, it is at first hard to tell whom it is he considers his rival for her affections.

> "Look upon me, for I am far better and more handsome than this sorcerer! I have riches and honour, and all recognize that none has such a lineage as I. But thou art my riches and my honour, thou art my family and kinship—and lo, he is taking thee away from me!" When Charisius said this, Mygdonia said to him: "He whom I love is better than thee and thy possessions. For thy possession is of the earth and returns to earth; but he whom I love is heavenly, and will take me with him into heaven." (Hennecke-Schneemelcher, *New Testament Apocrypha*, v. 2, 505).

Actually, in the context of the story, these words could refer either to Jesus or to his "twin brother" Thomas (or to any of the other encratite apostles), but eventually things become clear, when Mygdonia explains that "Thou art a bridegroom that passes away and is destroyed, but Jesus is a true bridegroom, abiding immortal for ever" (509).

Aegeates, estranged husband of Maximilla, certainly seems to understand Andrew, not Jesus, to be his rival for the affections of Maximilla, as it is Andrew whom he calls "the one whom you love more than me" (410).

The tradition of the apostles being martyred through the intervention of jealous husbands was widespread and appears even in the so-called 1 Clement, where we read,

> Let us bring before our eyes the good apostles!—Peter, who because of unrighteous jealousy endured not one or two, but numerous trials, and so bore a martyr's witness and went to the glorious place he deserved. Because of jealousy and strife Paul pointed the way to the reward of endurance; seven times he was imprisoned, he was stoned, [et cetera,] and bearing a martyr's witness before the rulers he passed out of the world and was taken up into the holy place, having proved a very great example of endurance (5:3–7, Goodspeed's translation.)

Scholars confess themselves puzzled as to the jealousy references. Can we really imagine the spite between Christian parties prompting rival Christians to have Peter, then Paul, arrested and executed? Such an absurd suggestion, made by Cullmann (*Peter: Disciple, Apostle, Martyr*, Philadelphia, 1953, 99–103), only results from a too-quick reading into the apostolic examples a situation parallel to the one the writer invoked the examples to meet. He doesn't say Peter and Paul succumbed to the same variety of jealousy he seeks to correct among the Corinthians.

The only kind of jealousy associated in the tradition with the deaths of the apostles is the *romantic* jealousy of the husbands of their female converts. Of course if one admitted this, it would place 1 Clement much later than most scholars want to place it. It would mean the letter was written in the second or third century, not at the end of the first, since it presupposes traditions otherwise met with only in second and third century documents.

Stevan L. Davies (*The Revolt of the Widows: The Social World of the Apocryphal Acts,* Carbondale, 1980) argues cogently that the protagonists of these Acts, though they bear the names and personae of the apostolic figures of first-century renown, actually represent the itinerant charismatic apostles of whom the Didache treats, and whose radical ministries were eventually smothered by the growth of ecclesiastical institutionalism. And it is striking that of these Gnostic and encratite apostles we read of the very same scandalous suspicions Charisius and Aegeates seem to voice against Thomas and Andrew.

It is of such dubious workers that the Pastor writes in 2 Timothy 3:6–7, "for among them are those who make their way into households and capture weak women, burdened with sins and swayed with various impulses, who will listen to anybody and can never arrive at a knowledge of the truth." Dennis Ronald MacDonald has convincingly shown that such polemics in the Pastorals are written precisely to confute the sort of apostles we read of in the Acts of Paul, and that the Pastorals even employ the very same complex of traditions that we find in the Pauline Acts (*The Legend and the Apostle*, Philadelphia, 1983).

What had once been the noble ideal of apostolic poverty (at least affirmed in the circle of the itinerant charismatics) later came to be viewed by suspicious ecclesial authorities as shiftlessness. The pseudonymous author of the Clementine Epistles on Virginity voices his suspicions of the itinerant charismatics, borrowing the terms used by the Pastor: "Such are the ways of all those who do not work, but go hunting for tales, and think to themselves that this is profitable and right. For such persons are like those idle and prating widows 'who go wandering about among houses' . . . without fear of God . . . they traffic in iniquity in the name of Christ—which it is not right for the servants of God to do" (chapter XI).

Could it be that these suspicions of the itinerant charismatics as so many Cagliostros corrupting Christian wives found their way into the Apocryphal Acts? There they appear as the groundless ravings of unregenerate husbands who, like the devil whose tools they are, fume at losing their wives to Christ. This is what I think happened. And furthermore I am going to argue that these suspicions may have been in large measure well-founded.

First we must note the fact that as a genre the Acts are based on the Hellenistic romance novels. This would in itself mean little. Other hagiographic works, like Philostratus's *The Life of Apollonius of Tyana* and Pseudo-Callisthenes's *Alexander Romance* have employed many of the conventions of the romances as well, such as Dickensian tricks of Providence, travel narratives, exotic sights, imprisonments, and intrigue. The Acts, too, make abundant use of all these fictive props. But unlike the other hagiographies, the Acts have maintained the central feature of novels like *Chaereas and Callirhoe*, *Theagenes and Charikleia*, and *Leucippe and Clitophon*, namely that of star-crossed lovers, who fell in love at first sight and must overcome many torments and trials of virtue before being reunited with each other in holy matrimony.

Most scholars of the novels and the Acts note how this structure has been retained, only with the modification that now the lovers are Jesus Christ the heavenly bridegroom and women encratite converts like Thecla, Mygdonia, Maximilla, and Xanthippe. They hear the preaching of the apostle and are struck with love at first sight, but it is Jesus they love. The love-sick malaise afflicting Callirhoe and the religious daze of Thecla (recalling that of Franny Glass in Salinger's *Franny and Zooey* or of Sharon in the 1991 Michael Tolkin film *The Rapture*, both of whom also leave their dumbfounded men, by the way) are virtually indistinguishable. Neither family members nor fiances/husbands can understand it.

Callirhoe, newly stricken by the sight of her immediately-beloved Chaereas, "lay on her bed, her face covered, crying and uttering not a word" (B.P. Reardon, *Collected Ancient Greek Novels* [U. of California P., 1989], 23). Thecla, obsessed with the preaching of Paul on the virgin life, "for three days and three nights . . . has not risen from the window either to eat or to drink, but gazing steadily as if on some joyful spectacle" (Hennecke-Schneemelcher, 355). The mooning and pining of Charikleia, Leucippe, Anthia, and the rest are described in the very same terms.

The apostles are Jesus' stand-ins on earth, so it is the preacher of Jesus that the starry-eyed convert follows with maudlin devotion. When the apostle is imprisoned for having converted her, the woman visits him in prison, bribing the guards if need be, suffering persecution along with him, just so she may never be separated from the author of her salvation. If Paul leaves for another town, Thecla goes off in search of him. All this, of course, parallels the exertions of the lover on behalf of the beloved in the romance novels.

Why this almost embarrassingly close resemblance between the Acts and their prototypes, the novels? One might answer simply that the encratite element, once present, would necessitate the theme. But this is hardly the case. I believe we would have been justified in expecting no more than the persecution of the encratite apostle by the deprived (but not necessarily jealous) husband. But we could not from the simple fact of encratism expect the element of the woman's maudlin devotion to the apostle.

Davies suggests that we may have here reflected the emotional focus of encratite women on the preachers who converted them, these last, again, furnishing the prototypes for the apostles in these stories. He notes the importance of the fact that in the Acts Christ is sometimes said to appear to the women converts in the form of Peter, Paul, Andrew, John, or Thomas, and on the basis of this observation Davies suggests this explanation for the romantic theme:

> Visions reported in the Acts indicate that these men were seen to be like Christ by widows, and indeed Pseudo-Clement reports that they "took upon them the name of Christ" (1 Epistle 11). If they were in some fashion apprehended as being like Christ by "brides of Christ" and if they departed from those "brides" soon after having arrived and established a relationship with them, the women could be in the position of lovers deserted by their beloved. This facet of the apostles' impact might account, to some extent, for the reports in the apocryphal Acts of persons desolated by the fact that an apostle departs (93).

What Davies seems to be envisioning is a kind of Freudian dynamic of "transference" by the encratite convert of her newfound infatuation for her heavenly bridegroom Jesus onto Jesus' representatives on earth, the encratite apostles, wearing the literary guise of the biblical apostles in these texts. I am convinced he is correct, but only partially so. He has not seen what I suspect is the full meaning of the claim that the apostle is the mirror image or earthly twin of the Christ that he preaches. I strongly suspect that this claim justified exactly what the enraged husbands suspected: sexual intercourse between the encratite preacher and his female converts. In this case the infatuated devotion to the apostolic guru would be no surprise at all, nor would be the survival of the romantic theme in the Acts. The Acts would really be romances in the fullest sense, just as their pre-Christian prototypes were.

I do not mean to suggest that the doctrine of the apostle as the twin of Christ was either first invented or later employed as a mere pick-up line, though either is possible. Rather I am suggesting that in full religious seriousness (though perhaps with as much pious self-deception as clergy sex-abusers even today) the itinerant apostle and his convert would have what they considered chaste intercourse, both believing that the former had for the moment been transubstantiated into his heavenly counterpart. Then they entered together into the "bridal chamber," the esoteric initiatory sacrament that prompted so much suspicion among the Church Fathers, and perhaps for good reason. We really must at least suspect something of the sort when we read statements like that made to Thomas by his convert Mygdonia: "Truly, my lord [Thomas as the Lord Jesus?], I have received the seed of thy words" (491).

Andrew says to Maximilla, "I rightly see in you Eve repenting and in myself Adam being converted: for what she suffered in ignorance, you are now bringing to a happy conclusion because you are converted" (410). Can the point be that Maximilla did what Eve did, i.e., having intercourse with her Adam (= Andreas ="man" or husband), but without incurring guilt because she did it according to knowledge?

The whole picture as I am painting it would be a close parallel to the theology and practice of Hindu-Buddhist Tantra. Tantric and encratite cosmogonies are closely parallel. Just as encratites (including many Gnostics) believed that our world of sin, pain, death, and division came about from the sexual Fall of Adam and Eve, so do Tantrics believe that the phenomenal world of duality (which is but *maya*, illusion) stems from the primordial intercourse between Siva and Sakti, Siva's "bride" or "power," Kali. From this primal union of opposites came the division of perceived reality into sundered halves, illusory distinctions (such as that between conventional good and evil), half-truths.

Soteriologically, the encratites sought to regain "the image of the androgyne" (Wayne Meeks), regaining the blissful monism of Eden by undoing that Original Sin that had expelled their first ancestors from it. It was their "making the male as the female and the female as the male so that there is no more male and female" (Gospel of Thomas, logion 22; Gospel of the Egyptians, fragment 5), that freed women from the domestic servitude to which they had been condemned in the wake of eating from the tree of carnal knowledge (Genesis 3:16).

Thus in the encratite movements of early Christianity women could take leadership roles denied them in orthodoxy since they had shed the sexual distinctives that led to their debarment. And thus they withdrew sexually from their mates. They were now "one spirit" with the Lord, and could no more become "one flesh" with any mortal man.

Tantrics, too, sought to overcome the manifest world of plurality by mystically transcending it in their own persons. They practiced Hatha yoga, the yoga of bodily disciplines, indulging in the practices of "the left-handed path." These practices, shunned by the more conventional and faint-hearted yogis, involved consumption of "the five forbidden substances," meat, fish, beans, wine, and sex. The point was to leapfrog the differences into which the world had been divided by the primal sex-act of Siva and Kali. One acted as if the differences between piety and blasphemy, between the forbidden and the permitted, did not exist, a kind of "realized eschatology."

One could do this because one would by means of the practices have entered into a unitive state of consciousness utterly without worldly lusts and motives. Thus these ordinarily odious acts would incur no bad karma. One Tantric scripture announces that "By the same acts that cause some men to boil in hell for a hundred thousand eons, the yogi gains his eternal salvation!"

One of those acts was ritual sexual intercourse with a woman who must not be one's wife. With a psychological detachment St. Augustine would have envied, the yogi enacted intercourse in a state of spiritual transport in which he became the embodiment of Father Siva, his partner taking the persona of Mother Kali. As sexual climax was reached, the Tantric mystic called breathing, sense perception, and ejaculation to a screeching halt. The resulting spiritual shock catapulted him to the primordial oneness of the All before the embrace of Siva and Kali had sundered it. (Further on Tantric yoga, see Mircea Eliade, *Yoga: Immortality and Freedom,* Princeton, 1958, esp. "Mystical Eroticism," 254–258; Agehananda Bharati, *The Tantric Tradition*, Garden City, 1970, 179).

In the Tantric system intercourse without passion or consummation was the key to regaining paradisiacal Oneness. In encratism, it was a different but analogous redefinition of intercourse that accomplished the same end: earthly celibacy as the price for a spiritual *hieros gamos* with the heavenly bridegroom, this time not Siva but Jesus.

This much would not be controversial among scholars, though none to my knowledge has noticed the encratite-Tantric parallel. However, I am proposing we trace the parallels one crucial step farther, all the way to positing encratite ritual sex in a spiritual state of mind. Such seems to be the suggestion of the romance-patterns in the Acts between the apostle and his female convert anyway.

Can we point to any parallels closer to home? Yes, indeed. First we might point to a literary precedent. In the *Alexander Romance* we find a particularly interesting sequence in which Nectanebus, once Pharaoh of Egypt, now mage and astrologer in the service of Olympias of Macedon, predicts that the Queen will have a dream of the god Ammon who will beget a divine child by her. By power of suggestion she does have the dream, but it is followed by a nocturnal visit from her old confessor Nectanebus himself, accoutered in the traditional trappings of ram-horned Ammon. The two have intercourse, and Alexander the Great is the result. In the course of the novel Alexander seems to be considered as truly being the son of Ammon, so the ruse of Nectanebus does not seem to be mere trickery. Rather, the aged magus seems to function as the earthly stand-in for the heavenly bridegroom.

We do find chicanery pure and simple in an episode recorded by Josephus in his *Antiquities of the Jews*, XVIII.13.4. There we read of a Roman matron named Paulina who is deceived by the priests of Isis who have been bought by the amorous rogue Mundus. He has bribed them to tell Paulina that the god Anubis has hatched a passion for her and wishes to appear and have intercourse with her in the darkness of his adytum. Paulina and her husband are delighted at the honor. It cannot be considered adultery as long as her suitor is one of the gods. Alas, it is only Mundus. He has his way with her but cannot resist kissing and telling. Once he boasts of his trick and triumph, Paulina and her husband see to it that his doom is sealed. Here I think we have a fair parallel to the situation presented in the Acts as I understand it, though, let me hasten to add, only as seen from the perspective of the alienated husband.

Finally, let me suggest that there may even be a biblical precedent for the behavior of the encratite apostles whose Tantric-style escapades may underlie the romances of the Apocryphal Acts. Here I must refer to the neglected study *Angels and Ministers of Grace* by M.J. Field (1972). Field was an anthropologist working for many years in West Africa, where he noticed several surprising parallels between Old Testament practices and African folkways (something that has recently claimed the attention of missionary theologians as well).

From clear similarities Field began to reason to less clear but possible similarities. He noticed several puzzling supernatural phenomena in the pages of the Bible that would make new sense on analogy with certain aspects of traditional African and Arab societies, as if the supernaturalist biblical versions might reflect early, non-supernatural experiences or practices that managed to survive without the mythological clothing elsewhere.

Among these biblical phenomena were the several stories in which an angel or a "man of God" visits a barren woman to announce she will after all bear a son. Field notes that it was not unknown, and in some societies it was quite common, for a man to seek children by having his wife share a bed with a shaman or itinerant holy man. From our perspective there would be nothing supernatural about it, since success would only mean, so to speak, that it was the husband who had been barren, not the wife. But in a male chauvinist culture (is there any other kind?) this would never be admitted. So in such cases the newborn child was believed to be the product of a divine visitation. An angel had visited to announce a miracle birth. In fact a holy man had come to facilitate a natural one. In the course of time, the tales would grow taller, the woman's age increasing, etc.

Field suggests such a practice as the historical basis for the angelic or prophetic visits, later to yield children, to Sarah (Genesis 18:10), Mrs. Manoah (Judges 13:3), Hannah (1 Samuel 1:17–20), the Shunammite (2 Kings 4:14–17), Elizabeth (Luke 1:13, 24), and Mary (Luke 1:31, 34–35).

Field's thesis is surely speculative and in the nature of the case unproveable. But if we judge it plausible, then perhaps some of that plausibility rubs off onto my suggestion that the encratite apostles, the itinerant charismatics whose exploits lie at the base of the Apocryphal Acts, engaged in sexual intercourse with the women to whom they ministered on the basis of a theological rationale that no doubt both of them believed. It was no mere mortal, but the heavenly bridegroom, albeit under the aspect of his "twin brother" on earth, who joined the "bride of Christ" in the sacrament of "the bridal chamber."

25

TENDENTIOUS TABLE TALK:
A REVIEW OF CRAIG L. BLOMBERG'S
CONTAGIOUS HOLINESS: JESUS' MEALS WITH SINNERS

New Studies in Biblical Theology 19. InterVarsity Press, 2005. 216 pp.

Though the series to which this volume belongs usurps the title of the venerable SCM Press series Studies in Biblical Theology, it represents a tragic retreat from the fearless and innovative scholarship that marked its predecessor. As editor D. A. Carson says right up front, the books in the series "are written within the framework of confessional evangelicalism" (p. 9). As the bland and preachy themes of the other volumes in the series make plain, what we are dealing with here is in-house sectarian, parochial exegesis, abandoning the dangerous public forum of ideas, retreating into a "safe" and comfortable community of like-believing interpreters, all inerrantists who use the term "criticism" as a self-esteem-building euphemism for what they are really doing, apologetics aimed at edifying tender evangelical readers. It is especially ironic for Blomberg to be lionizing Jesus and his supposed fellowship with sinners when the whole point of the book is to help insulate conservative seminarians within the safety of the pre-critical flock, away from non-kosher ideas of genuine critics.

Blomberg's main goal seems to be to refute E.P. Sander's (admittedly peculiar) thesis that Jesus welcomed sinners, not caring whether they repented, as well as Dennis C. Smith's claim that Jesus' meals as depicted in the gospels must be understood as Greek symposia transplanted onto Jewish soil thanks to pandemic Hellenization. To Smith's symposium business Blomberg returns again and again like a refrain, though it is difficult to see why it is that important.

But by far most of the book (as Jacob Neusner would say, the shank of the book) is a completely pointless side-trip into every conceivable reference to meals and eating in the Old Testament, the Dead Sea Scrolls, the Apocrypha, and the Pseudepigrapha, plus Classical Greek and Roman references. The pregnant mountain thus scaled brings forth a mouse of a contrast: as we already knew, Jesus seems not to have superstitiously avoided people on the basis of likely ritual impurity or even if they were Gentiles. Yes, yes, Dr. Blomberg is a learned fellow, all right. It's not that he is trying to impress anybody. Anyone who is even mildly acquainted with him knows better than that. But he is reinforcing the evangelical notion of what New Testament scholarship is: a command of ancient data and being conversant with the views of commentators. It is an essentially uncreative enterprise of guarding the store to prevent "shrinkage" of merchandise, lest real critics erode the stock-in-trade of Orthodox Protestant preaching by whittling away the reliability of the Bible.

It is written plainly on every page that Blomberg has forgotten the genuine critical axioms of Bultmann and the form- and redaction- critics, whose methods he facilely assures his readers are passé ("The form-critical analyses assume a fallacious and now- outmoded kind of historical research," p. 22). This is like a chiropractor informing a patient that no one bothers with "mainstream" medicine anymore.

So completely does Blomberg (like the mutually sustaining circle of intra- Evangelical commentators he quotes) mean "apologetics" when he says "criticism" that he deems blatant harmonization to be a "critical" axiom: "demonstrating that a theme is crucial to a Gospel writer's literary purposes bears no relation to the probability of its historical authenticity" (p. 22). "But the two passages [the two fish stories in Luke 5 and John 21] scarcely need to be pitted against one another. Each is intelligible in its own context" (p. 126). As to the lampoons of John's fasting and Jesus' conviviality, we need not choose between them, for as R. Stein says, "Both are valid expressions of different aspects of God's kingdom, and if either is totally ignored, an unbalanced portrayal will result" (p. 118). How nice.

Blomberg and his ilk bear the same relation to overt, admitted apologists as today's "Intelligent Design" advocates do to yesterday's Flood Geology partisans. They seek respectability by trying to associate their efforts with an earlier generation's scientific consensus. In Blomberg's case, he wants to go back in time to the conservative critics of an earlier generation, like T.W. Manson and Vincent Taylor. They often repaired to "epicyclical" devices to explain variant versions of a saying or story. If there are two stories or sayings that sound significantly alike but have equally important differences, what should we infer? It seems the least assumption-ridden suggestion would be that oral tradition has produced mutant, word-of-mouth versions, or that the evangelists have simply rewritten material they thought they could improve. But either solution disturbs apologists, so they like to say evangelist A was following one tradition, evangelist B another. Or that Matthew was using one "source" with one version, while Luke used another, with another version. For Blomberg and company, "oral tradition" itself becomes an additional, purely accurate "source" alongside already-written ones. "The Lukan parallel (Luke 9:10-17) diverges from Mark a little more than Matthew did. Even where the two texts contain similar information, there is less verbal parallelism, suggesting greater influence of the oral tradition on Luke's form" (p. 107). Matthew (in Matt. 15:32–39) "also rearranges the sequence of a few details, so that one wonders if oral tradition has influenced his structure" (p. 111).

This approach implies what Blomberg eventually admits: Jesus said or did it twice, and each version is a literal, accurate report. "This much variation in wording and sequence, even granted the verbal parallelism that remains, suggests the possibility of two separate teachings of Jesus on two distinct occasions" (p. 115). It seems never to occur to Blomberg and his colleagues that the very source analysis they adopt (Markan Priority, Q, etc.) was made necessary only by the recognition that pure oral transmission could never yield the degree of verbal similarity we find when we compare the gospels. Apologists everywhere take for granted that a tradition is a transcript, so different versions must be different, accurate reports of different events/speeches. Blomberg doesn't need Q; he appeals to it only because real critics do and he wants to try to beat them at their own game. If we were playing *his* game, there would be no talk of gospel sources at all.

Blomberg will not even admit that Mark has used two versions of the same miracle story, the multiplication of bread and fish: "The feeding of the four thousand is often viewed as a doublet of the multiplication of the loaves for the five thousand. From Mark's perspective, however, the two incidents are clearly distinct, inasmuch as Mark 8:1 indicates that 'another large crowd gathered'. The Greek uses the adverb *palin* ('again'). The dialogue in 8:14–21 will also refer back to both episodes as separate" (p. 109). Of course anyone can see that Mark means to narrate two separate, similar miracles. The question, of which Blomberg seems to be entirely oblivious, is whether Mark is perhaps making virtue of necessity, being stuck with two versions of the same story, like the Genesis redactor who was faced with three variant versions (12:10-20; 20:1-18; 26:1-17) of the patriarch (Abram/Abraham/Isaac) lying to the king (Pharaoh/Abimelech) about his wife (Sarai/Sarah/Rebecca). Just as the Genesis redactor decided to use all three versions *of the same story* by separating them and arbitrarily positing that one took place during *another* famine (26:1), so has Mark *obviously* used both versions, like a pious scribe who does not dare exclude any textual accretion lest he omit some words of God. It does not occur to Blomberg to recognize a redactional seam. There can be none, for he is an inerrantist: if the details of Paul's conversion stories do not match, he must have been converted three times.

Blomberg treats us to a similar harmonizing spectacle when he gets to Luke 7:36–50, the Lukan version of the Bethany anointing, or rather, as he thinks, Luke's account of a *different* anointing, as if Jesus had to expect this sort of attention from female fans as often as Elvis had them ripping his clothes off. "The striking similarities, most notably the use of an alabaster jar of perfume, could suggest that the two divergent accounts have influenced one another in some small ways, but there are no compelling reasons for not treating Luke 7:36–50 as primarily a separate incident" (p. 131). "Luke clearly believes it to be a separate incident" (Ibid.). Unless Blomberg is gifted as a mind-reader or a necromancer, the assertion is grossly circular. How do we know Luke believed he was (merely) reporting a separate incident? We "know" it only if we are persuaded of the inerrancy of scripture, whereby any assertion in the text must be taken literally.

Otherwise we might have to wonder if Luke is exercising literary license and wholly rewriting Mark's story. But we wouldn't want that, because then we might have to recognize that Luke and Matthew have rewritten Mark's Easter story, too, and in rather drastic fashion. And then we could not pretend the gospel Easter stories are "evidence that demands a verdict."

How do we know that the saying "Many will come from east and west to recline with Abraham, Isaac, and Jacob in the kingdom of heaven" (Matthew 8:11-12) refers to Gentiles? Well, Jesus says it to recognize the faith of a Gentile, so that's that, right? Again, inerrantism. Does it not even occur to Blomberg that the saying circulated independently, only to have been "framed" by the story of the Centurion? It may well have first referred to Diaspora Jews. Blomberg's "argument" that it doesn't mean that amounts to no more than a fundamentalist assertion, with stopped-up ears, "No, it happened just like the Bible says!"

Against Dennis Smith, Blomberg decrees that "the very literary-critical approach to which Smith… appeals has demonstrated that one cannot strip unhistorical layers from a historical core of Gospel pericopae, as once was thought" (p. 22). Blomberg doesn't get it. As Frank Kermode pointed out long ago, the more literary a passage appears, the less likely it is to be historical. And as D.F. Strauss (who knew what criticism was) said long before that, once one recognizes the tendency of a pericope, the reason it is told, and one sees its artificiality, no reason remains for trying to salvage historical remains (as, e.g., Gerd Lüdemann still does in his Acts commentary). For instance, Blomberg is happy to recognize that the evangelists mean to cast Jesus as a new Moses and a new Elijah, even that the depiction of the audience as seated in groups of fifty and a hundred is meant to recall the arrangements of the Israelites in the wilderness (p. 104). Doesn't he see what that means? The whole scene is a midrashic fiction. Or do we imagine Jesus as Schonfield's scheming messiah, choreographing the whole scene to make a point to future gospel readers?

The most damning objection to there having been two distinct bread miracles is the impossible obtuseness of the disciples who, having seen such a miracle once, could not conceivably be stumped at how to feed the crowd when the exact same circumstance arose again. But Blomberg has an "answer": "the point may be that they think Jesus is asking *them* to replicate the earlier miracle" (p. 109). This is worthy of Gleason Archer and his encyclopedia of apparent Bible contradictions.

But the most comical cases of Blomberg's "criticism" amounting to apologetics of the most contrived sort concern the spectacular character of the miracles. The fact of their enormity phases him not in the least. "The distinction in the locations of the two feeding miracles, combined with the obscurity of the geographical references, supports the conviction that both were separate events in which Jesus was actually involved" (p. 110). You mean, these throat-clearing attempts to *make* the stories seem to be those of different events outweigh the likelihood that both versions are merely rewrites of the Elisha story in 2 Kings 4:42–44, where that prophet does the same thing? What would William of Ockham say? Is it more likely that a man magically increased the mass of some fish and barley rolls one day (or two days)? Or is it more likely that the teller of such a tale has merely copied it from a well-known prototype? A stubborn refusal to countenance the possibility of genuine miracles (which

Blomberg ascribes to historical critics) has nothing to do with such a judgment. Just because God *can* do anything doesn't mean he in fact *did* everything every ancient (or even every biblical) writer says he did. Unless, of course, there is good prior reason to believe in biblical inerrancy. That is the issue. Blomberg and his coreligionists do not just want us to admit miracles might happen; what they want is for us to believe in biblical inerrancy as they do. When they say this or that consideration vindicates a miracle story as "likely," they do not mean this is why they have come to accept it with more or less provisional confidence. No, they already believe it as a point of doctrinal duty. They are just engaging in apologetics to defend what they already believe.

If anyone needed more evidence, look at Blomberg's treatment of the water-into- wine miracle (John 2:1–11). "The miracle thus admirably satisfies the criterion of coherence with teaching generally recognized to be authentic elsewhere" (p. 122). Was Blomberg absent on the day they explained that such criteria are relevant only to *sayings*? To make "coherence" with a teaching theme the deciding factor whether a man magically changed one chemical substance into another is just perverse. It is not coherence but *analogy* that is the relevant criterion here: is this miracle, so similar to that of Dionysus and so unparalleled in all creditable history, to be judged more probably a myth like the Dionysus version, or as a credible historical report? Again, even the pious believer in miracles (if piety even requires such) can, even *must*, decide: no, insofar as we can judge, not having been there, it is surely more likely to be a fiction, a legend, told for theological reasons. "The clearest redactional or theological overlay in the passage comes at the end, when John describes this miracle as the first of Jesus' signs (*semeia*)—the standard expression in the Fourth Gospel for Jesus' mighty deeds – but the historicity of the core miracle itself is unaffected by this label" (p. 123). Oh dear.

The Emmaus story strikingly parallels the story (attested for the fourth century BCE) of Asclepius in disguise, catching up with two crestfallen believers who sought his healing in the holy shrine at Epidauros but left disappointed. Coaxing out the reason for their glumness, he reveals himself, performing the healing on the spot. When we read a very similar story about the Risen Jesus, what are we to conclude? I suppose an omnipotent deity could rise from the dead. No dogmatic bias to the contrary can allow me to disqualify the Emmaus tale as an historical report. But neither can I discount the possibility that poor Sostrata may have actually been healed by the power of a very real Asclepius, son of Apollo. What business have I, as a historian, "presupposing" that Asclepius did not exist and perform miracles? But if we feel pretty safe in classifying the one story as a legend (and the earlier one at that), why do we not assess the other as likely to be a holy legend, too? That is the way the historian reasons. But this is the way the covert apologist for biblical inerrancy reasons: "The generally restrained nature of the narrative... particularly surrounding the meal, and the ambiguity created by Jesus' immediate disappearance after the disciples recognized him, all support authenticity. A purely legendary story would disclose Christ far more clearly and fill in the obvious gaps Luke has left in his narrative (as in fact the apocryphal Gospel accounts regularly do)" (p. 160). There is no ambiguity. There are no gaps. There could be no clearer revelation of the Risen Christ. And the restrained character of the narrative is simply the mark of better writing, not necessarily of reporting. And just because there may be even grosser legends, wilder fictions, does not mean more subtle ones are to be judged historical.

Very little of *Contagious Holiness* is spent demonstrating that Jesus probably did seek the company of sinners so as to influence them for good. But then the book is not really about that. As with all such monographs by Evangelical scholars, the book is a mass of historical apologetics.

CREDITS

CRITICIZING CHRISTIANITY

1. "Must We Take a Leap of Faith? (Have We Already?)" *American Rationalist* 26, no. 6 (March–April 1982).

2. "Masochism and Piety," *Journal of Religion & Health* 22, no. 2 (Summer 1983).

3. "Plaster Sanctification," paper presented at the 2013 American Atheists National Convention.

4. "Protestant Hermeneutical Axiomatics: A Deconstruction," *Christian*New Age Quarterly* (April–June, 1997).

5. "The Psychology of Biblicism," *Humanist* (Spring 2001).

6. "A Mighty Fortress Is Our Mentality" (unpublished sermon).

7. "On Having Your Head up Your Assumptions," *Free Inquiry* 24, no. 1 (December 2003/January 2004).

8. "Damnable Syllogism," *American Atheist* 45, no. 6 (July 2007).

9. "A Mess of Miracles," *Secular Nation* 12, no. 2 (2nd Quarter, 2007).

10. "The Marginality of the Cross," *Journal of Unification Studies* 6 (2004–2005).

11. "Nothing Bespeaks the Divine Inspiration of the Bible," *American Rationalist* (January/February; March/April 2012).

WORLD RELIGIONS

12. "Kosher Pigs and Jews for Jesus," *Secular Nation* 5, no. 4 (October–December, 2000; National Jewish Post & Opinion, February 6, 2002.

13. "If You Dislike Christianity, You'll Hate Buddhism!" *Christian*New Age Quarterly* (October–December, 1996).

14. "Of Myth and Men: A Closer Look at the Originators of the Major Religions— What Did They Really Say and Do?" *Free Inquiry* 20, no. 1 (Winter 1999–2000).

RADICAL THEOLOGY

15. "What Is (and Is Not) Postmodern Theology?" paper presented to the American Academy of Religion (unpublished).

16. "Postmodern Unitarian Universalism," *Religious Humanism* 31, no. 1 & 2 (Winter/ Spring 1997).

17. "Loose Canon: A Proposal for a New Biblical Canon," *Christian*New Age Quarterly* 19, no. 3 (Summer 2010).

FREETHOUGHT

18. "Errors of the Elohist: An Appreciation of Ingersoll's *Some Mistakes of Moses*," *Free Inquiry* 21, no. 2 (Spring 2001).

19. "Is the Bible *Mein Kampf*?" *Secular Nation* 8, no. 3 (3rd Quarter, 2003).

20. "Humanisms: A Theological Classification," *Secular Nation* 9, no. 1 (1st Quarter, 2004); *Secular Nation* 9, no. 3 (3rd Quarter, 2004).

21. "The Return of the Navel: The 'Omphalos' Argument in Contemporary Creationism," *Creation/Evolution Journal* 1, no. 2 (Fall 1980).

BIBLICAL EXPLORATIONS

22. "How the Gospels Subvert Apologetics," opening statement for a debate with James R. White, May 6, 2010.

23. "Acts 14 and the Equinox of the Gods," paper presented to the Acts Group of the Jesus Seminar, Spring 2003.

24. "Heavenly Bridegrooms: The Sex Acts of the Apostles," *Journal of Higher Criticism* 8, no. 2 (Fall 2001).

25. "Tendentious Table Talk: A Review of Craig L. Blomberg, *Contagious Holiness: Jesus' Meals with Sinners*," *Journal of Higher Criticism* 12, no. 2 (Fall 2006).

ABOUT THE AUTHOR

Robert M. Price is a freethought advocate who has written on many subjects in many venues, and for many years. *Atheism and Faitheism* collects a good number of these essays from various stages of his career. He has been at various times an agnostic, an exponent of Liberal Protestant theology, a non-theist, a secular humanist, a religious humanist, a Unitarian-Universalist wannabe, an unaffiliated Universalist, and a Fellow of the Jesus Seminar. Any way you cut it, his name is Legion. The initial section, "Criticizing Christianity," is three times the size of any of the others. These pieces document Price's self-extrication, step by step, from the Born Again Christianity in which he dwelt for some dozen years.

Not your typical atheist, Price continues to love the various great religions as endlessly fascinating creations/expressions of the human spirit. He loves theology, too. Some of these essays reveal Price as an adherent of the radical Deconstructive, or Death-of-God theology. Price prefers Nietzsche's proclamation that God is dead to the straight-laced party line of purely secular atheism. But there are old-time Freethought pieces here, too. Bob Price hosts The Bible Geek podcast, and indeed the Bible is his main focus of interest, so you will find a sample of his biblical studies here.